COMPREHENDING COLUMBINE

RALPH W. LARKIN

COMPREHENDING COLUMBINE

TEMPLE UNIVERSITY PRESS
Philadelphia

TEMPLE UNIVERSITY PRESS
1601 North Broad Street
Philadelphia PA 19122
www.temple.edu/tempress

Published 2007
Printed in the United States of America

∞ The paper used in this publication meets the requirements of the American National Standard for Information Sciences—Permanence of Paper for Printed Library Materials, ANSI Z39.48-1992

Library of Congress Cataloging-in-Publication Data
Larkin, Ralph W., 1940-
Comprehending Columbine / Ralph W. Larkin.
p. cm.
Includes bibliographical references and index.
ISBN-13: 978-1-59213-490-8 ISBN-10: 1-59213-490-4 (cloth : alk. paper)
ISBN-13: 978-1-59213-491-5 ISBN-10: 1-59213-491-2 (pbk. : alk. paper)
1. Columbine High School (Littleton, Colo.)
2. School violence—Colorado. I. Title.
LB3013.33.C6L37 2007
373.17'820978882—dc22

2006020365

2 4 6 8 9 7 5 3 1

To Andrew and David

CONTENTS

FIGURES

1

ARMAGEDDON (WELL, ALMOST)

NOTHING HAPPENED. It was 11:19 A.M., April 20, 1999. By 11:09 A.M., Eric Harris and Dylan Klebold had hauled into the Columbine High School cafeteria two bombs hidden in large duffel bags and placed them near the tables where the athletic crowd ate lunch. Each bomb was a twenty-gallon propane tank wired to a one-gallon can of gasoline that was attached to a detonator and a timer set to go off at 11:17 A.M. The duffel bags blended in with the backpacks strewn all over the cafeteria floor by the approximately 480 students who were eating lunch at the time.

Eric was in the junior parking lot, southeast of the main entrance, and Dylan was in the senior parking lot, southwest of the main entrance. Each was strategically located approximately forty-five degrees from the south entrance of the high school so they could shoot at fleeing students without endangering each other. Klebold was dressed in cargo pants, a black T-shirt that said "Wrath," and a black trench coat. Underneath his coat was an Intratec TEC-DC-9, 9-mm semiautomatic handgun attached to a strap slung over his shoulder. His cargo pants had large pockets that allowed him partially to conceal a Stephens 12-gauge double-barreled shotgun, particularly since the barrel had been cut down to approximately twenty-three inches. Harris, also wearing a black trench coat, wore a white T-shirt underneath that said, "Natural Selection." Both wore combat boots. Harris hid a

Hi-Point 9-mm carbine rifle on a strap under his coat. He carried a Savage Springfield 12-gauge pump shotgun in a duffel bag that also held numerous explosive devices, including pipe bombs and CO2 canisters, and ammunition. The shotgun's stock and barrel had been cut off, reducing it to twenty-six inches. In addition, the boys were armed with several knives, including a nine-inch kitchen knife, a dagger, and two combat knives, one a folding blade knife about four inches long, and the other having a hatchet blade of about 3 1/2 inches in length, the handle of which doubled as brass knuckles with ten sharp spikes protruding outward. Their cars were booby-trapped with bombs timed to explode later in the day when the parking lot would be filled with emergency personnel.

By 11:19 A.M., nothing had happened. The bombs did not explode. No ball of fire ripped out the cafeteria windows. No dismembered body pieces were propelled through the air. No mortally wounded students were lying on the cafeteria floor, groaning and calling for their mothers. The ceiling above the cafeteria did not collapse, dropping the fifty-six students studying in the library above, the debris from the floor, and the tables, chairs, stacks, and other equipment onto the unsuspecting students in the cafeteria below. The ground did not reverberate; thick black smoke did not emanate from the cafeteria. No chaos had broken out as students ran from the scene. No flood of students ran for safety through the south entrance to the high school only to be mowed down in a withering crossfire from semiautomatic weapons. Harris and Klebold's apocalyptic vision of the destruction of their high school was thwarted only because the detonators they had purchased were defective.

The Columbine massacre was the most important news event in 1999; throughout the 1990s, only the O. J. Simpson trial received more media coverage (Muschert 2002). Despite the overwhelming media coverage and the subsequent national debate over youth violence, precious few attempts were made to analyze the causes of the shootings. As Downs (1998) has shown, the media have a very short attention span, moving from excited involvement to loss of interest in a short span of time. Because of the magnitude of the story of the Columbine shootings, daily reportage lasted for a full month. Despite the salience of the story, the vast media presence, the large number of local, state, and national investigators, at the close of the investigation, nobody could offer a coherent explanation as to why Eric Harris and Dylan Klebold set out to kill their peers and destroy their school. Even though there was agreement, for the most part, about the facts of the case, the question of "why" has never been adequately addressed. This study examines personal, local, and societal factors that propelled Harris and Klebold to attempt to kill 500 of their fellow students and destroy their high school.

THE ASSAULT

Months of preparation and meticulous planning culminated in that moment. Over the past year, the boys had collected weapons, made and tested pipe bombs, wrote to-do lists, drew up plans, conducted field research, and fantasized about the coming revenge that they were going to exact from Columbine. In his Trenchcoat Mafia web site, Eric Harris opined that he could kill 500 students. If the bombs had exploded as the two boys had originally planned, the number of dead and wounded may well have approximated that number.

With their watches and the timers synchronized, they waited in the parking lot for an explosion that never happened. They had apparently walked to the top of the stairs that led to the west entrance of the school. When they realized that their plans needed revision, they looked at each other, and one of them said, "Go, go!"

It was a warm spring day, and Rachel Scott and Richard Castaldo had decided to eat their lunch on the grass beside the west entrance. When Harris and Klebold reached the top of the stairs, they saw Rachel and Richard. Rachel was killed in a hail of bullets, and Richard was seriously wounded. The assault had begun. Then they turned and started shooting down the stairs at students who were behind them and who were apparently walking to the "smokers' pit," a congregating place in Clement Park just to the north of the school where smokers gathered to have a cigarette. They shot Daniel Rohrbough, Sean Graves, and Lance Kirklin. Rohrbough died instantly, but Kirklin and Graves survived. Then Harris and Klebold turned in a more westerly direction and began shooting at five students on a grassy slope. As they ran away from the gunman, two were hit: Michael Johnson was able to run up the hill and hide behind a shed containing athletic equipment; Mark Taylor was seriously wounded and could not move.

Dylan Klebold ran back down the stairs toward the rear entrance of the cafeteria. On his way, he shot Lance Kirklin at close range. Klebold entered the cafeteria and stood at the rear, apparently trying to figure out why the bombs did not explode. He stood there for less than a minute, exiting the cafeteria and running back up the stairs to Eric. By that time, Eric had taken off his trench coat. He shot down the stairs at Ann Marie Hochhalter and hit her several times as she struggled to run for cover into the cafeteria. One of the gunmen shouted, "This is what we always wanted to do! This is awesome!" The boys threw pipe bombs onto the grassy area, into the parking lot, and onto the roof of the school, creating several explosions.

At about this time, teacher Patti Nielson, who was on hall duty during the lunch period, heard a commotion outside the west entrance to the school. Thinking that students using toy guns to film a video were making too much noise, she intended to tell them to "knock it off" as she approached the doors of the west entrance. She and a student, Brian Anderson, who was told by a teacher to get out of the school because of the shooting and the bombs, were hit with metal and glass as Eric Harris shot through the doors of the west entrance. Both Nielson and Anderson were caught between the inner and outer doors. Nielson suffered abrasions to her shoulder, forearm, and knee from the fragments. Anderson was hit in the chest by the flying glass and metal. Neither was wounded seriously, and both retreated from the doors, running in a southerly direction toward the library. Nielson ran into the library, hid in a cupboard under the librarians' counter, dialed 911 on the school phone, and informed the police of the assault.

At 11:22 A.M., Sheriff's Deputy Neil Gardner, who was in his patrol car eating lunch and monitoring students at the smoking pit in Clement Park, received a panicky emergency call from a custodian at Columbine High School. The deputy was needed on the south side of the school. While moving from the north to the south side of campus, he heard over the radio that a girl was down in front of the high school, apparently in reference to Ann Marie Hochhalter. As Deputy Gardiner drove from Clement Park to the south parking lot, he received a second call: A shooter was in the school. He pulled his cruiser to the end of the south parking lot where he had a clear view of the west entrance to the high school. Eric Harris saw him and began shooting. The deputy shot back at Harris four times without hitting him. Harris and Klebold then ran into the school.

News was spreading that the school was under assault. People could hear the gunfire and explosions of the pipe bombs. Teachers and students were flooding from the school in panic. In addition, five other deputies from the Jefferson County Sheriff's Department arrived on campus. The scene was chaos. The sheriff's deputies tried to get information from the students and teachers. This is what they reported:

> As the first deputies arrived on campus, they were met by chaos and hysteria. Terrified students and teachers were fleeing in all directions from the high school in the suburban neighborhood. Others were still inside. The deputies could hear explosions coming from inside the school. The students were telling them about bombs, guns and hand grenades, and about gunmen with assault rifles and semiautomatics. There were other

> reports of possible terrorists, four shooters, six shooters, seventeen-hostages. There was a man wearing a trench coat; there were two guys in trench coats. There was a guy in a white T-shirt, with a hat, not with a hat. The gunmen had changed clothes to blend in with the other students. There was a shooter on the roof. The gunmen were in the auditorium. No, they were in the cafeteria. (Jefferson County Sheriff's Office 1999)

A female student observed Brian Anderson staggering down the hall toward the library and Patti Nielson ducking into the library. She informed science teacher Dave Sanders, who was standing at the top of the stairs that led from the cafeteria to the upper-level of the school where the library and the science classrooms were. Sanders told the female student to go downstairs. At just about this time, Harris and Klebold entered the building through the west doors. They began shooting and walking in an easterly direction, laughing as they were shooting.

A teacher and several students were in the hall. Klebold suddenly ran down the hall shooting, wounding student Stephanie Munson in the ankle. She escaped by running past the administrative offices through the eastern entrance of the high school into the teachers' parking lot. Klebold stopped in front of a bank of telephones, turned around, and returned to where Harris was standing at the intersection of the halls. At this point, Sanders and the custodians were frantically trying to herd kids away from danger. As Sanders rounded the corner into the West Hall, he saw Harris and Klebold, who also saw him. He turned around in an attempt to retrace his steps back towards the stairs that led to the cafeteria. However, as he did so, he was shot twice in the back. He staggered around the corner and collapsed on the floor. He then crawled to the science hallway. Several students pulled him into a science classroom and administered first aid.

By this time, the halls were empty. Students were either hiding in rooms with the doors blockaded or had fled from the building and were being redirected toward Leawood Park, which was across Pierce Avenue, to the east of school. Harris and Klebold, apparently uncertain about what to do next, began walking up and down the library hall shooting their weapons and randomly throwing bombs.

At 11:29 A.M., they stopped in front of the library doors. The fifty-two students in the library had been told by Patti Nielson to hide under the desks. Nielson, hiding under the front counter, was on the phone to the 911 operator. Harris and Klebold entered the library, shouting, "Get up! All athletes stand up," and "Anybody with a white hat [part of the uniform of the athletes] or a sports emblem on it is dead. Today is your day to die." When nobody stood up, Harris said, "Fine, then I'll just start shooting." He fired his shotgun across the front counter. Flying splinters injured Evan Todd, who was hiding behind the copier machine at the end of the counter. Harris and Klebold then walked from the front counter of the library toward the windows. As they passed Kyle Velasquez, who was sitting at the computer table, Klebold shot him, killing him. The two gunmen set down their duffel bags, which were filled with pipe bombs, Molotov cocktails, CO_2 canisters, and ammunition. The boys then fired through the windows at fleeing students and law enforcement personnel. Fire was returned, forcing them to back away from the windows.

At this point, Harris and Klebold began their killing in earnest. In the next 7 1/2 minutes, they killed ten and injured twelve of their fellow students. After backing away from the windows, Dylan Klebold turned to his left and fired his shotgun, wounding Daniel Steepleton, Makai Hall, and Patrick Ireland, all who were hiding under a table. Patrick Ireland, although wounded, began administering first aid to Makai, whose leg was gushing blood. Ireland was shot again. All three boys survived their wounds. Patrick floated in and out of consciousness. After the assault was over, he crawled to the window where he was helped out by firemen and placed onto the top of a fire emergency vehicle that had been driven there to rescue him.

Klebold then took off his trench coat and dropped it on the floor. Harris turned to his right and shot Stephen Curnow at close range, killing him instantly. He also shot at Kasey Ruegsegger, injuring her. The boys were laughing and enjoying themselves immensely. Some girls were overheard to ask, "Why are you doing this?" They answered, "We've always wanted to do this. This is payback. We've dreamed of doing this for four years. This is for all the shit you put us through. This is what you deserve" (Jefferson County Sheriff's Office 1999; Zoba 2000, 34).

Harris turned to his left and walked to a nearby table. Rapping it with his knuckles, he taunted, "peek-a-boo," and stuck his shotgun under the table. With a single blast, he killed Cassie Bernall. However, the gun recoiled and smashed into Harris's face, breaking his nose. He was momentarily stunned, and blood began to flow from his nose. He then turned to Bree Pasquale and asked her if she wanted to die. As she was pleading for her life, he laughed and said, "Everyone's gonna die. We're gonna blow up the school anyway." Meanwhile, Klebold had moved to a table adjacent to the one under which Cassie Bernall was hiding. He spied Isaiah Sholes, a black student. Klebold said, "Hey look, there's that little nigger," and began pulling Isaiah out from underneath the table. This comment seemed to snap Eric Harris out of his daze, and he walked over to the table and shot Isaiah point blank three times, killing him. Dylan stated, "Man, I didn't know black brains could fly that far." Dylan then shot under the table several times, killing Matthew Kechter. Eric Harris threw a CO_2 canister underneath the table where Daniel Steepleton, Makai Hall, and Patrick Ireland were lying wounded. Makai Hall grabbed the canister and threw it in a southerly direction where it exploded without injuring anybody.

Harris and Klebold then walked toward the stacks in the middle of the room. Eric jumped on a table. He grabbed the top of one of the bookcases and attempted to tip it over, cursing at his failed effort. Harris shot his gun into a southerly direction between the bookshelves at nobody in particular. Klebold headed toward the library door, turned to his right, and shot out the display case just to the south the library door. Then he walked around the display case and shot at Mark Kintgen who was hiding underneath the table nearest the case, injuring him. Klebold then noticed Lisa Kreutz, Valeen Schnurr, Jeanna Park, Kelly Fleming, Diwata Perez, and Lauren Townsend huddled together underneath the next table. The first shot injured Lisa Kreutz and Valeen Schnurr. Dylan shot his gun as fast as it would fire, killing Lauren Townsend.

Eric, walking toward Dylan, looked under a table where two girls were hiding, and said, "Pathetic." Valeen Schnurr, who was seriously wounded, was crying, "Oh my God, oh my God." Overhearing Valeen's pleas, Dylan asked, "Do you believe in God?" She responded, "Yes." He said, "Why?" and walked away

Harris and Klebold then headed south along the eastern side of the library. They stopped at a nearby table, and Harris shot underneath, wounding Nicole Nowlen and John Tomlin. Tomlin crawled out from under the table, and Klebold shot him dead. The boys then turned, traversing back toward the table where the girls were hiding, and shot under it several times, killing Kelly Fleming and injuring Jeanna Park and Lisa Kreutz.

The shooters then walked to the middle of the library between the stacks, where they reloaded their guns. Eric Harris noticed somebody under an adjacent table. He shouted, "Who is under the table? Identify yourself!"

It was John Savage, a former friend of Dylan and a boy both shooters knew. He identified himself and asked Klebold what he was doing, to which Klebold responded, "Oh, just killing people."

Savage asked, "Are you going to kill me?"

Klebold hesitated and told Savage to leave, which he did. Another student under the same table did not fare so well. Eric Harris went over to the table and shot Daniel Mauser dead. The boys moved south to a table under which several students were hiding. One of the young gunmen said to the other, "I have been waiting to do this for a long time." The other responded, "You know what else I want to do?" His partner responded, "Yeah, to stab someone."

They opened a barrage of fire, killing Cory DePooter and injuring Jennifer Doyle and Austin Eubanks. It was 11:35 A.M. Harris and Klebold left the library and walked into the science area. Their actions now seemed disjointed and random. They shot into empty science rooms. They saw students who were hiding and apparently did nothing. They taped a Molotov cocktail to a science room door, which started a small fire that was later put out by a faculty member. They then walked down the stairs to the cafeteria.

The apparent reason for Harris and Klebold's return to the cafeteria was to explode the propane bombs that they had made and to create a conflagration of serious proportions. Upon entry into the cafeteria, Eric knelt on one knee, resting his rifle on the banister of the stairs leading into the cafeteria, and fired several shots at one of the bombs. Again, nothing happened. Dylan went over to the bomb and fiddled with it. He then stepped away from the bomb and threw either a pipe bomb or a CO_2 canister toward it, which exploded and started a fire. Still the propane bombs did not explode. The boys left the cafeteria, taking drinks of water from containers left by fleeing students. The fire in the cafeteria was eventually extinguished by the sprinkler system.

The boys returned to the library at noon, which was deserted with the exception of the dead and those wounded who could not move. According to the coroner, the boys committed suicide by firing bullets through their heads. Although the rampage lasted about forty-five minutes, because of the confusion and slowness of the police to secure the premises, some researchers mistakenly reported that it was four hours long (Newman 2004, 154).[1]

AFTERMATH

The fallout from the Columbine shootings was immediate and terrifying. The country was horrified. The attack on Columbine was unprecedented in its magnitude, body count, and viciousness. President Bill Clinton addressed the nation, stating that he was shocked and saddened by the shootings and offered condolences to the members of the Columbine community (Stout 1999). Vice President Al Gore was dispatched to Colorado to attend the April 25th memorial services for the victims of the Columbine massacre. The shootings lead network news programs for several days. Talk shows were inundated with telephone calls from people expressing opinions about the shootings and the state of today's youth.

On National Public Radio, listeners called in to relate how they, too, were bullied and terrorized as high school students.

The country was convulsed into fits of self-reflection and finger-pointing. Debates on bullying, access to guns, violent video games and television shows, rock-and-roll music, parenting, and school security were renewed. Blame for the assaults focused on gun culture and the ease by which weaponry could be obtained, the so-called goth youth subculture, lack of parental supervision, and of course, a general lack of values (Gibbs and Roche 1999; Staten 1999; Verhovek 1999).

Harris and Klebold hoped that their act would generate a massive revolt. In one of the videotapes, Harris said, "We're going to kick-start a revolution" among the dispossessed and despised students of the world (Gibbs and Roche 1999). Although they did not engender a revolution, their acts resonated among students who had been bullied and humiliated by their peers. In the weeks following the Columbine High School shootings, schools across the country experienced thousands of bomb scares, scores of attempted bombings, and several attempted copycat killings (Emergency Net 1999). The two self-styled revolutionaries partially achieved their apocalyptical vision of a nationwide revolt. The most serious incident occurred in Taber, a farming community of 7,200 people, located about 110 miles southeast of Calgary, Alberta. On Wednesday, April 21, the day after Columbine, a student opened fire with a sawed-off .22-caliber rifle at W. R. Myers High School, killing one student and seriously wounding another. On April 23, in a town outside Baton Rouge, Louisiana, two fourteen-year-old boys were arrested for shooting and wounding a fellow student at a middle school. Four boys were charged with planning a rampage killing at Hollins Woods Middle School in Port Huron, Michigan, on May 15. On May 20, a boy upset with his girlfriend brought a gun to Heritage High School in Conyers, Georgia, and attempted to shoot her.

Terrified school administrators hardened their school environments by increasing hall patrols, installing metal detectors and security cameras, recording all incoming telephone calls, meeting and coordinating security policies with local police, and mandating zero tolerance antiviolence policies, many of which abrogated the First Amendment rights of students. The American Civil Liberties Union (ACLU) was swamped with telephone calls from students and parents complaining about the arbitrary suspensions and expulsions of students for writing satirical essays, wearing trench coats, black clothing, or Marilyn Manson T-shirts to school. Many expressed opinions that might have been construed as sympathetic to Harris and Klebold (Graves 1999).

Since the initial reaction, numerous other school shootings have occurred, including a rampage killing by Charles "Andy" Williams in Santee, California, on March 5, 2001, in which he killed two students and wounded thirteen others. Williams claimed to be exacting revenge for the bullying and intimidation he received from his peers (Roth 2001). Less than three weeks later, on March 22, 2001, at neighboring Granite Hills High School, former student Jason Hoffman shot and wounded five persons before he was shot and disabled by a school security officer. Between those two shootings, on March 7, Elizabeth Bush wounded a fellow student in the cafeteria at Bishop Newman High School, in Williamsport, Pennsylvania. She was a victim of teasing by her peers. Of the twenty school shootings in which persons were injured or killed since 1996, this was the only one perpetrated by a female. On September 24, 1993, Jason McLaughlin killed two fellow students at Rocori High School in Cold Springs, Minnesota. McLaughlin claimed that one of the victims had bullied him; the second death was the result of a stray bullet.

On March 22, 2005, Jeffrey Wiese, the grandson of the former tribal police chief of the Ojibwa nation, killed his grandparents, five fellow students, a security guard, and himself in a rampage shooting at his high school on the Red Lake Indian Reservation in northern Minnesota, in the worst shooting since Columbine (Wilogoren 2005b). Wiese patterned his attack after Columbine by wearing a black trench coat to the school and asking a fellow student if he believed in God before killing him. Wiese, like Eric Harris and Dylan Klebold, flirted with Nazism, posting messages on Nazi web sites under the names of "Native Nazi" and "Todesengel," German for "angel of death." He complained of lack of pride and advocated racial purity among members of his tribe (Wilogoren 2005a). At the time of the shootings, he was being home-schooled because of threats that he had made toward the school.

Columbine is arguably the most famous high school in America. Its name is synonymous with the rampage killings of Harris and Klebold. In the wake of the shootings, a new term, the "Columbine effect," has emerged, which refers to the increased willingness of students to inform authorities when they hear of an act of violence about to be committed by their peers. Prior to Columbine, this did not happen. In the post-Columbine period, numerous plans of violent adolescents have been disrupted, including the capture of Al Joseph DeGuzman, on February 1, 2001. DeGuzman planned a shooting rampage at De Anza College in California and had stockpiled weapons and bombs in preparation for the assault, which was planned for February 2nd. In November 2001, an attempt at a rampage shooting in New Bedford, Massachusetts, was foiled because a student overheard the plans and reported them to authorities. The planned attack was conspicuously modeled after Columbine (Butterfield and McFadden 2001).

Meanwhile, in Columbine, just to the west of Littleton, Colorado, what was once just another newly-developed affluent suburb with its tracts of three-, four-, and five-bedroom houses on winding streets with a spectacular view of the Rocky Mountains, emotions ran rampant. Three processes were occurring simultaneously and mutually contradictorily. First was the necessary gathering together and mourning of a community in great pain over the loss of its children and a teacher. Second were recriminations, assessment of blame, and questioning of the behavior of authorities, both prior to and subsequent to the attacks. Third was the media circus.

From the moment the shootings began, confusion reigned. News of the shootings was communicated rapidly throughout the valley. Within the first minutes of the attack, children inside the school were calling parents and 911 on their cell phones. The news media were alerted and had crews on the scene by 11:30 A.M. Brooks Brown, a friend of Eric Harris, had encountered, by pure happenstance, Eric in the parking lot just minutes prior to the assault. Harris told him to go home immediately and not look back. He went to smoke a cigarette, unaware of what was happening. When he realized that Eric and Dylan were attacking the school, he phoned first the police and then his father, and again he called the police. Panicked parents approached the school and were told by police officers that they would not be allowed near the school and that they were to pick up their children at the Leawood Elementary School gymnasium, which was located a few blocks away. Anxious parents had to wait as school buses ferried students from Columbine High School to the elementary school. As each school bus pulled up, relieved parents hugged and kissed their children in tearful reunions. However, confusion and apprehension grew later in the afternoon as waiting parents were told that more buses were coming. When it was determined that no more buses would be arriving from the high school, horrified parents understood that their children was either dead or seriously wounded. They were inconsolable; several parents walked out of the gymnasium and vomited.

Harris and Klebold compiled hit lists that numbered sixty-seven students against whom they had grudges. Their behavior during the rampage seems to indicate that if they came across people they actually disliked, they would have killed them, but they encountered only two persons who were specifically mentioned in their hit lists. The names on their lists have not been revealed by the police, although they revealed that apparently one person on a hit list was wounded in the assault. Apparently, the other one was not hurt. Specific targets were not the goal of Harris and Klebold; they were there to inflict pain on the entire community. If that was their goal, then they surely succeeded.

Columbine High School was not just a good school; it was one of the best schools in the state. Its students won academic honors. Its sports teams, especially its football and soccer teams, were perennial contenders for state championships; their football team, the Rebels, won the state championship in their division in 2000, 2001, and in 2003 (Tobias 1999). Their marching band had recently marched in the Fiesta Bowl and Rose Bowl Parades; the band finished sixth in state competition. Columbine High School cultivated an image of clean-living, God-fearing, virtuous youth. The school won Jefferson County's Paul Davis Sportsmanship Award two years running (Kurtz 1999). Columbine students averaged in the seventy-first percentile in reading and the seventy-sixth percentile in math nationwide; 82 percent of its seniors go on to college. Ninety-one percent of the teachers at Columbine are teaching in their own area of expertise (*Columbine High School* 2001).

The shootings came as a terrible shock to what had been a self-satisfied community. On television, on April 20, 1999, a burning image of the shock of the community was portrayed by a teacher, her keys hanging from a blue and white Columbine Rebels' lanyard around her neck, crying out over and over, "How could this happen here?"

Because Columbine is in unincorporated territory, government seems to be at arm's length. Governmental services, including education, are provided by Jefferson County whose offices are located in Golden, about fifteen to twenty miles away. The city of Littleton is several miles to the east and is in neighboring Arapaho County. Southern Jefferson County has no town hall, no post office, and no police department. Much closer, the local community is held together more intimately by its many religious institutions. It is not surprising that the clergy were the most visible leaders in the healing process. Churches were opened to anyone who needed comforting; youth groups gathered daily. A major response to the horror of the shootings was to present Columbine as a majority of residents viewed it: patriotic, religious, and unified in its opposition to the evil perpetrated by Harris and Klebold. Beginning with the memorial service five days after the shootings, Americans became familiar with the call and response, "We are...Columbine!"

From President Clinton to Jerry Nelson, the pastor of Southern Gables Evangelical Free Church, people called for a time of reflection and healing. Prayers were given for the souls of the dead and for the recovery of the wounded. People prayed publicly and privately. Jonathan and Stephen Cohen, Columbine students, composed a song of comfort, entitled "Columbine, Friend of Mine." An excerpt reads:

Can you still hear raging guns
Ending dreams of precious ones.
In God's sun, hope will come,
His red stain will take our pain.
Columbine, friend of mine.
Peace will come to you in time.
Columbine, friend of mine.

Few communities in America are as culturally homogenous as Columbine. As in all communities, however, an event as momentous as a shooting is bound to create divisions. As time passed, the reflection and healing process looked more like the eye of a hurricane. Controversies broke out about the actions of the SWAT teams and the decisions made by Jefferson County Sheriff Stone. Residents asked how Harris and Klebold were able to arm themselves with semiautomatic weapons. Accusations about the harassment of students at Columbine High School by athletes and the laissez-faire attitude of the staff toward such behaviors were trumpeted in the media. The question of the culpability of the parents of Dylan Klebold and Eric Harris was raised. Lawsuits proliferated: the parents of Isaiah Sholes filed suits against the Klebolds and Harrises; the school district and the sheriff's office were sued for negligence because of failure to provide sufficient security at Columbine High School and failure to act on the early warning signs of Harris's and Klebold's violent attitudes. The Klebolds and Harrises sued the sheriff's department over the ownership of their sons' videotapes made prior to the assault. Additionally, the sheriff's department was being sued by numerous complainants, including the parents of Daniel Rohrbough, who contended that their son was shot not by Klebold but by law-enforcement fire. The wife of Dave Sanders, the murdered teacher, sued over the delay in allowing emergency medical services personnel to minister to her husband's wounds, which resulted in his bleeding to death. Parents of the victims sued the three persons who procured weapons for Harris and Klebold.

In addition, whispers were heard among members of liberal Protestant sects concerning the evangelical cast of the memorial service. Reverend Jerry Nelson's veiled anti-Semitism in his sermon during the memorial service created controversy. The myth that Cassie Bernall was murdered because she said she believed in God caught on and spread through the evangelical community like wildfire. Tensions between evangelicals and liberal Protestants that had hitherto been suppressed emerged.

Columbine was the largest mass murder on American shores between the Oklahoma City bombing in 1996 and the attacks on the Pentagon and the World

Trade Center on September 11, 2001. It received extensive coverage for months in national media. After the initial coverage, local news outlets, especially the *Rocky Mountain News*, the *Denver Post*, and *Westword* (a local weekly), kept their readers updated on the police investigations, the various lawsuits, and reactions of the local communities to the shooting.

The Columbine shootings were the most intensively reported and investigated act of violence in the history of American education (Muschert 2002). To this day, there is no coherent explanation as to why Klebold and Harris took it upon themselves to try to destroy their high school and kill as many of their peers as possible. After months of investigation, John Stone, Sheriff of Jefferson County admitted:

> In preparing this report, we have relied on the work of approximately 80 investigators from all levels of government. Under the direction of the Jefferson Sheriff's County Office, the investigators contacted students, teachers, and others who may have had information about the crime. In all, investigators concluded about 4,400 leads. They examined videotapes, 911 recordings, posted reports, medical and autopsy reports, and physical evidence collected at the scene and the conspirators' residences. …
>
> While this report establishes the record of events of April 20th, it cannot answer the fundamental question—WHY ? That is, why would two young men, in the spring of their lives, choose to murder faculty and classmates? The evidence provides no definitive explanation, and the question continues to haunt us all (Jefferson County Sheriff's Office 1999).

Because of its magnitude, the assault on Columbine High School has become an important sociocultural event. In the wake of the shootings, a variety of pundits have suggested numerous causal factors: harassment and bullying, video games, television violence, homophobia, religious hatred, mental illness, political liberalism, lack of values, easy access to weapons, rock-and-roll music, the goth youth subculture, lack of parental supervision, and even Jewish conspiracies. Some explanations are counterfactual, others may have some basis in fact but their influences may be different than originally thought, and still others may be suggestive but misguided. In addition, contributing factors, such as the influence of a paramilitary culture, have not been explored. As an example of counterfactual arguments, in the wake of the shootings, several web sites sprouted, suggesting Klebold and Harris's rampage was a Jewish conspiracy because Klebold's mother is Jewish, although the family occasionally attended

Lutheran services. Although Zoba (2000) rightfully maintained that religious hatred motivated the shootings, she failed to analyze why the boys hated evangelicals in the first place. If the boys were seeking retribution, the question arises, "Retribution for what?"

Despite all the speculation, there is no comprehensive understanding as to why it happened and why it happened where it did. What is it about Columbine that created a climate in which two boys could hate so much, define themselves as superhuman, and reserve for themselves the right to kill as many people as they possibly could? Although investigators repeatedly indicated that Klebold and Harris were equal opportunity haters, they were not equal opportunity killers. They went after their peers, their school, and their community. In order to piece together the reasons why Klebold and Harris engaged in their rampage, we need to investigate not only those factors that impinged upon their lives in the immediacy of family and peer relationships, but we must examine the institutions of our society and the cultural trends that contributed to their behavior.

In this book, several sources are explored, including interviews my wife, Debra Larkin, and I conducted with reporters, members of the community, Columbine students, religious leaders, and experts in the field, as well as media reports, books written about Columbine, and police investigation documents, in order to piece together a comprehensive understanding of the factors leading to the Columbine shootings. As a consequence of the investigation, several explanations could be ruled out immediately because of the lack of supporting data or because they were unverifiable assertions that could not possibly be explored empirically. In the former category were explanations such as political liberalism and lack of parental supervision. In the latter category were lack of values and the presence of Satan. It was obvious from the outset that the boys had easy access to a high-powered weapons and explosives. However, such access did not cause the shootings; rather, it enabled the shootings and bombings to occur. Another enabling factor was the use of violent video games, although not in the way alleged in the media. Rock-and-roll music and goth subcultures gave vent to feelings of alienation; however, whatever links there were between German industrial music, the boys' favorite genre, and the shootings were, at best, tentative.

In this book, four major themes are explored in relation to the shootings:

(1) the presence and tolerance of intimidation, harassment, and bullying within the halls of Columbine High School and on the streets of the larger community
(2) religious intolerance and chauvinism in southern Jefferson County

(3) the rise and popularity of paramilitary culture in Western states in the 1990s

(4) the culture of celebrity in postmodern America. Subsumed within these four major themes are the roles of video games, television, rock-and-roll music, adolescent subcultures, and mental illness.

2

GOD'S COUNTRY

COLUMBINE IS GOD'S COUNTRY in at least two ways: first, it is nestled into the foothills of the Rocky Mountains. To the east is 1000 miles of plains. From the mile high city of Denver, the eastern escarpment of the Rocky Mountains rises another mile and a half in altitude. Running north and south for as far as the eye can see is the magnificent mountain range that forms the continental divide of this country. The vistas fare breathtaking and spectacular. Few suburbanites are as fortunate as those in southern Jefferson County who can sit on their patios and have a majestic view of the mountains, many of which are snowcapped year-round. Figure 2.1 is a view of the Rockies in the spring, a few miles north of Littleton.

The second reason that Columbine is God's country is because it is literally viewed that way by the many evangelical Christians who live in the area. Columbine is openly and sometimes aggressively religious. It has one the largest concentrations of Christian evangelicals in the country. Perhaps the clearest expression of the fusion of physical and spiritual expressions of the divine is in the pulpit of the West Bowles Community Church, an evangelical Presbyterian congregation that sits at the western end of southern Jefferson County. The Church is laid out so that the parishioners are facing west. In the center of the pulpit is a twenty-foot-wide, forty-foot-high window that faces the Rocky Mountains. During services, the window is

FIGURE 2.1: *A view of the Rockies from near Golden in late spring*

sometimes fully covered with a curtain. When the curtain is opened, congregants are exposed to an unobstructed view of the Rocky Mountains in front of which is superimposed a simple outline of a cross.

Before proceeding, geographical confusions need to be cleared up. Columbine is an unincorporated territory in southern Jefferson County. It is west of Littleton, which is separated from Columbine administratively because it is incorporated as its own city and because it is located in Arapahoe County. In Littleton, housing is older and more modest than in Columbine. Just to the west of Littleton is a small, mostly uninhabited area called "Columbine Valley." Further west is the Columbine High School catchment area. Between Littleton on the east, Chatfield Reservoir on the south, State Highway 470 on the west, and the city of Lakewood on the north, three high schools, Chatfield, Columbine, and Dakota Ridge, serve students in that region of southern Jefferson County. Because the Jefferson County schools allow for a certain amount of choice of schools, mobility of students between high schools is common. However, the catchment area of Columbine High School is in the eastern area of the territory closest to Littleton, referred to by the Jefferson County schools as the "Columbine articulation area" (Jefferson County Public Schools 2004). Thus, the geographic term "Columbine" refers specifically to the catchment area of Columbine High School, which runs from the Littleton and Arapahoe County line on the east to the Chatfield Reservoir on the south, Wadsworth Boulevard on the west, and Lakewood on the north. For the purpose of this study, the term "Columbine" will be used to designate the territory in southern Jefferson County bounded by Arapahoe County on the east, Route 470 on the south and west, and Bowles reservoir and West Bellevue Avenue on the north.

Although typically suburban in terms of housing developments with serpentine roads set off, sometimes in the form of a gated community, from broad straight streets that are populated by strip malls, it has an aura of squeaky cleanliness. Housing developments are separated from each other by uncultivated open spaces, parks, rivulets, and ponds. It is common to see developments separated from each other by several acres of prairie grass.

Because the county seat is in Golden, twenty miles away in northern Jefferson County, the major evidence of government in the area is the schools. Much more prominent noncommercial social institutions are the numerous churches that populate the area. The self-image of southern Jefferson County is that of peaceful Christians living in harmony with each other and with their environment. The people of Columbine are deeply religious. The Littleton-Columbine area contains about 60,000 residents and seventy Christian churches, including one Eastern Orthodox congregation. If we assume an average family size of four persons, that means that there is one religious institution for every 200 to 250 families. Of the seventy churches, twenty-three are mainline Protestant churches,

TABLE 1.1 HOUSING STATISTICS FOR COLUMBINE AND UNITED STATES

	COLUMBINE	U.S.
Housing Occupant (%)		
Owner	85.05	66.19
Renter	14.95	33.81
Number of Bedrooms (%)		
None	0.70	3.25
1	5.81	14.70
2	15.01	31.20
3	31.64	42.16
4	40.93	15.18
5 or more	8.22	3.40
Median Value of Owner Occupied Houses	$232,625	$115,012
Year House Built (Columbine Only, %)		
1990–2000	24.77	
1980–1989	16.77	
1970–1979	44.46	
1960–1969	12.06	
1959 or earlier	1.94	

Note: data are drawn from the U. S. Bureau of Census, 2000 decennial census for the United States total population excluding Puerto Rico and for the eight census tracts that cover Columbine (Jefferson County Census Tracts 120.48-120.55).

including Methodist, Presbyterian, Lutheran, and Episcopalian; four are Catholic. The most popular sect by far, however, is the Baptist Church, with ten separate congregations. Other fundamentalist congregations include the Assembly of God, Calvary Chapel, Disciples of Christ, Church of Christ, Gospel (Four Square and Full), Holiness, Church of the Nazarene, and Pentecostal. In addition to these are numerous evangelical congregations, with the West Bowles Community Church (Evangelical Presbyterian) one of the largest and most successful congregations in the area.

Columbine is a new community, developed over the last thirty years. According to the United States Census Bureau, nearly one-quarter of the buildings in the area are ten years old or less (Table 1.1). Nearly half of the houses built in Columbine were constructed in the 1970s. In addition, and can be seen in Table 1.1, the vast majority of homes are owner-occupied and are quite large, with virtually half of them having four or more bedrooms, according children their own private spaces. The median value of houses in Columbine is twice the national average ($232,625 compared to $115,012 in 2000).

Visual observation of the Columbine High School catchment area reveals two major types of housing: detached single-family dwellings and town houses. Some townhouse developments feature modest two- and three-bedroom homes, while others tend to be much larger. Similarly, nearly all single-family dwelling units are parts of large developments. Some older developments, such as those at the eastern boundary of Columbine near Littleton, tend to be older and smaller than those built to the west. These developments contain three- and four-bedroom single-story ranch-style houses. The developments further west and closer to the mountains are more likely to be two-story homes with a greater number of rooms. An aerial view of southern Jefferson County suggests that real estate is being developed from east to west and from north to south. Residential areas closest to Littleton are fairly dense with little in the way of undeveloped territory. To the south and west, residential developments become sparser with more tracts of undeveloped acreage. Some developments to the south and west are surrounded by open fields. Southern Jefferson County is still in the process of being developed as it spreads south and west.

Columbine is a bastion of upper-middle-class whites. The graphs below tell the tale. Columbine is over 90 percent white (Figure 2.2). The second largest category, Latinos, with slightly more than 5 percent, is virtually invisible as a separate ethnic category. My observations of Columbine suggested that the majority of Latinos are white persons with Spanish surnames; I did not see many persons with Latino features. Similarly, black people were quite rare. The only time I observed Asians was at an all-Asian pickup basketball game in Clement Park;

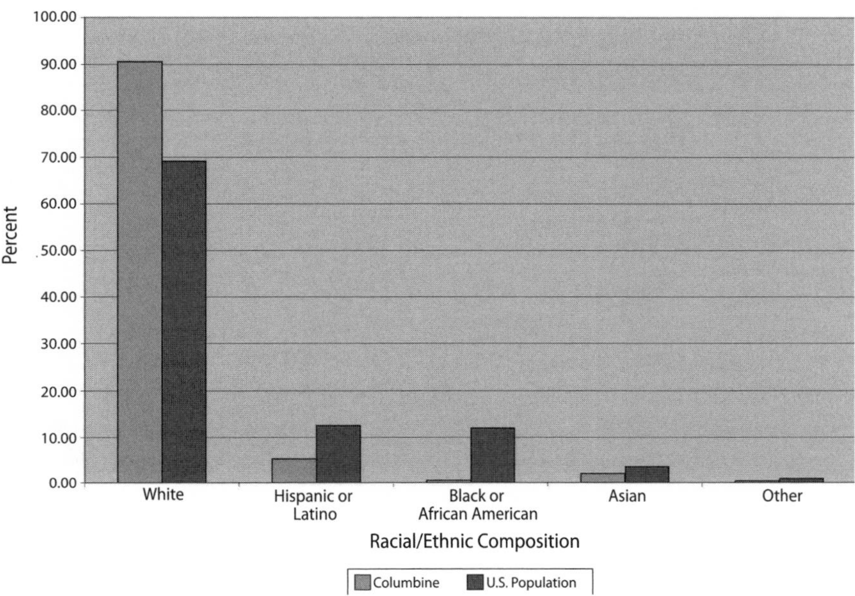

FIGURE 2.2: *Racial composition of Columbine and the United States*

two carloads of Asian teenagers drove into a parking space near the basketball court and played a game among themselves. No players from any other ethnic group were involved.

Some students commented on the overwhelming whiteness of the area. On his web site, Eric Harris commented, "Littleton, Colorado, isn't a great place to grow up as a white boy. If I had my druthers, I'd be anywhere else at all, even in some place with lots of malt-liquor-drinking, rhyme-busting, ass-capping Negroes and perhaps a few squinty-eyed, dog-eating Chinese people!"(Harris's web site now defunct.) When I interviewed four females, formerly students at Columbine High School, they mused about how white Columbine was and wondered whether it prepared them for living in a more racially and culturally diverse world. Jeff Stark, former Columbine student and writer for Salon.com, wrote that he and his friends called the place, "Little fun" because nothing ever happened there. It was boring.

Not only is the populace of Columbine overwhelmingly white, they are also overwhelmingly native born. Figure 2.3 compares place of birth for Columbine to the total U.S. population. Columbine is 97 percent native born compared to 89 percent of the general American population. Although 40 percent were born within the State of Colorado, 55 percent were born outside the state. This suggests that Columbine is a place of choice for its adult residents.

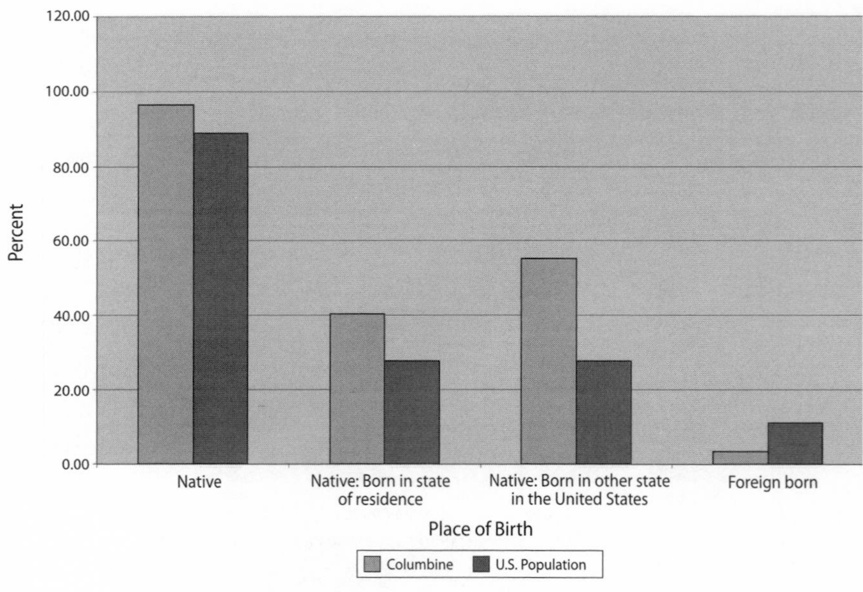

FIGURE 2.3 *Nativity for Columbine and the United States*

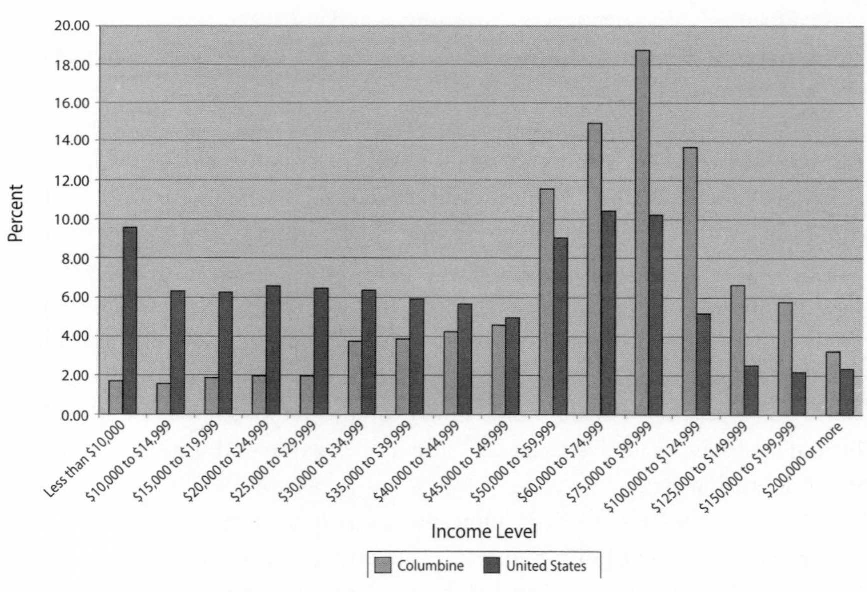

FIGURE 2.4: *Income distribution for Columbine and the United States*

Socioeconomic indicators demonstrate the nearly exclusively upper-middle-class character of Columbine. Figure 2.4 presents the income distribution for Columbine compared to the United States population as a whole. Nearly 60 percent of U.S. families have incomes between $50,000 and $125,000 a year; an additional 15 percent make more than $125,000 a year. The median income for Columbine's families is $61,005, 30 percent higher than the national family median income at $42,690. Approximately 80 percent of the Columbine families have incomes above the national median.

Not surprisingly, Columbine residents have more education than the national populace (Figure 2.5). The U.S. population is split about equally between those persons who have had at least some college education and those with a high school education or less. Slightly more than 50 percent of the national population has completed high school; nearly 80 percent of adults in Columbine completed high school. Twice the proportion of Columbine residents has baccalaureate degrees as the national population (32% to 16%). Compared to 8 percent of the nation as a whole, 13 percent of adult Columbine residents have master's degrees.

The statistics on educational attainment present two surprises: first, the proportion of the population with doctorate degrees in Columbine is smaller than

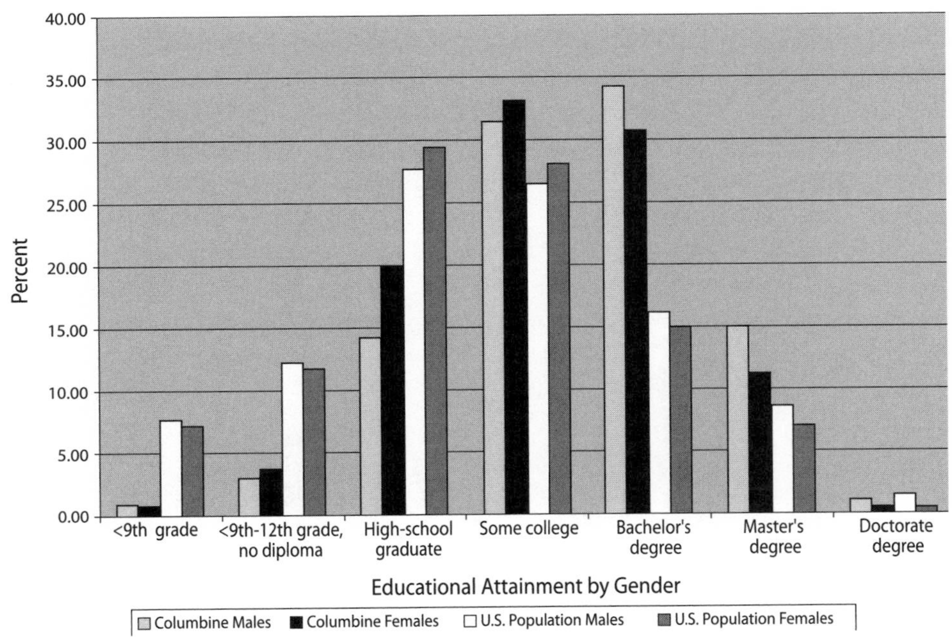

FIGURE 2.5: *Educational attainment for Columbine and for the United States by gender*

in the national population (1.08 to 1.38 for males; 0.43 to 0.58 for females). These data suggest that Columbine is an upper-middle-class community; however, when compared to other upper middle-class communities, it has fewer high-end professionals, such as medical doctors, college professors, Ph.D.-level psychologists, and other professionals with doctorates (e.g., doctors of education, social work, or business administration). This may be because there are no large hospitals in the area, although the Colorado Mental Health Institute at Fort Logan is about five miles away, University of Denver is about ten miles away and the downtown Denver educational complex housing the University of Colorado Denver campus, Denver (Metro) State College, and Denver Community College is about twenty miles to the north.

The second surprise is that the differential between educational attainment of men and women in Columbine is greater than that in the general population, especially among college graduates and those with master's degrees. In the general population, the difference between males and females is slightly more than 1 percent in favor of the males. In Columbine, the percentage differences between the genders in those two categories are between 3 percent and 4 percent, with a greater portion of the males having higher degrees. Slightly more than 50 percent of the adult males in Columbine are college educated; only 42 percent of the females have bachelor degrees, a difference of 8 percent. This

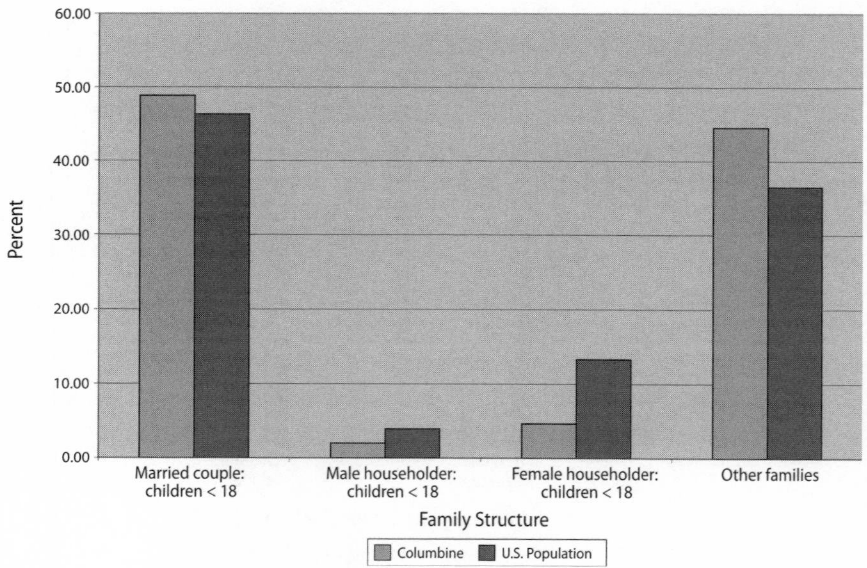

FIGURE 2.6: *Family composition for Columbine and the United States*

differential is more than twice that of the national population, in which 26 percent of the men and 23 percent of the women have a college education, a difference of about 3 percent. These statistics suggest that Columbine, relative to the nation as a whole, may have a smaller proportion of professional women than other upper middle-class communities. Columbine has an aura about it of having intact nuclear families characterized by stay-at-home moms. Indeed, this image is bolstered by statistics on family composition (Figure 2.6).

Although Columbine is fairly typical of the nation in its proportion of married couples with children under eighteen (49% to 46%), dramatic differences are found between Columbine and the national population in single householder families: Approximately 5 percent of Columbine families are headed by a single female; the national rate is nearly three times that (14%). Similarly, households headed by a single male constitute 2 percent of Columbine families and 4 percent of the total population.

The demographics bear out media impressions of Columbine: it is a solidly white, affluent suburb that takes a certain amount of pride in its political and cultural conservatism. It has more intact families than most places in the United States. It is a place where families move to raise children; it has a reputation for excellent schools. Recreational facilities and open areas abound. Within a mile of Columbine High School are the Southwest Plaza Regional Mall and Bowles Crossing Shopping Center, constituting one of the largest shopping areas in the region.

The economic basis for the Littleton-Southern Jefferson County area is primarily high-tech corporations. The largest employer in the area is Qwest Communications, with 47,000 employees, 3,000 of whom are employed in Littleton (City of Littleton 2004). Qwest is a telecommunications company that provides satellite and landline telecommunication services. The second largest private employer is EchoStar, a national company of 15,000 employees, of which 1,900 are headquartered in Littleton. The company maintains eight orbital satellites and sells receiver dishes to clients for telecommunications, including television. The third largest private employer is Lockheed Martin space systems, with between six and seven hundred employees. It was featured prominently in Michael Moore's film, "Bowling for Columbine." Moore noted that the facility was involved in secret defense research and was part of the military-industrial complex. The fourth-largest private employer is Norgren, a company of six hundred employees that makes pneumatic valves. The remainder of the employers have fewer than five hundred employees. Of the remaining employers that have between one hundred and five hundred employees, six are car dealerships; the Mercedes-Benz dealer has one hundred employees, and the local Lexus dealership employs 150. The success of the dealerships can be witnessed on the roads. My informal observations suggested that about half of the private vehicles on the roads are either late model SUVs or pickup trucks. The only place where I saw more sedans than SUVs was in the teachers' parking lot at Columbine High School.

Here is the embodiment of the American dream: spacious suburban homes, strip malls, schools, large recreational areas, and churches. Columbine might be considered Colorado's Bible belt. Fifty miles to the south of Columbine is Colorado Springs, the very heart of the Christian right, headquarters of Focus on the Family and home to one of the largest chapters of the Christian Coalition in the country (Cooper 1995). A Mormon regional center that serves several states is located in Littleton (Cullen 1999a). Columbine residents view themselves as hard-working, morally upright, patriotic, American citizens. Most are Republicans and proud of it. They believe in racial tolerance even though in their community there are very few racial minorities to tolerate. They see themselves, as nearly all Americans do, as good people. They view their lives of privilege as evidence of the goodness of an American society that rewards virtue with material well-being and strong communities of like-minded individuals.

COLUMBINE HIGH SCHOOL, APRIL 19, 1999

Columbine High School is a comprehensive high school that serves about 1800 students on a sprawling campus, which is part of a large educational and recreational complex that contains Robert F. Clement Park, Johnson Reservoir, and the Columbine Public Library. The school campus occupies about one-fourth of the territory located just south of Clement Park. The school itself consists of a single building surrounded by play fields. Figure 2.7 shows Rebel Hill, behind the playing fields, where the fifteen crosses were first placed following the shootings. Figure 2.8 shows the Columbine High School sign at the Pierce Avenue entrance to the school.

Columbine High School was described to this researcher by Frank DeAngelis, the principal, as a typical suburban high school. He described the school in glowing terms:

> D: Probably about 80 percent of our students go on to college. Academics are very important. We have a majority of our students that take at least three or four years of math, in addition to the other requirements—three or four years of math aren't required. Our students do

FIGURE 2.7: *Rebel Hill*

very well academically: not only do they attend college in the state of Colorado, but around the nation. As far as test scores on standardized tests, we're always near the top. Jefferson County, the school district, we're near the top in the state.

RL: Are you talking about SATs?

D: SATs, ACT … in Colorado within the last five or six years, CSTAPT scores, which are Colorado State Assessment Program, and once again our students did very well as freshmen and sophomores on that standardized test. I think it's really a great comprehensive educational program. We're a very traditional school, eight periods a day, fifty-minutes a period; we're not on block schedule. [We have] a very established staff. Now that's changed a little bit over the past few years since we've been losing a few teachers due to retirement. The majority of our staff members have master's degrees. We have over thirty-one clubs where the students can participate. There can be full curricula clubs, there's forensics, and debate, we have an outstanding performing arts program, our vocal music and instrumental programs are large programs. We have three full-time staff members in the music area, and over forty kids are involved in our music program.

FIGURE 2.8: *Columbine High School sign, Pierce Avenue*

Mr. DeAngelis's characterization of the quality of the instructional program was corroborated by the state accountability report (Colorado Department of Education 2003), which ranked Columbine High School as "high" in academic performance, using a five-category scheme with the following ranks: unsatisfactory, low, average, high, and excellent. However, most of the comprehensive high schools in the Littleton-Southern Jefferson County area were similarly rated. Heritage High School, located in the city of Littleton and serving approximately the same number of students, was ranked "excellent." Typically, high schools serving upper-middle-class white populations, such as Columbine, have an academic program that is quite good and apparently up to the expectations of the community. Following the shootings, *Rocky Mountain News* reporter Lynn Bartels (1999) interviewed Columbine student Elsa Coffey-Berg who had been sitting next to one of the unexploded bombs left by Klebold and Harris. Elsa, the reporter noted, was planning to study international relations at Colorado State University. The following characterization of Columbine High School was excerpted from the interview:

> Elsa Coffey-Berg's parents checked out Jefferson County schools before they moved to Colorado from Idaho in 1998. "We chose Columbine because of its academics," Elsa said. "We had chosen this school because it was so, like, perfect."... Over the years, she's wondered where the

> stories are on the good things about Columbine, the choir singing in nursing homes or National Honor Society members performing community service. "I'm really glad I'm at Columbine. There's no place that [I] would rather graduate from. There are great teachers[,] and I have great friends. I love it here."

In a letter to the editor of the *Phi Delta Kappan*, an educational journal, Marilyn Salzman (2001) spokesperson for the Jefferson County Schools, characterized Columbine High School as follows:

> Columbine High School has a 26-year history of excellence. Last year, its students had the highest SAT scores of the 16 neighborhood high schools in Jefferson County, Colorado. About 85% of Columbine students go on to college. The daily attendance rate is 95%, and the graduation rate is 93%.
>
> The school has an award-winning forensics team, a world-class band, a model peer-counseling program, and state championship sports teams. Seven of the past eight years Columbine has won the Paul Davis Sportsmanship Award for Jefferson County. The winning school is chosen by a vote of every varsity athletic coach.

The extent of student participation in extracurricular activities characterized by Principal DeAngelis was supported by student interviews. The debate team had between thirty and forty members. The Drama Club was large and had an enthusiastic following; their productions were highly successful and included a sophisticated repertoire. Columbine High School was characterized not just as a good school, but one of the best in the state. Even students who were harsh critics of the school spoke of its academic program positively. Typically, students divided teachers into those they loved and those who were "assholes." However, according to the students, Columbine High School certainly had its share of gifted teachers. For example:

> Mr. [X] ... would send you to the principal's office for swearing in class, and I mean saying "hell" or "damn," period, swearing. If you were late, if you ditched, he called your parents. He took away a letter grade. He did not fuck around. And we loved his class more than anything. My favorite class[es] I've ever had was his philosophy class, and my history class I had with him. He was the most hard-ass teacher. So it has nothing to do with being a hard ass. A lot of teachers think, "Well, I'm not as

easy-going so the kids are going to hate me." He was a super hard ass. He was a *brilliant* teacher. He knew what he was talking about. The requirement for the philosophy class, as far as curriculum in Jefferson County goes, because they'd just started philosophy classes [was that] we had to learn and understand and be able to discuss intelligently Plato and Aristotle, all these western philosophers. So [X], instead of having us waste time on all these Western philosophers that you really don't need to know any more, we spent six weeks on them, we learned them, we had them memorized, we did them, and then we went on to Eastern philosophy. Then we spent maybe six or seven weeks doing tai-chi in class, learning Lao Tzu, all these brilliant philosophers that weren't even part of the class. And he didn't just know them; he knew everything about every one of these philosophers. He could discuss it with us.

He [Mr. X] didn't make fun of kids. He never said anyone had a wrong answer. He knew to direct them and show them how they could be "more right" is how he put it. And even kids who were the dumbest sons-of-bitches I ever met in my life, like this one kid on the football team, [K], he was probably the stupidest person I ever met intelligence-wise, he was just lower. He could not hold a conversation about anything. It was sad. And he raised his hand in Mr. [X's] class, this kid who never talked. He raised his hand, and he and I had debates in class. I mean he reached kids, like freakish. He knew, he cared, he got to them—brilliant. The best teacher, the way all teachers should be, is Mr. [X], above and beyond all things (Recorded May 13, 2003).

Another student revealed the following:

I thought I got a good education [at Columbine High School] for the most part, and anything that was for my disadvantage was my own fault. The big thing as far as my education at Columbine was that there were two math programs at Columbine. You could chose the traditional math program, where you do problem after problem after problem, and there's the interactive math program which is word problems where you have to show that you know what you're doing with the equation rather than solving it a million times. Which is good in its own right, but there's not a lot of repetition and I fell behind in math. I took four years but then I had to take remedial courses in high school to catch myself up. But as far as the English department, they were all wonderful. Science department was wonderful. Social science department was wonderful, gym was

> wonderful—I couldn't have asked for much better. I would have liked a few more advanced placement opportunities and Honors programs but you know, it's public school and it's hard to offer much of that, especially when you're Jefferson County. . . . We had AP classes, but you couldn't really get into anything until your senior year. The only option that you had before senior year was that you could take accelerated chemistry or accelerated physics (Recorded April 10, 2003).

A student who attended the University of Colorado, the state's premier public educational institution, had this to say about her education at Columbine High School:

> RL: Now how well did you feel you were prepared for college?
>
> EK: Since I took a lot of, you could say, "tough courses"—I took AP English, AP History, statistics, Spanish, and stuff life that, I took a lot of the harder, more demanding classes my senior year, rather than slacking off, so going into college—granted, I felt I was prepared in some aspects; in other aspects I wasn't. You know, from the educational level I'd say I was prepared for it, but for going from, I'd say, an overprotective mother to having a lot of independence, that was a big change. Based on academics, I felt I was prepared.
>
> RL: Did you see much change in your grade point average between high school and college?
>
> EK: No [giggle], it stayed exactly the same.
>
> RL: That's interesting.
>
> EK: I was really scared, because at orientation at CU they told us that your grade point average would drop a whole point from high school to college. And I was like, "Oh great, I'm going to go from a 3.7, 3.6, down to a 2.7, 2.6." I mean it would fluctuate, based on the semester, but I went out pulling a 3.3 (Recorded May 5, 2003).

EK continued to talk about a favorite teacher at Columbine High School who retired and only substituted at Columbine:

> EK: He would only really substitute at Columbine. I actually invited him to my college graduation party, but he was unable to attend. So that's how memorable he was to me.
>
> RL: And it sounds like he's got a real allegiance to Columbine.
>
> EK: Yeah, he did.

RL: And why was that, do you think?

EK: He said because of the students. The atmosphere at Columbine is because of—he said the students because of their behavior, that they were there to learn rather than just to, you know, screw around. He got the impression that the students really cared (Recorded May 5, 2003).

A consensus existed among students, faculty, and Principal DeAngelis that Columbine offered students a rigorous academic program that prepared them for higher education. In addition, a wide range of student clubs and programs existed that allowed students to participate in numerous academically related activities such as forensics, drama, music, computers, and so forth. The level of student participation in what C. Wayne Gordon (1957) called the "semicurriculum" of sports, clubs, interest groups, and school activities was extremely high. In my study of a suburban high school in 1976 (Larkin 1979), I found that the motivational and communal basis for participation in high school activities had been decimated; students tended to view school as unpaid labor. Therefore, the vast majority withdrew from voluntary participation. The club structure in that suburban high school had withered away to the point of nonexistence. Students who participated in clubs did so cynically, with an eye to putting such participation on their college applications.

This was not the case with Columbine High School, which had a rich club structure and high levels of student participation. In the quotation above, Principal DeAngelis characterized Columbine High School as "traditional." In another interview, he described the high school as "conservative" with a highly religious student body. Indeed, Columbine High School seems to be a throwback to the 1950s in many ways: overwhelmingly white, strong academically, sports crazy, with a high level of school spirit, heavy participation in school clubs, and well-behaved students. Prior to the shootings on April 20, 1999, Columbine High School was a source of community pride; today, it still is a source of pride, perhaps even more fiercely than before the shootings. On this researcher's first visit to Columbine High School, every member of the office staff was dressed in Columbine High School insignia wear: It was Columbine Pride Day, and staffers took it seriously. However, there is a defensiveness to that pride as a consequence of the negative publicity associated with the Columbine High School shootings. In the spring of 2003, this researcher happened upon a group of one female and four male Columbine High School seniors at a restaurant who were anticipating the end of the school year. Suggesting that they were members of the leading crowd, they claimed that all students were treated equally at Columbine High School by the administration, and that the administration does a great job in controlling harassment. They claimed that harassment of low-status students by student athletes was more reminiscent of middle school conflicts. A reporter returning from the fifth anniversary memorial of the shootings informed this researcher that although students from neighboring Chatfield, Heritage, and Dakota Ridge High Schools were critical of their schools, Columbine students simply could not find anything negative about their school. However, two parents who were interviewed in 2003 and a student who had a younger brother in Columbine High School stated that the harassment had returned and was every bit as strong as before.

LM: [My youngest brother] is a senior now, and he tells me every day Columbine is worse than it's ever been, ever.
DL: In what respect?
LM: In every respect.
JN: Which is scary because my brother graduated in 2001, and he said it was the worst it's ever been.
LM: My brother comes home with new stories every day (Recorded April 30, 2004).

This was corroborated in a story in *Newsweek* magazine on Columbine High School's returned to normality (Meadows 2003), that stated, "One indication that the school is reaching a new normality is that bullying is back" (57).

As much as Columbine High School and the community it served were culturally reminiscent of the 1950s, the intrusion of postmodern culture created anomalies and contradictions. In an interview with a former Columbine student who transferred out prior to the shootings, the following conversation transpired:

RL: So what were your most memorable experiences at Columbine?
ED: Ahh … memorable experiences?
RL: Either positive or negative.
ED: There were a lot of them that I've actually been trying to forget most of them, because it's … I'm sure that like most people's high school experiences, it wasn't pleasant.
RL: What wasn't pleasant?
ED: The complete lack of respect that people show, which I know is standard in all high schools, but I'm not certain if it's standard for the faculty to show that little respect.

RL: To you personally, or just generally?
ED: To anybody who didn't have, who didn't quite fit [in]. …
RL: How'd you find the academic program?
ED: I thought it was absolutely atrocious.
RL: Why?
ED: Because it seemed to me that they taught everybody at the lowest common denominator. They found the slowest learner, and taught at that level (Recorded April 10, 2003).

This was not the only time that students indicated that they felt they were not respected as members of the Columbine community. An evangelical Christian student related the following:

> I've been bullied by more in high school, it's not my peers, and it's not by kids who don't like me, it's by teachers. Maybe it's because I would say [I was] an outspoken kid, but I would say a lot of us, teachers rip you apart. I walked into philosophy the first day: "So, isn't anybody going to tell me they're Christian. Isn't anybody going to tell me that God is what's ultimately real?" And he just went on. And then I had a history teacher that was the same way… . It's like I've learned to be able to go up to that teacher and say, "Listen. During class I didn't feel that you were very fair towards me," and you know that teacher might talk and I was always wrong… . I've had meetings with the principal and teachers, and I still came out wrong, even though it's plain and clear that I'm right. I've had a teacher say in front of myself and my parents and the principal, he said, "I just don't—you know, you're a great kid in your work. I just don't like the way that you live." He said that, and he still has his job. (Recorded May 12, 2003)

The vast majority of Columbine High School students were typical upper-middle-class white students who essentially conformed to the norms of the school. This status pyramid pretty much replicated those of other high schools (Wooden and Blazak, 2001). At the top were athletes and "soches," the popular students who ascended in the peer culture by virtue of athletic feats, physical attractiveness, family status, social skills, and clique membership. In the middle was a vast agglomeration of students differentiated from each other by neighborhood, interests, participation in school clubs and activities, academic achievement, rock-and-roll music tastes, and so forth. At the bottom was a miniscule collection of outcast students: stoners and goths, the latter group consisting of fewer than twenty students.

> RL: So let me ask you this: In Columbine High School—you described yourself as kind of an outcast—and there are a number of high school outcast subcultures—what proportion of the student body at Columbine when you were there would you consider members of the disaffected students, the kids who were outcasts? The school has about 2,000 students in it. About how many students would you say didn't fit into the mold?
>
> ED: Didn't want to be or refused to be?
>
> RL: Refused to be… .
>
> ED: I'd have to say less than 1 percent. Maybe, when I was there, there were 1800 students. There were maybe, maybe a dozen people that fit in that category… . I always thought it was very ironic that the mascot for Columbine was the Rebels because they demand absolute conformity (Recorded April 10, 2003).

Numerous students corroborated the observation of ED: the outcast student population at Columbine High School was minuscule. Although very small relative to the student population, their presence tended to be discomforting to the majority of students, the administration, and a great many of the faculty, with the exception of certain teachers who welcomed them. One student noted:

> Because the loser kids, if we liked the teacher, you can ask the teacher like Ms. A, Mr. X, Mr. B, and Mrs. C. You can ask any of those teachers [about loser kids]. They were the ones who were loved by the loser kids (April 30, 2003).

Thus, within Columbine High School was a very small subculture of disaffected students. To the credit of the faculty, these students, such as ED and others like him who saw themselves as intellectuals not willing to conform to the expectations of the majority, were able to find teachers who liked them and offered support. However, within the mainstream of Columbine High School, nonconforming students were perceived as a blot on the reputation of the high school. They did not fit in, and they did not want to fit in. Their presence made others feel uncomfortable. For some evangelical students, this small group was perceived as evidence of evil.

SPORTS AT COLUMBINE

For the first twenty years that Columbine High School existed, its sports history was fairly typical. As Stark (1999) characterized it, "There were some state champion soccer teams... ." Apart from its outstanding boy's soccer program, in which Columbine teams were always at or near the top of their league and had won several state championships, some teams were good, some were bad, and most were mediocre. This was especially true of the football team. However, in the mid-1990s, at about the time that Frank DeAngelis was appointed principal, Columbine High School emerged as a major power not only in soccer but in football, basketball, and wrestling. DeAngelis, who was a social studies teacher prior to his promotion to principal, had been head coach of the baseball team, which had won state championships in 1987 and in 1991. According to Prendergast (1999), the school won thirty-two state sports championships in the 1990s.

Columbine won its first football state championship in the fall of 1999, the season following the shootings. The victory rally was portrayed in the media as bittersweet (Enlissen 1999). The football team, which had comeback victories from fourteen-point deficits in both the quarterfinal and championship games, was used by Principal DeAngelis as a metaphor for the school as a whole in their struggle to overcome the tragedy of the shootings. They persevered against adversity. DeAngelis said, "This team never quit... . It's about not giving up and that's what Columbine High School represents" (Enlissen 1999).

The Columbine Rebel football team won its second state championship in the fall of 2000. The victory was considered by many to be a part of the healing process (Enlissen 1999). In the following year, Columbine placed second in the Jefferson County 5A conference behind its sister school, Chatfield High, which won. In 2002, Columbine won the state championship with a perfect 14-0 record, and was ranked twenty-second in the United States, an accomplishment that made the front page of the sports section of the *New York Times*. Principal DeAngelis was quoted in the article:

> The team and the school and the community at large had every reason to quit, to give up, to descend into total despair, but we've come out of it to a great degree. The fact is, we'll never be totally back to normal. How can we be? We had every reason to quit, but we didn't let that happen. We showed amazing resolve and resilience, and maybe, in some way, we've given faith to others, who saw how we responded (Berkow 2003, 26 September : D1–D5).

The success of the football team and its national exposure were popularly characterized as evidence that Columbine had successfully transcended the tragedies of the shootings (Berkow 2003; Meadows 2003). The grit, determination, talent, and success of not just the football team but the entire athletic program seem to give Columbine the aura of success.

THE HIGH SCHOOL AND THE COMMUNITY

Southern Jefferson County was mistakenly identified as "Littleton" in the media. The Columbine shootings were described in the major media as "Terror in Littleton" (Stout 1999). Local media, such as the *Rocky Mountain News* and the *Denver Post*, did not make the mistake of identifying Columbine High School with Littleton. Although the closest incorporated community to Columbine, Littleton is not even in the same county. News reports were filed from Littleton because the United States Postal Service identifies that area as part of the Littleton postal zone.

The area in Southern Jefferson County that this researcher has identified as Columbine has no collective identity. It is nothing more than a series of residential developments, strip malls, and shopping centers. A pastor whose life was spent primarily in the Northeast and Midwest characterized the area as follows:

> You could not find community. And the only glue in South Jefferson County was Southwest Mall... . So that was the only sense of community, but there's no official [government] down there. It's unincorporated. So, I mean they can't have a parade anywhere because there's no place to coalesce. So that was kind of goofy. So, it's different getting used to the west. The selfishness in the west is unbelievable. Like Wyoming's barbaric, and Colorado isn't that much better (Recorded April 29, 2004).

Churches, however large, cannot provide a region with a collective identity. Even large churches are too small; congregations cross neighborhoods. Propinquity, social networks, and small ideological differences distinguish various congregations. Although the shopping mall may be a focal point of the area, people come to it as consumers in small groups and as isolated individuals. The mall does not provide a sense of collective identity. It is a place of commerce and not much else.

The only institutions that provide a sense of collective identity are the high schools. Many high schools that cater to an upper-middle-class suburban student population maintain strong academic programs. However, academics do not provide schools with a great deal of visibility. More than anything else, the football team gives a high school, and consequently its community, visibility. When the Columbine High School Rebel football team won the state championship in 2003, the team was featured as the lead article on the front page of the *New York Times* sports section (Berkow 2003) and in a feature article in *Newsweek* magazine (Meadows 2003). The championship game was attended by 7,500 spectators. Perhaps not as impressive as the 10,000 to 15,000 average attendance at Permian High School, perennial high school state champion contender in Odessa, Texas, population 94,000, reputed to be the most sports-crazed city in the country (Bissinger 1990), but certainly respectable.

Southern Jefferson County has no collective identity outside of Columbine High School. Nothing else distinguishes it from the thousands of suburbs ringing urban cores. Much to the dismay of its inhabitants, it is known to the rest of America as the place where the largest school massacre in American history took place. From the ashes of the Columbine shootings has emerged a successful football program that provides a more positive image of the school and the community. Principal Frank DeAngelis is the prime articulator of the spirit, resolve, and desire of the community to present a positive face of a dedicated, hard-working, religious, tolerant, and quintessentially American community.

3

CULTURAL WARS AT COLUMBINE

THE COLUMBINE SHOOTINGS generated a huge religious controversy. In the "basement videotapes" Eric Harris and Dylan Klebold made prior to the shootings, they vilified evangelicals. During their rampage, they insulted and attempted to humiliate students whom they knew were deeply religious. Although there is no evidence that they specifically targeted them, when they came across students who they knew were evangelicals, they were more vicious with them than with other students. Perhaps the most celebrated and bizarre aspect of the shootings was the beatification of Cassie Bernall as a Christian martyr who died proclaiming her faith.

The Columbine shootings provided the grist for a minor cottage industry of books about religion in Columbine. First were hagiographies of Rachel Scott (Nimmo and Klingsporn 2001; Nimmo, Scott, and Rabey 2000; Scott and Rabey 2001) and Cassie Bernall (1999), each of which had a parent as author or coauthor. Second came numerous books and articles written primarily for evangelical audiences and secondarily for the general public. These proclaimed the religious message of the Columbine shootings. Chief among these publications were *Martyr's Torch: the Message of the Columbine Massacre* (Porter 1999); *Day of Reckoning: Columbine and the Search for America's Soul* (Zoba 2000) and *Columbine: Questions That Demand an Answer* (Epperhart 2002). Most recently, Justin Watson, a professor of religious studies at Le Moyne College published *The Martyrs of Columbine: Faith and the Politics of Tragedy* (Watson 2002), an academic and dispassionate analysis of the religious overtones of the shootings.

Surprisingly, what began as a side issue overwhelmed media attention as evangelicals pressed the case that their children were being targeted because of their beliefs, alluding to the persecution of Christians in Rome prior to the conversion of Constantine in the fourth century. Rachel Scott and Cassie Bernall, unlike their fellow victims, were raised to the status of martyrs who died defending their faith (Watson 2002). The emergence of religion as an issue in shootings that occurred in a public school raises several questions. First, to what extent did Harris and Klebold target evangelicals in their rampage? Second, why did they evince hostility toward evangelical students? Third, why did religious persecution emerge as a major issue over the Columbine shootings?

CHRISTIANS IN THE CROSS HAIRS

Following the Columbine shootings, a struggle emerged between several factions over the ownership of the Columbine shootings (Cullen 1999e). That is, how should Columbine be defined and understood? In retrospect, it is clear that the antievangelical theme of the shootings received much greater play than the facts warranted. There are several reasons for this phenomenon. First, and most important, Columbine is situated in one of the most conservative areas of the country. Within fifty miles of Columbine are the headquarters of Focus on the Family, an evangelical organization that, under the guise of education, promotes a conservative political agenda, and the Promise Keepers, founded by former football coach Bill McCartney from the University of Colorado, that advocates a muscular Christianity whereby men are exhorted to take back the authority of their families that they have putatively ceded to their wives (Cooper 1995; Cullen 1999a). In addition, the Christian Coalition (The Christian Coalition 2003), one of the largest conservative lobbying groups in the country, which is opposed to abortion, cloning, and homosexuality and is hostile to political free speech, has in this area one of its largest chapters. Second, shortly after the shootings, rumors surfaced stating that Harris and Klebold had taunted some of their victims about their religious beliefs. When *Time Magazine* (Gibbs and Roche 1999) revealed the antievangelical comments of the boys in the basement tapes, the worst fears of evangelicals were realized. Third, the evangelical community, beginning in the 1980s, has built itself a universe parallel to secular society, consisting of churches, schools, communities, consumer goods, electronic media, book publishers, and social services that are affluent, self-contained, influential, and form the core of President Bush's "faith-based initiative" (Talbot 2000). Therefore, they had the institutional wherewithal to promote their view of the Columbine shootings.

However, one undeniable fact confronts conservatives and evangelicals: the shootings happened in their backyard, not in the Sodom and Gomorrah of San Francisco or New York. However much they declaim secular humanism, the lack of prayer in schools, failure to put the Ten Commandments in school rooms, moral relativism, permissiveness, progressive education, and other liberal bugbears (Huckabee 1998; Porter 1999; Zoba 2000), undeniably the most vicious school crime occurred in a conservative community that was overwhelmingly white and Christian in a school that had a reputation for having well-behaved students, good sportsmanship, and strong school spirit. As the Reverend Bruce Porter (Porter 1999), minister of the evangelical church attended by Rachel Scott and her family, put it, "[T]his slaughter of innocents ...occurred in MY town, down the street from MY church, and on MY watch" (68, emphasis in the original). Furthermore, rampage shootings have overwhelmingly occurred in conservative suburban and rural communities predominantly in the South and West (Newman 2004).

The evangelical and political right lashed out at secular society, especially the constitutional separation of church and state. Porter (1999) was fairly typical in his funeral oration for Rachel Scott:

> We removed the Ten Commandments from our schools. In exchange, we've reaped selfish indifference and glorified hedonism.... We removed prayer from our schools and we've reaped violence and hatred and murder. And we have the fruit of those activities before us now. I want to say to you here today, that prayer was established again in our public schools last Tuesday [N.B.: April 20, 1999]. What the judiciary couldn't do, what the churches couldn't do, the children did themselves. The Duke of Wellington once said, "If you divorce religion from education, you produce of race of clever devils" (32).

THE EVANGELICALS TAKE OVER THE MEMORIAL SERVICE

After the initial shock, the evangelical community sought to define the shootings in religious terms, as a Manichean struggle between good and evil. Zoba (2000) noted that the memorial service for the dead and wounded students and their families was taken over by evangelical pastors and turned into a revival service complete with threats of hellfire and brimstone. The memorial was supposed to be nondenominational and inclusive of educational and political leaders. Vice President Al Gore was there, representing the Clinton Administration. On the dais, and participating in the services were General Colin Powell; William Owens, the governor of Colorado; the superintendent of the Jefferson County School District, Jane Hammond; and Frank DeAngelis, the principal of Columbine High School. The service itself included a rabbi even though there are not enough Jews in the Columbine and Littleton area to form a congregation.

Following the comments of local political dignitaries, Jerry Nelson, pastor of Southern Gables Evangelical Free Church in Littleton, made the following remarks:

> It was during World War II, and Betsy Tambune of Holland was lying nearly dead in a Nazi concentration camp. In spite of her tragic circumstances, and because of them, she spoke with confidence of God's love for her and of God's control of her life. Lying nearby, a woman raised her recently crushed and deformed hands and fingers, and she snarled back at Betsy's confidence, "My name is Maria Pracik. I was first violinist of the Warsaw Symphony. Did your God of love control this?" With tears of empathy forming in Betsy's eyes she softly responded, "I don't know. I only wish you knew my Jesus." What Betsy was saying is this, there is only one rational way to live without despair in a world of such pain, and that way is to know the son of God, Jesus Christ. He loves you and he died for you.... He says, "For God [so] loved the world that He gave His one and only son, that whoever believes in Him will not perish, but have life everlasting" (Savidge 1999).

The rabbi was offended by the remarks, which implied that Christians had a better chance at survival of the Holocaust than Jews because of their faith in Jesus. To Jews, such a homily denigrates their suffering in the Holocaust and raises the genocidal behavior of German Christians to a glorification of Christ. If that was not sufficiently offensive, Franklin Graham, the son of the Reverend Billy Graham, followed Pastor Nelson with the following comments:

> Jesus said, "I am the resurrection and the life. He who believes in me will live, even though he dies, and whoever lives and believes in me will never die." Do you believe in the Lord Jesus Christ? Have you trusted

> him as your savior? Jesus said, "I am the way, the truth and the light. No man comes unto the father but by me."
>
> It is time for this nation to recognize that when we empty the public schools of the moral teachings and the standards of a holy God, they are indeed very dangerous places. My friends, to be prepared, we must be willing to confess our sins, repent of our sins, and ask God for His forgiveness and to receive his son Jesus Christ by faith into our hearts and into our lives. God will forgive us and He'll cleanse us of all of our sins. And He'll give us a new heart and a new spirit and a new beginning. And He will give us the hope and assurance that one day we will be with Him in heaven (Savidge 1999).

Franklin managed to invoke the name of Jesus Christ eight times in a nondenominational service broadcast to the entire country. He also lent credence to the myth that Cassie Bernall died defending her faith:

> A few nights ago, I was inspired while listening to Larry King interview a young girl, a student, from the high school, Mickie Cain. She told of her friend Cassie. As the killer rushed into the library and pointed his gun and asked her the life-or-death question, "Do you believe in God?" She paused and then answered, "Yes, I believe." Those were the last words this brave 17-year-old Christian would ever say. The gunman took her life, and I believe that Cassie went immediately into the presence of Almighty God. She was ready. She was ready (Savidge 1999).

Not only were Jews offended, but also members of liberal Protestant sects. They were particularly unhappy about the evangelical takeover of the supposedly nondenominational memorial service. The Reverend Don Marxhausen, pastor of St. Philip Lutheran Church in Littleton, who served as de facto leader of local Protestant churches and who officiated over the small, private funeral for Dylan Klebold, was quoted as feeling "offended," and "hit over the head with Jesus" (Cullen 1999a). Reverend Marxhausen related the event to me:

> The guy told one Holocaust story, only two-and-a-half minutes, and he managed to insult every Jew in America. The rabbi was such a gracious man—I was on the podium with him. But anyway, so, there was a reporter there from the *Denver Post,* and she said something like, "Do you have a quote to say?" And I said, "You mean, Hail Mary, we got hit over the head with Jesus?" And I said, yeah, that's what happened, 'cause

> I felt like I was getting hit. Then the hate mail came . . because you can't complain about Franklin Graham. But a lot of other people said, thank you, thank you, thank you. So, when you step out front you get it from both sides (Recorded April 29, 2004).
>
> Zoba (2000) relates that:
>
> "The consensus was that it [N.B.: the memorial service] was not inclusive to all the communities," said the Rev. Michael Carrier, president of the Interfaith Alliance of Colorado and pastor of Calvary Presbyterian Church in Littleton. "I felt like [Franklin Graham] was trying to terrorize us into heaven instead of loving us into heaven. The service was supposed to be for all people of Colorado and the nation to find solace, not an evangelical Christian service" (140).

Members of evangelical community defended the service as representative of the Columbine community. Some evangelical leaders admitted that the service was heavily evangelical. Zoba (2000) quoted an evangelical pastor who said, "I understand where [the critics] were coming from. I didn't disagree with anything that was said or represented at the service, but I might have disagreed with the timing" (141).

Also disturbing to many viewers was the fact that all of the participants in the memorial service were Caucasians, even though two of the victims were persons of color: Isaiah Sholes was African American and Kyle Velasquez was Hispanic (Cullen 1999a). The composition of the memorial service reflected the covert racism in Columbine, paralleling the vicious racism displayed by Klebold and Harris.

RACHEL SCOTT AND CASSIE BERNALL: FROM VICTIMS TO CHRISTIAN MARTYRS

The memorial service was held on April 25, 1999, five days after the shootings. Already, the religious overtones of the shootings were asserting themselves. Both Cassie Bernall and Rachel Scott had been elevated to Christian martyrdom. Earlier that day, Rachel was described by her peers in the service as "full of life, clever, confident, warm, and unfailingly kind" (Watson 2002, 52). Several testimonies referred to her middle name, "Joy," as emblematic of her because of her ability to bring happiness to others. Her reputation for being a good person transcended the evangelical community. A self-identified "outcast" student indicated extreme respect for Rachel and stated, "Rachel was a New Christian, and she did it the right way" (Recorded May, 13, 2003).

Rev. Bruce Porter officiated over Rachel Scott's memorial service, which was televised worldwide by CNN and MSNBC (Watson 2002). In addition to the savaging of the First Amendment cited above, he set the stage with the establishment of his "torchgrab ministry":

> Rachel carried a torch—a torch of truth, a torch of compassion, a torch of love, a torch of the good news of Jesus Christ her Lord, whom she was not ashamed of, even in her death. I want to lay a challenge before each and every one of you young people here today: the torch has fallen from Rachel's hand. Who will pick it up again? Who will pick up the torch again… ?
>
> I am hereby issuing a challenge to every student in every school across this nation. Pick up the torch that Rachel carried. Pick it up and hold it high and stop being a victim. Be proactive, speak to the culture you live in, declare a "cultural revolution" of compassion and mercy and love and forsake violence. You have the power within your hands, young people. We can't do it. We have failed (Porter 1999, 34–35).

Porter (1999) described his audience as enthusiastic and leaping to their feet when he issued that challenge. According to Watson, Porter's oration transformed Rachel into a figure to be venerated. He referred to her on his web site as "one of the Christian martyrs who died in Columbine High School" (Watson 2002, 54). In the days following the funeral, Porter stated that he received hundreds of e-mails, cards, letters, and telephone calls from people who heard his oration. He published numerous testimonials from Christians all over the world. A nonevangelical student who was at the service described Porter's oration as a crass attempt to use the media to expand his ministry. He noted that up until that point, the memorial service was about Rachel, but then it became about Bruce Porter.

Cassie Bernall achieved even greater celebrity as a martyr than Rachel Scott. Early in the police investigation, a student misattributed Dylan Klebold's asking Valeen Schnurr whether or not she believed in God to Cassie Bernall. An article in the *Rocky Mountain News* on April 23 was dedicated to Cassie's profession of faith in the face of a shotgun barrel. It was repeated in an article on April 25. On April 27, the *Rocky Mountain News* printed an article about Valeen Schnurr's miraculous recovery. In it, they noted that she had a confrontation with one of the killers in which she was asked the same question as Cassie Bernall and had answered it affirmatively, as had Cassie. National media picked up the story. During the month of May, *Time* and *Newsweek* ran cover stories on the Columbine massacres that mentioned her martyrdom; feature articles on Cassie appeared in the *Weekly Standard* and Salon.com.

Word of Cassie Bernall's supposed defense of the faith and subsequent martyrdom spread through the evangelical community. Christian rock pop star Michael W. Smith recorded "This Is Your Time" in Cassie's honor. Her parents appeared on Christian talk shows, such as the 700 Club, and mainstream talk shows, such as Oprah, Today, 20/20, and Larry King Live. During their appearances, they claimed that her death was a victory of Jesus Christ over Satan and an affirmation of the family's evangelical beliefs (*Cassie Bernall—Her faith has touched us all* 1999). Cassie's story spread in youth-oriented evangelical Christian web sites and chat rooms. As stories were retold, Cassie's defense became stronger and her image became bolder in the face of her executioners; in some cases, retellings had her scolding Harris and Klebold for their lack of religious convictions.

In her early teens, Cassie Bernall, according to her hagiography, *She Said Yes*, was a troubled and difficult child. She had apparently drifted into a goth subculture and with a friend had dabbled in Satanism. Cassie had experimented with marijuana and alcohol. She was apparently depressed and had contemplated suicide. She was so alienated from her parents that she, along with her friend, fantasized about killing them. Misty Bernall found out about her daughter's musings when she was rummaging through her drawers and found letters that Cassie had received from her friend espousing Satanism and advocating the killing of one's parents. Her parents confronted Cassie, who was outraged by the violation of privacy. They grounded her, forbade her to associate with her friend, enrolled her in a Christian school, and allowed her only to participate in the youth group at West Bowles Community Christian Church. Later, she transferred to Columbine High School. They weaned her away from her old crowd. In 1997, at a youth retreat, she apparently had an epiphany, was reborn, and dedicated her life to Jesus.

Since then, the Bernalls have established the Cassie Bernall Foundation, dedicated to providing funds for evangelical youth ministries and a home for Honduran orphans. Cassie's parents have established their own ministry to spread the word about Cassie's miraculous transformation from slacker to devout Christian and to promote their "tough love" methods by which they engineered Cassie's change of heart (Bernall 1999).

Within days of the tragedy, the Bernalls were approached by a representative from Plough Publishing, a small publishing house run by the Bruderhof, a

German-based sect, and asked to write a book about Cassie's conversion and martyrdom, to which they agreed. Early in the investigation, Jefferson County sheriff detectives Randy West and Kate Battan began to have doubts about the accounts that were reported in the media when they were interviewing students in the library who could not verify the claim. Students in the proximity of Cassie Bernall had no recollection of any conversation between her and either of the shooters. Most troubling was the testimony of Emily Wyant, a friend of Cassie's, who was right next to her under the desk and testified that was there was no conversation between Cassie and the killers. According to Zoba (2000), West and Battan gave the Bernalls a warning that the testimony about Cassie's behavior during the assault was conflicting. The investigators, on the basis of their interviews, concluded that there was no conversation between Cassie and the shooters and that the dialogue between Valeen Schnurr and Dylan Klebold had been misattributed to Cassie Bernall, who was killed much earlier in the assault. The representative from Plough Publishing and the Bernalls reinterviewed Joshua Lapp, Craig Scott (Rachel Scott's brother), and Evan Todd, whose testimonies in the presence of people who had a vested interest the affirmation of Cassie's defense of the faith were vaguely positive. Because of flimsiness of the evidence, Plough Publishers decided to insert the following disclaimer in their introduction to the book:

> Though the precise chronology of the murderous rampage that took place at Columbine High on April 20th, 1999—including the exact details of Cassie's death—may never be known, the author's description as printed in this book is based upon the reports of numerous survivors of [the] library (the main scene of the massacre) and takes into account their varying recollections (Bernall 1999).

It is highly unlikely that Cassie Bernall died defending her faith. The investigators understood that the events in the library were chaotic and that students' memories of the events would be distorted by their own emotional responses to a highly traumatic situation in which their lives were being threatened. Therefore, they had to be very careful in their reconstruction of the events in the library. They noted the following problems with student testimonies: distortions of time, impaired observations or recall when Klebold and Harris came within close proximity of their location, difficulty recalling the events in chronological order, and the influence of media coverage on their memory of events. In essence, students viewed media reports between the incident and the police interviews that colored their reportage of the actual events. The police investigation team concluded that such distortions were remedied by interviews of multiple persons. Because they had no interest in whether or not Cassie said "yes" and because they were sympathetic to the Bernalls, the police description of the events in the library stands as the most accurate and reliable.

Of the three conversations that Zoba claimed involved taunts about religious beliefs, only the conversation with Valeen Schnurr could be confirmed by investigators, and that was hardly a case of taunting. Neither Harris nor Klebold knew Rachel Scott or Cassie Bernall. Rachel was a year behind them in school. However, Harris and Klebold vilified a Rachel in the basement tapes. According to Judy Brown, the Rachel (along with "Jen," both of whom sat near "Nick") that they were identifying as "stuck up Godly whores" was in their psychology class. The reference to Rachel was mistakenly identified as Rachel Scott. According to the Jefferson County Sheriff's Department's report (1999), Klebold and Harris were fifteen to twenty feet away from Rachel Scott and Richard Castaldo when they shot them. If the boys had said anything to Rachel Scott, they had to have shouted it. Furthermore, Richard Castaldo, who was sitting right next to Rachel and the only living witness to her murder, could not remember Klebold or Harris saying anything.

In the case of Valeen, the exchange with Klebold was confirmed by several witnesses. An important fact disregarded by the defenders of the myth of Cassie Bernall's martyrdom was that Klebold's questioning of Valeen about her belief in God was in response to her cries of, "Oh God, oh God," after having been wounded. Also, according to testimony, after asking Valeen whether she believed in God, to which Valeen answered, "Yes," Klebold did not kill her; rather, he asked, "Why," and walked away.

No evidence exists that indicate that either boy knew Cassie Bernall or even knew that it was she who was hiding under the table. The testimony of Emily Wyant, who was the only witness to the killing of Cassie Bernall, was dismissed by Zoba because Emily was highly traumatized by the shootings. However, her testimony was maintained under pressure of the mushrooming myth and desires by believers to have her disavow her story (Cullen 1999f). The Wyant family became concerned about hostility directed at them by believers who had a vested interest in maintaining the myth. In the weeks and months following the publication of Cassie Bernall's story, Christian ministries had reported a dramatic increase in adolescents joining their youth groups.

According to Cullen (1999f), the *Rocky Mountain News* sat on the story for several weeks, citing sensitivity to the feelings of the victim's families for not releasing the debunking of the myth of Cassie Bernall's martyrdom until it was released by Salon.com over the Internet. Although Wyant had testified to the FBI about the death of Cassie Bernall and *News* reporters had known for months about the lack of a factual basis for the myth, they continued to report it as fact right up to the time that it was reported in Salon.com. The *Rocky Mountain News* was accused of unethical behavior in the treatment of the Cassie Bernall story because it feared a backlash by evangelicals.

Despite a lack of evidence of Cassie Bernall's defense of her faith in the face of the rampaging Harris and Klebold and the considerable amount of evidence indicating that the original attribution was mistaken in the chaos of library shootings, Misty and Brad Bernall, Cassie's parents, carry on their She Said Yes ministry. The book, *She Said Yes,* has sold over a million copies, Christian ministries still proclaim her martyrdom, and web sites dedicated to her encourage visitors to comment on her defense of the faith.

Once the myth was called into question, Bruce Porter, the Littleton evangelical minister who established Torchgrab Youth Ministry, which is dedicated to the memory of Rachel Scott, stated the following:

> It matters little in the end whether or not Cassie was quoted correctly in this circumstance. The fact that so many who knew her instantly accepted the initial reports that she said "yes" is a clear indication that, without any doubt whatsoever, she would have said it! Cassie's mother, Misty Bernall, in her highly recommended book, *She Said Yes,* made it clear that Cassie said, "yes" every day (Porter 1999, 7).

In a similar vein, Dave McPherson, youth minister at West Bowles Community Church where Cassie Bernall worshiped, is quoted by Watson (2002) as saying:

> The church is going to stick to the martyr story. It's the story they heard first, and circulated for six months uncontested. You can say it didn't happen that way, but the church won't accept it. To the church, Cassie will always say yes, period (159).

For the evangelicals, then, the story of Columbine has been interpreted as a vicious attack on evangelical students who became martyrs for the cause. Even though the factual basis for such claims is shaky, to say the least, what has happened is that the myth has been reprinted so many times that it has taken on a reality of its own. Among evangelicals, the martyrdom of Rachel Scott and Cassie Bernall has become an article of faith.

THE STRANGE JOURNEY OF THE CROSSES

The story of the evangelical attempt to define the Columbine shootings in their own terms would not be complete without a description of the saga of the crosses. Greg Zanis, a carpenter from Naperville, Illinois, a deeply religious man who was aware of the significance of his own occupation in Christianity, began placing wooden crosses around the country to commemorate victims of violence after he found his father-in-law murdered in 1996. His father-in-law taught him his trade, and the two were very close. The first cross he erected was in memory of his father-in-law. As he erected crosses to commemorate victims of violent crimes, he gained a reputation as a caring and compassionate healer, especially among conservative and evangelical Christians. By the time the Columbine shootings occurred, he had erected 200 crosses throughout the United States (Zoba 2000).

Brian Anderson, the student who was caught between the inner and outer doors of the west entrance of Columbine High School when Eric Harris was shooting into the school, had heard of Zanis's ministry, Crosses for Losses. He and some friends tracked down Zanis's ministry and asked him to place fifteen crosses on Rebel Hill overlooking the football field, one for each of the victims, including Harris and Klebold. As soon as Zanis received the message, he and his son purchased the wood, made the crosses, and transported them from Florida, where he was on vacation, and drove sixteen hours to Colorado. He arrived in Columbine on Tuesday, April 27, and began digging holes and placing the crosses in the holes on Rebel Hill, overlooking the play fields and the school. He was helped in his efforts by mourners who were sitting on the hill. He placed the fifteen crosses in a line, with the crosses commemorating Dylan Klebold and Eric Harris at each end.

The crosses, considered by Zanis as a symbol of Christian forgiveness, became an icon memorializing the victims of the shootings. In addition to the names of each of the dead, Zanis tied a pen to each cross so that mourners could inscribe their feelings on it. The crosses became a focal point for the mourning community. Mourners not only wrote inscriptions, but they placed flowers, toys, mementos, letters, poems, and other items that they thought were meaningful expressions of sympathy at the base of the crosses. According to Zoba (2000), 125,000 people visited the crosses during the next few days, even though most of the time it rained, and the hill became muddy and extremely slippery. Because of the uniqueness, popularity, and symbolic power of the crosses, the media latched onto them as a symbol of Columbine.

Not surprisingly, the placement of memorials for Harris and Klebold created a controversy among the mourners (Zoba 2000). On Rebel Hill, spontaneous debates broke out about the propriety of having memorials to the killers. The debates took on a religious cast. Those who opposed the inclusion of Harris and Klebold in the memorial thought it inappropriate to include the perpetrators because they were instruments of evil and should not be memorialized with innocent victims. Those who agreed with the inclusion of Harris and Klebold thought that it was a symbol of Christian forgiveness and the beginning of the process of healing the community. Some expressed the opinion that Harris and Klebold were victims of a society that lionized violence. The messages left on the crosses reflected the debate. Some mourners defaced the crosses of Harris and Klebold with messages like, "Evil bastard"; others wrote more comforting messages like, "Begin to forgive."

The crosses for Harris and Klebold were torn down by Brian Rohrbough, the father of Daniel Rohrbough, who was shot in front of the school by Dylan Klebold. When Rohrbough found out that there were crosses commemorating the killers on Rebel Hill, he was outraged. He called the parks department and demanded that they remove the two offending crosses. When nothing was done, he called CNN, and on April 30, with the media present, he tore down Klebold's and Harris's crosses, cut them into pieces, and threw them into a dumpster. He then announced to the media, "'We don't build a monument to Adolf Hitler and put it in the Holocaust Museum—and it's not going to happen here'" (Zoba 2000, 49).

Zanis was very upset about the controversy surrounding the fifteen crosses and the desecration of the crosses for Harris and Klebold. He immediately drove his pickup truck from Illinois to Colorado, pulled out the crosses, and returned home. After returning home, Zanis started receiving telephone calls by the hundreds asking him to return the crosses. This act enraged Brian Rohrbough even more because he thought that Zanis should have left the thirteen crosses commemorating the victims. Rohrbough claimed that Klebold and Harris did not deserve crosses because they did not repent their sins, and because of that failure, they were going to hell.

Zanis drove eighteen hours back to Colorado, and replaced the thirteen crosses on Rebel Hill at the behest of Steve Schweitzberger, a real estate developer from Littleton. The attempt to replace the crosses on the hill was to create a permanent shrine for the Columbine victims and establish a record of their story for Light Force TV, a Houston-based Christian network, which was on site filming the proceedings (Westword 1999). The Parks and Recreation Department removed them almost immediately, citing safety issues. The hill was steep, and at that time of year it was muddy. During the previous incarnation of the crosses, many people had slipped on the hill, and one person had been pushed over the hill in an apparent dispute over whether the killers should be part of the memorial. The county did not want to be sued for negligence. Zanis was supposed to have a meeting with Bob Easton, executive director of the Foothills Park and Recreation District, concerning the placement of the crosses; however, when Zanis entered Clement Park at 8 A.M., the media person from Light Force TV whisked him away, and he never attended the meeting with Easton.

Apparently accepting Rohrbough's rationale, Zanis apologized to Rohrbough in a meeting arranged by the Light Force TV. However, Rohrbough, a confrontational man who complained that his son was actually shot by police fire and sued the Jefferson County Sheriff's Department for the wrongful death of his son, at first did not accept Zanis's apology. He shouted at Zanis and claimed that he was crazy to memorialize the killers. Finally, Zanis said to Rohrbough,

> "Listen, I've asked you as a Christian brother to forgive me and you haven't. I'm tired of you yelling at me. I put up with all I can take. I'm going to pack my crosses and go back Illinois. But I want to ask you one more time, are you or are you not a Christian brother? And are you going to forgive me or not?"(Zoba 2000, 50–51)

With that, the two men embraced and Rohrbough forgave Zanis. The episode, of course, was filmed by Light Force TV. When commemorating Columbine outside Colorado, Zanis, believing that there should have been fifteen crosses, displayed fifteen, two smaller than the other thirteen.

During the interim in which the crosses were removed from Columbine, Will Ambrose of Littleton erected thirteen memorial crosses at the northern edge of Clement Park to replace those removed by Zanis. Zanis's crosses were placed within a few feet of those erected by Ambrose, creating a spectacle of twenty-six crosses in close proximity. Finally, Zanis's original thirteen crosses were permanently placed in a local cemetery in Littleton, where they can still be viewed. The second set of memorial crosses was removed.

However, that was not the end of the crosses controversy. Steve Schweitzberger claimed he had organized a fund drive to raise $1.6 million in order to purchase Rebel Hill from the government so that they could place crosses on the hill. Even though the plan had the support of powerful members of the Columbine and Littleton political community, including U.S. Representative Don Lee (Republican), who represents Columbine's district, it never materialized.

Beginning with orations at the memorial service, a concerted effort was put forth by evangelical community to define the Columbine shootings in religious terms with Klebold and Harris as the embodiment of evil, whose innocent victims were killed because of their devotion to Christianity. Of all the books written by Christian evangelicals about the Columbine shootings, only Zoba (2000) acknowledged the possibility that one of the motivations of the boys was revenge for the bullying and harassment they received at the hands of their peers. For all the rest, Klebold and Harris were evil incarnate, and to them, evil exists *sui generis*, as an intervention of the devil into human affairs, and, therefore, needs no explanation. According to a reporter who covered the story, outspoken members of the community continually emphasized the evilness of Harris and Klebold, as if they were subhuman. This particular orientation was evidenced when this researcher asked Principal DeAngelis for his explanation as to why the boys attacked the school. The core of his response was, "They were just *evil* kids" (emphasis his).

Certainly, the attack on Columbine High School was an evil act. What the evangelical ministers and Principal DeAngelis failed to acknowledge was the role of the school and the community in the generation of that evil. In their rush to distance themselves from the acts of Harris and Klebold, and in some sense to cover themselves and deny culpability, they placed the shootings under the mantle of evildoing, failed to ask the hard questions, and focused on the healing process without any attempt to ascertain what caused the shootings in the first place.

CHRISTIANS VERSUS CHRISTIANS

In one of the first interviews conducted for this study with a news reporter who lived in the neighborhood, I was informed that real estate agents steer evangelicals into southern Jefferson County where Columbine High School is located. The reporter also indicated that tensions existed between evangelicals and members of liberal Protestant sects. Evangelicals were characterized by this informant as arrogant and intolerant of the beliefs of others. The reporter also indicated that evangelicals viewed themselves as more Christian than non-evangelical Christians:

> There is a big influence [of evangelicals in Columbine] which can be very destructive, especially in the hands of teenagers who say "we're saved." They were so smug. "We know about Jesus. Jesus loves us...." It can be vicious, hypocritical, and exclusionary (Recorded November 6, 2000).

In Columbine, non-evangelical Christians and nominal Christians were perceived by the evangelicals as insufficiently religious. Even though evangelicals are a numeric minority in southern Jefferson County, they regard themselves as the cultural elite of the territory. The testimony of this reporter seemed to be in consonance with the comments of evangelical pastors in the controversy over the memorial service held on April 25, 1999.

In addition, the evangelical community is powerful in the area and is not afraid to use its power. The reporter I interviewed stated that evangelicals often used tactics of intimidation. She stated,

> Evil, evil, evil. Hate, hate, hate. There is a great separation there. There is them [the evangelicals] and there is the rest of us.... Things happen to you if you speak up with a different point of view. You get hate mail and you get threats and stuff, you know. You just be quiet. You just be quiet. But I know that there are people in the community who are just heartbroken for those two boys and their families (Recorded November 6, 2000).

Liberal Protestants were also appalled by evangelicals using the tragedy forrecruitment. In addition, they were upset about the superficial nostrums being proffered to grieving Columbine families by well-meaning but naïve evangelicals. Reverend Marxhausen, who, by his own testimony, has dealt with tragedy in his own life and with his parishioners, stated the following:

> People would prey upon youth in the park. "Just pray to Jesus, and this'll go away." Hell no. God put grief into the system to remind us that we're all important to each other, so you just can't brush that off. Anyway, so that's just sort of another piece of all the other pieces (Recorded April 29, 2004).

This feeling was reflected in the hesitancy of local newspapers to report information at variance with the evangelical belief that Cassie Bernall died defending her faith, the pressure placed on Emily Wynant and her family to disavow her testimony to Jefferson County Sheriff's Office investigators, and their successful attempt to force the Lutheran minister Don Marxhausen, a vocal critic of their tactics, to leave town. An informant told this researcher that Marxhausen was "run out of town."

Harris and Klebold were exceedingly hostile to evangelical students. In the basement videotapes they made in the days prior to the shootings, they indicated that they were very proud of their hatred towards evangelical Christians, along with everybody else (Gibbs and Roche 1999). Zoba (2000, 131–32) retold the following conversation between Klebold and Harris from one of the tapes made prior to their rampage:

> H: If we have a fucking religious war …we need to get a chain reaction going here…. Shut the fuck up, Nick [an apparent reference to a classmate]. And those two girls sitting next to you, they probably want you to shut up, too. Rachel and Jen and whatever.
>
> K: Stuck up little bitches, you fucking little Christianity, Godly whores.
>
> H: Yeah, "I love Jesus, I love Jesus." Shut the fuck up!
>
> K: "What would Jesus do?" What would I do? Boosh! [he points his finger as if it were a gun at the camera]. [NB: "What would Jesus do" refers to bracelets that evangelical Christian girls wore with the initials WWJD engraved on them as a reminder to behave as Jesus would in any given situation.]
>
> H: I would shoot you in the motherfucking head! Go Romans—thank God they crucified that asshole.
>
> Both: Go Romans! Yeah!

In a slap at evangelicals, Harris apparently reconfigured the video game Doom so that when victims were killed, they cried out, "Lord, why is this happening to me" (Hubbard 1999).

The unasked question by evangelical writers was why Klebold and Harris were so hostile toward evangelical students. According to a friend of the two boys, the halls of Columbine High School were used by some evangelical students to proselytize their faith. In my interviews with Columbine students, most could not recall being proselytized by evangelical students. However, goth students could usually relate a story about being proselytized. They tended to be dismissive of such efforts. Brooks Brown (Brown and Merrritt 2002), a nonconformist student stated the following:

> I never made it a secret in high school that I wasn't a religious person, and devout Christians used to come after me and tell me I was going to hell. They would use quotes from the Bible to throw insults to me. I'd seen them try to force their beliefs on other students, guilting them into it, pressuring them to join up. They didn't want to hear what you thought about God, or the world. All they wanted to hear was "Jesus Christ is my Savior"—and if we didn't agree we weren't worth associating with (148–49).

In a personal interview, Brooks Brown stated the following:

BB: Christians do not treat you well in this town. And I was told I needed to be saved by Jesus Christ. That I was going to Hell because I didn't. There's like maybe twenty or thirty of them. And all they did was carry around their bibles during school, their teen bible, which increases the fun of religion so much, apparently, and they'd tell us we were going to Hell. All the time, all the time, all the time. The youth group became part of the school. It did.... It was Youth Group, it was Young Life.

RL: [Would you explain that]?

BB: Young Life was like seriously 150 kids would go a week. It became this massive like cult, it was sick. And because I never went, I was therefore a pure sinner.

RL: I assume they [hassled] Eric and Dylan.

BB: All the time. All of us. We were more outspoken. We were in a little group and were more outspoken about the fact that we were not Christians. I haven't been a Christian since I was seven. Eric and Dylan I think had never been. Dylan I know was raised very differently, religionwise. I know his father was a Methodist, I think, and Sue was Jewish. So he was raised very openly religiously. Kind of letting him pick his own thing (Recorded May 13, 2003).

According to a student who identified himself as a conservative and an athlete, but not a jock, and as a fellow member of the debate team with Brooks Brown, the relationship between Brown and evangelicals was mutually hostile:

RL: I see. I understand, and there's a lot of evidence, and I guess you're probably familiar with it, that there was a lot of hostility on the part Klebold and Harris toward evangelicals.

J: Yeah. And I haven't seen all the stuff that came out before the shooting happened, like their website and stuff like that, because a lot of that stuff was closed down, because of the evidence stuff. But evangelical or Christian students, I never saw them harassed. I mean they would do prayers around the flagpole every so often, there was a group that the Christians belonged to called "Young Life." They all got together and did their Young Life thing—I wasn't a part of it so I don't know what happened. The Mormon students met in the house right south of the high school, where they had their seminary, and stuff like that. Religion I really didn't feel was a big deal as far as the whole school went, whether certain people held hostilities toward religious students, that remained pretty much in their own minds, but nothing came out.

The only, only time I ever saw anybody attack somebody for their beliefs was in debate class, and a certain famous individual whom we all know, Brooks Brown, liked to disprove the theory of God. What he would do in debate class was if someone brought up, he'd do like the Lincoln-Douglas debate where they were debating ethics, and if somebody tried to use the Bible, or Christianity or something as a philosophy, in order to prove their point, he'd go and prove that God didn't exist. And he'd get these people to the point of tears. And then he'd brag about it. And that's really the only thing I saw.

RL: Did you see any proselytizing on campus?

J: Not really.

RL: Because Brooks mentioned in his book that sometimes evangelicals would chase down students and tell them that they were living in sin and would go to hell.

J: God, I never saw that!

RL: Okay.

J: I never saw that! That seems a little bit ridiculous to me. I mean, people know the boundaries, I would say. I really don't think anybody would go up to anybody else and say, "You're a sinner. You're going to hell. Repent now!" Not in high school, I mean, come on! Yeah, there were public displays of religious stuff going on, I mean like prayers around the flagpole, and Young Life meetings were sometimes announced over the announcements. But I really don't think anybody was trying to proselytize, trying to convert people right then and there. That seems a little bit over the top to me, but he's one to exaggerate, so ...(Recorded May 1, 2003).

However, J was not the only student who was aware of the Young Life Bible study group. In an interview with a group of four female students who were freshmen at the time of the shootings, the following was stated by one of the young women:

Well, I noticed in Columbine there was a youth group of very cliquey people. They were people who were in the morning Bible study. And they were very [all start laughing]. They were not nice. They were nice

> if they wanted to convert you and stuff, but they were very, they were some of the worst there.... And that had nothing to do with their religion. It just came from the fact that they were in on some little secret that they were better than other people (Recorded May 13, 2003).

In the quotation above, the other girls laugh at the mention of the morning Bible study group in instant recognition and in anticipation of what was going to be said. All four young women agreed with the comments. The evangelical students, apparently infused by the teachings and attitudes of their parents and their churches, constituted themselves as a moral elite in Columbine. A student reported the following:

> My little brother went with a friend of his, B.; he's a Jew, one of the three Jews that went to the school. Went to the memorial for the kids who'd [been killed] ...and the preacher actually had the gall to say that only three of the kids who were killed that day were in Heaven. They were the only born-again Christians. It makes me sick. It's not surprising (Recorded May 5, 2003).

The moral elitism of the evangelical clergy influenced the attitudes of their young parishioners. Because they perceived themselves as right and infallible in their religious beliefs, they were intolerant of other people's beliefs and were incapable of viewing alternatives to their own beliefs as having any validity. Brooks Brown, viewing himself as an iconoclast, took great pleasure in debunking their beliefs, displaying his hostility toward their moral elitism through debate and disputation. Klebold and Harris were willing to pick up the gun.

The students I talked to disliked, in addition to moral elitism, certain evangelical students for two other reasons: hypocrisy and moral rigidity. One of the girls in the group quoted above stated the following:

> And I remember seeing the What Would Jesus Do? bracelets on the [evangelical] girls in the choir class, saying the meanest things about people. And I remember saying, "What's your bracelet for? Why do you wear that? It doesn't make sense" (Recorded May 13, 2003).

Another student who was quite sympathetic with evangelical students made the following observation:

> What I found really interesting was that a lot of the [students] known to be Christians, some of them were very "Christian," didn't drink, didn't

> have sex and all that good stuff. And those were the people that I would hang out with too, because they had the same ideals as I did.... And I respected them because they followed the rules and values and ideals of their religion. Granted, I wasn't a very religious person, but those were the same ideals that I had. But some people claimed to be religious, but basically in some way I guess it was like a title for them. Because they would go completely opposite of the ideals and values of their religion (Recorded May 5, 2003).

I had the following conversation with a student who claimed he was a former member of the Trenchcoat Mafia and is a self-defined goth:

> T: Maybe the problem with the evangelicals is that they are another one of those entities in society that tries to force conformity. That's always been my problem. Anybody that tries to force their beliefs on me, I have a problem with.... You either are going to have Jesus as your savior, or you're going to Hell. Those are your only choices. We are right; you are wrong. And I really hate the word "pity," but I really pity people that can't open their minds to accept that maybe they're wrong.
>
> RL: Or, a slightly different way, not so much they're wrong, but that other people have valid perspectives.
>
> T: That's where I was going. I personally am a religious existentialist, so I personally believe that if you believe it, it's as true as anything else. I really don't think that anybody's wrong. At the same time, I think that I am right. I think that everybody's right (Recorded April 10, 2003).

In defense of the evangelical students, T indicated that it was a very small minority of students who actually attempted to proselytize other students. More typical was the following response from a student who was in the popular crowd:

> RL: Now, according to media reports, Harris and Klebold seemed to be hostile to evangelicals. Do you know if other students shared their hostility toward evangelical students?
>
> AM: No. I've never heard anything like that. I've never heard that from regular students; I've never heard about anybody that was part of the Trenchcoat Mafia or anything like that. I've never heard anything like that....

RL: Oh, okay. And did you ever witness evangelical students telling other students that if they didn't [believe in Jesus], they were born again that they would go to Hell?

AM: No. There were definitely church groups at the school but they definitely hung out with one another and there was never any preaching or anything like that, to anybody else that I saw (Recorded May 20, 2003).

Similar to the harassment, efforts to proselytize tended to occur underneath the radar of members of the leading crowd. Although such acts occurred rarely, what seems to be more important was the attitude of certain evangelical students of their moral superiority by virtue of the fact that they were members of evangelical sects, regardless of their personal behaviors.

Although many evangelicals may be humble and focus their lives on doing good deeds, the response of that community to the Columbine shootings revealed a darker side of aggression and intolerance. People who disagreed with them were intimidated, memorial services for the larger community were subverted in efforts to proselytize and spread evangelism, and efforts were made to scapegoat political liberalism as a cause of the tragedy. Given the mind-set of evangelicals, it is not surprising that they failed to look within their own community for causes of the Columbine shootings.

MORAL ELITISM

Ironically, Harris and Klebold saw themselves as morally superior to mere mortals in an almost Nietzschean view. In the videotapes made by the boys prior to their rampage, Klebold stated the following (Zoba 2000): "I know we're gonna have followers because we're so fucking godlike. We're not exactly human—we have human bodies but we've evolved into one step above you fucking shit. We have fucking self-awareness" (131–32).

Apart from his megalomania, it seems as if Klebold had appropriated the self-righteousness and moral superiority of the evangelicals. Harris and Klebold had apparently convinced themselves of their evolution into superhumans who could sit in judgment of others. The intolerance that Harris and Klebold showed toward not just evangelicals but to all others is a mirror image of the intolerance of evangelicals toward those who do not believe as they do. Although certainly not the prime cause of the Columbine shootings, the intolerance of evangelical students in Columbine contributed to the anger and hatred evinced by the boys.

In an ironic twist, the moral elitism evidenced by the evangelicals was incorporated by Klebold and Harris into a justification for their murderous rampage.

It is not surprising that as evangelicals assumed the mantle of moral superiority in Columbine and used the mass media to proselytize, that their children would accost their peers and tell them that if they were not born-again, they would burn in hell. In most cases, this would be merely annoying. However, in combination with the brutalization and harassment dished out on a regular basis by the school athletes, it only added to the toxicity of the student climate at Columbine High School.

4

THE PEER STRUCTURE OF COLUMBINE HIGH

ONE SIGNAL ASPECT of the shootings at Columbine was that the prime targets were Harrris and Klebold's peers. Although Kate Battan and John Kiekbusch, the investigators of the Columbine shootings, characterized them as "equal opportunity haters" (Cullen 1999c), twelve of the thirteen people they killed, besides themselves, were fellow students. The one teacher who was killed, Dave Sanders, seemed to be in the wrong place at the wrong time. In his writing, Eric Harris vowed retribution for the harassment he received at the hands of his peers. In his diary, he wrote: "After I mow down a whole area full of you snotty ass rich mother-fucker high strung God-like-attitude-having worthless pieces of shit whores, I don't care if I live or die" (Cullen 1999b). Throughout the shootings, the boys made comments such as, "This is for what you did to us," and "We are going to kill you all" (Jefferson County Sheriff's Office 1999; Zoba 2000). The bombs were placed in the cafeteria near the tables where the athletes sat and were timed to go off when the maximum number of students would be present. Whatever motives they may have had for the shootings, the evidence overwhelmingly suggests that the major targets were their peers and their school.

Their planning and their behavior were consistent in targeting fellow students. Administration, teachers, and staff were considered, if anything, collateral damage. Much has been made (Cullen 1999b) about the issue that if they wanted revenge on those responsible for Klebold's and Harris's nearly daily harassment and humiliation, why did they not seek out the so-called jocks who terrorized them? Why did they go to the library instead of the gym? None of the victims was on the hit list that Eric Harris compiled, which contained, for the most part, the names of some of the harassers; however, it also contained the names of girls who refused to date him, especially those girls who strung him along before finally refusing. During their rampage, the boys were obviously looking for athletes, but not necessarily hunting them out. What Cullen failed to point out was that the bombs were planted in the cafeteria underneath the tables where the athletes congregated for lunch.

It was clear from the outset that the target for Harris and Klebold was their peers. It did not matter whether they were innocent or guilty, jocks or nerds, males or females, or evangelicals or atheists. There are three reasons why they did not set out to target specific peers: first, they were interested in body count. They planned a massive killing that would have easily exceeded the death toll in the Oklahoma City bombing. Second, and related to the first, they wanted to do something spectacular that would make them famous because of the notoriety of their act. The third reason why they did not target specific peers was that they apparently wanted to target the entire peer structure, in which they were at the very bottom. Although they were harassed by a small minority of the student population, they blamed everybody in the school for their own degraded social status. Therefore, it is important to examine the peer structure in Columbine High School.

The structure of peer relations at Columbine High School was trifurcated: The "in crowd" was at the top and the outcast students were at the bottom, with the bulk of students in a vast middle ground. The shape of the membership in the peer group structure could be likened to a diamond with very small numbers of students at the top and at the bottom. Students in the middle could be differentiated by activities and sports participation, musical tastes, religiosity, and drug habits. The peer group structure of Columbine High School was quite typical of suburban high schools, with the athlete and cheerleader crowd at the top of the heap (Eckert 1989; Wooden and Blazak 2001). Across the country, football is the dominant high school sport and often the only basis for community solidarity and identity (Bissinger 1990); football players are the local heroes not only within the school but in the larger community as well. The literature on social status in the high school has been consistent over the last fifty years in identifying athletics as the defining factor in adolescent subcultural status (Coleman 1961; Gordon 1957). The one deviant case (Larkin 1979) tends to prove the rule. In a suburban high school that was known to have a football team that was continuously at the bottom of the league and which had a very active dissident student subculture, the so-called jock/rah-rah crowd did not have hegemony over the peer subculture. Rather it contested it with the intellectual/politico students. But this was 1976, in the wake of student political activism in a school known for its student political activism.

The bottom of suburban high school subcultures tends to be much more pluralistic and localized than the top. The outcast student groups can vary greatly among schools, although anti-intellectualism seems to be a commonality. Wooden and Blazak (2001), in their case study of the peer structures of four Southern California suburban high schools in the late 1990s, found high academic achievers (known as "brains" or "smacks") at the bottom of the peer structure in all four high schools. Band members and ethnic minorities ("cholos," a disparaging Anglo term for Mexican American gang members, and Asians) were at the bottom in two high schools, along with a variety of other subcultures, based upon such criteria as social skills (nerds/geeks/loners), musical tastes (metalheads/punks), or, for girls, sexual promiscuity (sluts). At Columbine, the bottom of the student social structure included Asians (who were not mentioned by other students but were observed by this author to be isolated from the rest of the student population) and "dark kids," or goths. The Trenchcoat Mafia was considered a collectivity of dark kids.

For an area that was solidly upper-middle-class, socioeconomic background played an extremely important part in the structuring of peer relationships, especially among the girls. Not surprisingly, the most visible status groups within the peer structure were the jocks and "preps" at the top and the outcasts at the bottom. The jocks were visible by virtue of their celebrity, their reputation for partying, and their aggressive behavior toward others of lesser status. The outcasts were particularly visible because of their ostensible lack of conformity in dress, behavior, and musical tastes.

Among the students interviewed for this study, there was a consensus about the nature of the peer structure of the school. All students who were interviewed were able to locate themselves within that peer structure, suggesting that it was visible to all. One student characterized the peer structure of Columbine as follows:

> JZ: The major cliques are like—it's really weird, it's different than it was four years ago or whatever, because the football, you know, the jocks and the stoners, are [friends] because the jocks like to get high.
>
> RL: And the stoners supply them?
>
> JZ: Oh yeah, of course. And so we're—I don't mean we; I don't do that—they're all like one big group of friends. And then I would say if I

had to break it down, the jocks and stoners are friends, and then you have your band kids, and then your drama kids, and then you have your choir kids, and it just kind of breaks down like that. It doesn't necessarily break down as it used to, with the jocks versus the stoners and that kind of thing. ... And then you have the dark kids.

RL: Goths?

JZ: Yeah. The kids that they don't care about anything, they're into your hardcore substances and that kind of thing. That's kind of how it is now.

RL: [I see.] That's kind of interesting. And where [do] you fit into this?

JZ: I, um, smoke weed [laughter breaks out] ...no, I'm just kidding. It's funny that this is recorded.

RL: There's a kind of undifferentiated middle here that can go any way?

JZ: Yeah.

RL: That's pretty standard.

JZ: Most of my friends are in a group and I just kind of, I found it easier to live in high school without a group. As soon as you don't have a group any more, you don't have to worry about the drama, the high school drama of arguments and fights, of "you did this" and "well I think that." You know, that kind of thing. You don't have that any more as soon as you step back, and say, "Why do I have to be part of a group when I can be friends with everyone?"

RL: What about your closest friends?

JZ: Who are they?

RL: Yes. What kind of group?

JZ: I'd say probably the cheers and the poms and the football players. ... I don't talk to too many band kids; they don't like the ... things [I like] (Recorded May 1, 2003).

In the Columbine peer group structure, the term "choir kids" has a special meaning because the choir has an overrepresentation of evangelical students in it. Although there are members of the choir who are there because they like to sing in a group, many of the choir members also sing in church choirs. Unlike other high schools that have been studied by sociologists over the years (Eckert 1989; Larkin 1979; Wooden and Blazak 2001), at Columbine High School, the religious factor played an important part in the stratification of student subcultures, although, like ethnicity, it tended to be hidden. One student noted, "Simply by not being Christian, you were tossed by the popular group." What that student meant by "Christian" was that evangelical students tended to be openly and sometimes aggressively religious, calling themselves "Christians" to differentiate themselves not from Jews, Moslems, or Hindus, but from nominal or secularized Christians and those from liberal Protestant sects.

THE IN-CROWD

At the top of the social structure of Columbine High School was the in crowd, consisting of the "cheers and the poms and the football players," as characterized by one female student who identified herself as a member of the leading crowd by virtue of her being a prep. A prep, in adolescent parlance, is a student who makes good grades, may participate in athletics but is not a jock, and is popular among peers. She characterized the position of the in-group thus:

> I went in, and I was a prep, as they would call them, and so that's different that I fit in with, and I came to church, so I kind of stayed away from that kind of mentality of parties, but there was definitely diverse groups when I was there. I think it kind of changed as the years went on. It was always like the rich, the popular kids, always had more, more like, what you'd say was favoritism from teachers, a lot of favoritism than other peer groups. And other peer groups too. You knew who they were. I didn't know who the band kids [were], I don't know who the goths, the dark kids, were ... (Recorded May 12, 2003).

In Columbine High School, because of its heavy emphasis on sports, preps played a minor role in the in-crowd. Most students viewed the in-crowd as primarily consisting of football players and the cadre of girls who hung out, dated, and supported them. As one student said, "The peer group structure, it was kind of weird. You've got the typical football player, cheerleader deal."

A consensus existed among the students that the leading crowd consisted primarily of jocks, cheerleaders, and their friends. The leading crowd was approximately as ethnically and racially diverse as the rest of the school. African Americans and Hispanics were represented in the leading crowd although it was predominantly white. One student characterized the ethnic makeup of the leading crowd as follows:

> RL: Now, this leading crowd, what you seem to be telling me is that they tended to ... I think you've already told me, their attitudes toward people who were different–Jews, Blacks, Hispanics, Asians–this was

revealed in racist and anti-Semitic remarks. Was this true of many members of this leading crowd?

EK: Not that I know of because some of them actually were African American or Hispanic.

RL: Members of the leading crowd?

EK: Yes.

RL: And why were they members of the leading crowd? Were they just good people, or were they jocks, or what? Or both, or what?

EK: Yeah. Basically, throughout my career, there were three African Americans total that were in the leading crowd. And they were older than our crowd too. Then some of the Hispanics or—basically the Hispanics, they were either jocks or they had been friends with people in the leading crowd since elementary school. And I know some of them, for the girls, they were cheerleaders. Which would fit into the leading crowd too, because they would date the jocks. ...

RL: Right, right. Now how [about] kids from different ethnic groups? Did they hang together, did they eat at separate tables in the cafeteria or anything like that?

EK: Yeah, from what I can remember, yes. All the Asian kids would pretty much stick together, all the Hispanic kids would pretty much stick together, and all the African Americans would pretty much stick together. There might be some intermixings among them, but, I mean not, they'd sit at their own lunch table but they wouldn't be spread out over a bunch of different groups (Recorded May 5, 2003).

The racial and ethnic inclusiveness of the peer structure at Columbine High School provided the outward appearance of tolerance. In southern Jefferson County, there was little, if any, tension between racial and ethnic groups. Issues of racism, ethnic exclusion, and anti-Semitism emerged only after the shootings, especially after the racism of Klebold and Harris was revealed in the killing of Isaiah Sholes, and the anti-Semitic remarks of Eric Harris on his Trenchcoat Mafia web site. The implicit and embedded nature of racism, ethnic exclusion, and anti-Semitism was revealed more starkly in the nationally televised memorial service on April 25, 1999.

Several students identified jocks as a clique within the in-crowd. A typical description follows:

IG: To me there ... were the jocks and there were the athletes. Jocks were the jerks who made fun of people and ...they were just ignorant and

> stupid; they didn't use their brains like they should have. Athletes, on the other hand, participated in sports and used their brains and were nice caring people. The jocks would walk around saying things like "gay!" and "fag!" and "sex" and stupid things, stupid words like that that really made no sense. To show you the brilliance of some of these minds, one of the jocks asked my friend [Z] one time if he was gay, and it came out: "Are you gay? I think you're gay. Are you gay? I think you're gay," blah, blah, blah. "Are you gay, fag?" It's just like, give it a rest, man. (Recorded May 1, 2003)

A parent who was interviewed offered a similar characterization of the jocks:

> There's a difference between athletes and jocks in my opinion, and the ones that are, basically the jocks is what I am talking about here. But absolutely no respect for anyone; all they think about is themselves … (Recorded May 12, 2003).

The differentiation between athletes and jocks was confirmed by an outside researcher who, in the wake of the shootings, conducted a study of the internal climate of the school (Huerter 2000). In her report she stated, "There was a clear distinction made by several people that there were 'jocks' who were involved in bullying, and there were 'athletes' who were not" (2). In Columbine parlance, the term "jocks" referred to a specific group of predators.

In the media blitz following the shootings, reporters interviewing Columbine students focused on what they referred to as "the cult of the athlete" that pervaded the high school (Adams and Russakoff 1999). Within that cult was a group that I have termed "the predators." Whether or not students were themselves victims of intimidation, harassment, or physical abuse, everyone knew who the abusers were: They were primarily members of the football and wrestling teams, although according to some people, some soccer players also may have been involved. This group was fairly cohesive and easily identifiable in the school; they constituted their own status group. The size and membership of this group varied on an hourly and daily basis, depending on who was hanging with whom, the time of day, and who was around, but was estimated to consist of about twenty members (Prendergast 1999). The core of this group consisted of three or four members who were known to administration, faculty, and students. Although their targets could be anyone, they tended to focus on the small group of outcast students. Obviously, not all members of the in-crowd were predators. Also in the leading crowd were scholar-athletes and student-leaders. It was the predators, however, who set the tone in the halls of Columbine High School.

The predators, who were male, had their female counterpart. Although not as openly violent, the females at the top of the social hierarchy at Columbine High School were highly covetous of their social status, which was tied to the socioeconomic background of their families and was also linked to the neighborhood from which they came. In an interview with four female Columbine students, the following discussion of the leading group of female students transpired:

FS1: I remember when I first got to Columbine I thought people here are so nice, because everybody has a smile on their face. The popular kids, you know, they all smiled. [Burst of laughter from all. N.B.: The laughter was cynical and knowing.] Yeah, smiles [sarcastically]. They talked horribly about one another behind their backs. In my middle school, people would openly get in fights and stuff and just say what they thought. In Columbine, everybody wore that little smile, but you know, you learned to discern …

FS2: Who was real and wasn't.

FS1: Yeah. So many of them. They had that smile and … I remember being in choir—I was with this group of [high status] girls, and every girl who'd walk by,they'd say [stage whisper], "Go away, go away, what does she think she's wearing?" They'd talk to the person [face-to-face] because there was this game, this status game, where they had to be nice to the right people, so they could get ahead.

RL: How would you know that you're getting ahead?

FS2: It's a jealousy/gossip game. It went, "Oh, hi! I have more money than you do, but I need to keep my status, so I'm going to pretend like I like you, that I like these other people who have more money than I do." It's like just a whole stupid— "My parents have more money than yours" or "I have more money" or "I drive a Mustang; you don't have a car." It's a stupid game. It's like everybody's jealous of what everybody else has. And there's these horrible gossips, like these girls who would spread horrible gossip about everybody. And I never—I was never there long enough to see the whole game, and understand the purpose of it, but I did hang out with this girl who hung out with a lot of the very popular girls, and so I'd be around them, and they would talk and say horrible things about her, and she would go and say horrible things about them, and it's just like I never understood it but it's a whole status thing. …

FS3: Where you try to slander someone else's name to [raise your own status].

FS2: It's like a whole game, and even if it's good gossip or bad gossip, if people are talking about you, you're popular. Even if it's bad—"Oh my god, what is she wearing? Did you hear what she did the other night?" and stuff. And I think that's part of it. It's a whole stupid game. It's like people with nothing better to do than to try and make gossip about someone else so they can have status in our school.

FS4: I picked up on part of it. I think it's a funny thing. Whenever I'd appear, one of the first things people would ask was, What neighborhood do you live in? Like no one could ask me that before, you know. Whenever I was the new kid in school.

FS2: I got that too.

FS4: They wanted to know …

FS3: And these condos [have] just been built, and I didn't know what neighborhood it was. I'd just moved here. "Well, I live off of Coal Mine. I'm not sure." And they're, "How can you not know which neighborhood you live in?" Like that's some really important thing.

FS4: You know, one thing that I noticed that really affected me about it afterwards, was that even the people that hated me before, after the shooting happened, when we saw each other, when we basically recognized, you just, all of those grudges went away. Everything went away. You just hugged that person. And you felt that they were really happy to see you. Then all of a sudden there's talking about moving on and [burst of laughter from other girls] then it was back to the same thing, back to the same thing. And I think that that's a bad thing. I think that it happened for a reason, and I think that I've changed as a person—I don't hold grudges—I can't hold a grudge because you never know when's the last time you're going to see a person (Recorded May 13, 2003).

FS3 was very much aware of how one's neighborhood of origin played into the status struggle among the female students of Columbine High School; she was one of the privileged ones from Governors Ranch. This perception was corroborated in an interview with SK and CL:

RL: I talked to some other girls, and they said that when they first entered Columbine, one of the first things they were asked by other girls was, Where do you live?

CL: Yup. It was very important to live in Governors Ranch, which is where I live now.

DL: Where's Governors Ranch.

CL: It was the nicer neighborhood. … It had a nicer elementary school.

SK: It's got the Brady Bunch vibe so deeply it's scary. … It's one of the feeder elementary schools. Governors Ranch, Leawood, Normandy, Columbine Hills, Dutch Creek. Five elementary schools, and they all go into Ken Caryl [Middle School]. That's the only feeder junior high is Ken Caryl, so six years with the same fucking kids.

CL: Junior high was absolutely horrible for me 'cause I was a Leawood kid at the time, I was a poor kid. I got it horrible there.

SK: I was a Normandy kid, so I was like in the middle.

CL: The girls would not, as much as I wanted to have friends in junior high, they would belittle me and they were always making fun of me, they wouldn't include me in their things because I lived in the poor neighborhood. I mean that was the bottom line. I wasn't cool enough for them because I lived in the poor neighborhood.

DL: Is there really a poor neighborhood around here?

CL: No. (Recorded April 30, 2004)

The gossip played on the sense of paranoia of female students. It was always carried on behind the victim's back, only to be learned about later. An interview with a female student who was a member of the leading crowd, well-known for her physical beauty and a favorite among football team members, and who was perceived as so high in status as to be unapproachable by an outcast student, revealed the following:

SK: This is weird. CL was the girl who was so hot and popular she didn't need to be on the cheerleading squad.

CL: But I wasn't popular in the sense that I had a lot of friends; it's just everybody knew who I was, but I really didn't have any friends. It's just people knew who I was 'cause of the way I dress and the way I look. People thought I was in the popular crowd, but I really hated all of them. And I didn't hang out with people on the weekends. I wasn't associated with that crowd. If anything, within the popular crowd I was known for arguing with them and causing a ruckus and being hated by them because I wouldn't put up with their, whatever they did. I didn't pretend like I was happy.

DL: But CL, you dated this guy who was a jock, right?

CL: I dated all the popular guys. But whenever they would go out on the weekends, I stayed home by myself. It's just those were the only guys asking me out. So if a girl's going to date in high school, how else is she going to go out with somebody? Those are the only guys that had enough guts to ask me out. SK never asked me out. Never, never, never ever.

SK: Remember the first time you came out here and we sat—you want to hear this story? This is going to be interesting. After math class, fourth hour, CL and I sat next to each other. I was like, I guess I was like the nerd guy who sat at her table.

CL: I never thought you were a nerd.

SK: We'd talk all the time, and we'd help each other with math, blah, blah, blah. And finally I did get the guts to start talking to her outside of class. ... We were friends. And a friend of hers, let's not name him what is real name is, the man you were talking about, and a few of his friends came up and told me that I shouldn't talk to her because I was a fag, and I should learn to suck cock instead.

CL: Was I there when you said that?

SK: You were five feet away with your back turned.

CL: So I didn't hear it, 'cause if I would have heard it, you know what I would have done if I would have heard that.

SK: So it shot my confidence for asking any girl out. I didn't date a single girl at Columbine after that, couldn't do it. So it wasn't that we didn't want to, it's that we'd get the shit kicked out of us if we tried.

RL: That's interesting.

CL: I didn't know that.

SK: Yeah, I know.

DL: That's more than interesting, that's horrifying.

RL: It's like property.

CL: Yeah, I always felt like property, always.

SK: You could tell. No offense to you, but you were definitely regarded as property. It was fucking horrible.

CL: Even when I didn't have a boyfriend, and even though I didn't, I wasn't friends with them, and I didn't hang out with them. I was property (Recorded April 20, 2004).

This conversation reveals several aspects of the peer culture at Columbine High School. First, although CL was perceived to have high status among her peers because of her physical beauty and the fact that she dated members of the football team, she was not a member of the female leading crowd. She characterized her relationship with girls in the leading crowd as one of mutual dislike, for at least three reasons: (a) She came from a family with a modest socioeconomic background; (b) She was Hispanic; and (c) Many were jealous of her physical beauty and attractiveness to the jocks. Because of the abuse she received from the girls in the leading crowd in junior high school, she decided that she was going to keep her distance from them in high school. In so doing, ironically, she found herself friendless and lonely on weekends even though she was regarded by her peers as having high social status.

The leading crowd of jocks, cheerleaders, and hangers-on were well aware of who they were and defended the boundaries between themselves and lesser mortals in the social structure of the school through intimidation and humiliation. This was as true for the girls as it was for the boys, although the techniques of intimidation and separation were quite different. The jocks were not afraid of using physical intimidation and rituals of public humiliation to maintain their supremacy in the peer social system. The leading group of girls defended their positions with as much viciousness as did the boys. However, their means were much less direct, with gossip that focused on sexual activities, the wearing of clothes, physical attributes, and so forth as methods of distinguishing themselves from other female students.

According to Columbine students, within the structure of peer subcultures, stoners occupied a relatively privileged position. Stoners were traditionally identified as those students who came to school stoned on marijuana. They were also identified as wearing jeans with black T-shirts emblazoned with the name of their favorite rock bands, usually bought at concerts where they played. They were also notorious for skipping school and missing classes, hanging at friends' houses, and partying during the day.

Wooden and Blazak (2001), in their analysis of four Southern California high schools, found that members of stoner subcultures, variously known as "dirtbags," "punks," "metalheads," and "burners," tended to have low peer status. Eckert (1989), classifying them as burnouts, viewed them at the bottom of the peer structure. Larkin (Larkin 1979) identified the precursors to stoners as "freaks," who carried on the hippie/freak radical (Foss 1972) cultural disaffection from dominant authority, at the bottom of the peer structure of the high school he studied in the mid-1970s.

The elevation of stoners as associates of the leading crowd is a unique discovery for researchers of adolescent subcultures. However, with the increasing acceptability of marijuana usage among adolescents in the 1990s (Marijuana Policy Project 1996), the stoners were received with greater favor within the leading crowd for apparently two reasons: First, marijuana usage was perceived as cool (O'Harrow and Wee 1996) and not necessarily associated with being a slacker; second, the stoners were the sources of marijuana for the leading crowd members who were not well connected.

The gender politics of the leading crowd were traditionally sexist. The jocks considered their girlfriends as their property and would let males of lesser social status know that to take an interest in girls who dated the jocks was to invite physical retaliation. For some, physical retaliation was not limited to the guys who may have poached on their property, but to the girls as well. I have heard, as did newspaper reporters (Adams and Russakoff 1999; Gonzales 1999; Kurtz 1999), stories of harassment, intimidation, and physical abuse of female students by members of the football team.

THE "INBETWEENERS"

In any large high school such as Columbine with its 1800 students in 1999, most of the students comprise a relatively undifferentiated mass. Although the majority of students may be identified, as JZ noted above, by their school activities—the band kids, the debate team, the choir students, the chess club—such categorization is amorphous, and many students did not easily fit into any category. IG, a student who identified himself not a member of the leading crowd though certainly having a certain amount of peer status in the school, characterized himself and his clique as follows:

> IG: You had your skaters, you had your stoners, you had your academics or nerds, I guess, and the crowd I ran with for the most part, we really didn't feel into anything. There was no real archetype for us. We called ourselves "the posse" and included eight guys from the school and then there were two guys who didn't go to the school. And one guy was a football player, a couple were stoners, some were academics or nerds, if you want to call them that. A couple of other guys were on the swim team with me. Another guy was a skater, all that kind of stuff. We were just the melting pot of different male cliques within the school.
>
> RL: Was your posse, was it … typical, or was it more diverse than most groups?
>
> IG: I would say it was more diverse than other cliques. We all had friends from different sides of the coin. Everybody, since they came from a different clique beforehand, had contacts with different cliques. Like Z, he was on the football team, so he got along with some of the jocks

a little bit better, and then D and L had more contact with the stoner type, more D than L. And L and B were academics, and my friend A and my friend M were on the swim team with me, and M was even on the debate team with me. L was the skater punk, and that kind of stuff. Then the other two, like I said, didn't go to the school.

RL: Did you guys share musical tastes?

IG: Yeah. That was one thing that brought us together. We all liked to get together and play music, and, in fact, Z and L were in that band that I was in, and one of the other guys that didn't go to the school was also in the band. Music was the big thing that brought us together. We liked hanging out together: everybody was really very cool with everybody else, so it was a good arrangement I guess [laughs] (Recorded May 1, 2003).

Another inbetween student described the peer social structure at Columbine High School and her place in it as follows:

RL: I wonder if you could talk about the various groups in your school. Now we know about the Trenchcoat Mafia, which was an identifiable subgroup. Were you familiar with them; did you know any of them?

EK: I didn't know them on a personal basis; I did know who they were. I could point them [out], and even if they weren't wearing the trench coats, it was not [hard to tell]. Two of them would come down the stairs or be off that same period and it's like, "Oh, here come members of the Trenchcoat Mafia." And some days they didn't even have their trench coats on. I mean, we knew who they were; they usually hung out in the same spots in the morning; and it's like I knew who they were since my sophomore year. They were around all the time until the point where I graduated.

RL: And were there any other identifiable groups that you would say, "Oh, there goes a member of—"

EK: They didn't have identifiable names. There was more of the Gothic crowd that would wear a lot of black. Then there was more of the skater crowd who kind of dressed in skateboard type clothes and would have their skateboards with them. There would be, of course, the druggie crowd that tended to, I guess, I don't know how hard core into drugs they got; I know they smoked a lot of marijuana—I never specifically watched them toke up before classes started in the morning. I'm

> trying to think who else. And then I guess some of the people I hung out with, we were more, I guess, floaters, you know, where we wouldn't be strictly stuck into one group. I didn't hang out with the jocks or anything like that, but, you know, I'd hang out kind of with the members of different groups of people (Recorded May 5, 2003).

The students in the middle tended to have greater freedom than either members of the leading crowd or the outcast students in the choice of their friends. Although many of the in-between students had friends who were in the leading crowd, very few of them associated with the outcast students. Of the several outcast students that I interviewed, all indicated that they pretty much associated among themselves and had very little contact with other students in the school. According to one Trenchcoat Mafia member:

> RL: I see. ... [W]hat would you say is your most common feeling as you look back on your time [at Columbine]?
>
> ED: I have to say frustration.
>
> RL: And what frustrated you?
>
> ED: Just the inability to learn anything at all, the complete caste system that they had. I was an outcast, and people just wouldn't talk to me because I wasn't in their group of friends. It just irritated me because it seemed to me that they were just too shallow to be able to, they're too shallow and stuck in their own little world to be able to see beyond it.
>
> RL: I see. So there was a lot of judgment on the basis of appearances; [is] that correct?
>
> ED: Not just appearances, but outward demeanor, basically anything. How you acted, the way you spoke, the certain little mannerisms you had, how you dressed, who your friends were (Recorded April 10, 2003).

This view was corroborated in a conversation recorded between two former students at Columbine High:

> SK: Don't look at me like that, SL. You remember how Columbine was. ... Littleton's that superficial. I just remember how people were treated based on their looks. I do (Recorded April 30, 2004).

Yet, one student who did hang out with the outcast students described herself as follows:

> JP: I don't know where I'd put myself … I was really into art, so I had a lot of friends from my different art classes. I never smoked in high school, but I hung out at the smoker's clique, which like most people who hung out there were kind of not generally accepted, so I don't know. I wasn't in the popular, crappy, Christian crowd … (Recorded May 13, 2003).

As can be seen by JP's comments, she was antagonistic and hostile to members of the leading crowd, primarily because of the hypocrisy she perceived in their profession of Christian values, their aggressiveness toward their fellow students, and their drug and sexual indulgences.

Eckert (1989), in her discussion of the antimonies of adolescent peer cultures in the school, noted that the relationships between the outcast students and the leading crowd were dialectical in that members of the leading crowd had no friends in the burnout subcultures and vice versa. However, students in the middle could have friends among both jocks and burnouts. In Columbine High School, relationships between jocks and outcast students were more polarized. Those students in the middle who had friends among the jocks tended to adopt the attitudes of the jocks toward the outcast students, even if tacitly. Although they may not have been as aggressive toward the outcast students, they were very much aware of their degraded status and tended to be disdainful of them and not associate with them. Those very few students in the middle who associated with outcast students tended to adopt the hostile attitude of the outcasts toward the leading crowd. Because of the domination of the peer group structure by a leading crowd that included not only jocks but was also Christian, there was greater antipathy toward the outcast students, especially because outcast students made religion an issue. They flaunted their atheism, agnosticism, or Satanism, in the case of some goth students, in the face of evangelical students, who were viewed by the outcast students as narrow-minded and hypocritical. Evangelicals were not viewed as "goodie-goodies" because the leaders of the predators were supposedly evangelicals.

THE OUTCAST STUDENTS

The outcast students, or in Brooks Brown's self-appellation, the "loser students," constituted an extremely small portion of the student population at Columbine, perhaps fewer than twenty students. Because they were such a small group and all experienced similar fates at Columbine High School, they knew and empathized with each other. This small group, who sometimes identified themselves as "nerds," tended to be bright students—many were intellectually pretentious—but tended to resist the conformity that dominated the student peer culture. Many, including Eric Harris, tended to consider themselves goths or dark people. In opposition to the clean-cut preppie, Abercrombie and Fitch dress of the vast majority of students, Gothic students tended to dress in black and were often unkempt. Of course, the most identifiable clique of the outcast students at Columbine High School in the late 1990s was the Trenchcoat Mafia. The emergence of the Trenchcoat Mafia is instructive about the status and experiences of the outcast students.

Joe Stair was the consensual leader of the Trenchcoat Mafia. He described its origins as follows:

> Stair: The Trenchcoat Mafia ... started out just as a group of friends; we didn't even call ourselves the "Trenchcoat Mafia," as I'm sure you've heard. We called ourselves the "Trenchcoat Club." It's just a group of friends. We thought we were being cool. We didn't really fit in with any of the other classic cliques. We were all pretty much outcasts; so we just clung together and gave ourselves this name, just for the heck of it.
>
> RL: And how many of you were there?
>
> Stair: Let's see, when I joined the Trenchcoat Club it was probably just four or five individuals. And then a bunch of my other friends, they saw me hanging out with this group of kids; some of them were wearing the dusters, [and] so they joined up. It just went from there. Kids started just calling us the "Trenchcoat Mafia" because some of our members, some of our friends wore dusters, so they started calling them that because a lot of us were interested in the military or wanted to join the military afterwards. Some of them carried themselves as if they were a member of the military. And they tried to use that term as a derogatory statement, I would assume. We thought it sounded cooler, so it was like, hey we'll go with that. That sounds good. I like that (Recorded May 1, 2004).

Brooks Brown (Brown and Merritt 2002) identified the naming of the Trenchcoat Mafia originating in a specific incident:

> While sitting at lunch one day, a few of the athletes were doing their usual routine, making fun of the kids they don't like. They saw this group of kids sitting together, all wearing black trenchcoats [*sic*] on a day when

> temperatures were in the 80° range. One guy commented that with the trenchcoats[*sic*], the group of outcasts look like some sort of Mafia.
>
> "Yeah, like the trenchcoat [*sic*] Mafia," said another.
>
> The term was supposed to be an insult. Instead, the group embraced it as a badge of pride. They were the outcasts and, rather than be ashamed of it, they were proud of it. In fact, they wanted to fight back against their antagonists. … (68)

This version of events was confirmed by another Trenchcoat Mafia member who stated:

> ED: It started out as a fashion thing, because it looks cool, and a bunch of people that were hanging out in the same groups picked up on the style, and just one day actually it was … I think it was actually Rocky Hoffschneider that coined the phrase. I think he said, "What are you guys? Some sort of Trenchcoat mafia? Well, we thought it sounded cool, so it sort of stuck (Recorded April 10, 2003).

Virtually every student at Columbine High School knew about the existence of the Trenchcoat Mafia, even though they may not have known any of the individual members. One student who did not identify himself as a member of the leading crowd but as having friends among the jocks described the Trenchcoat Mafia as follows:

> RL: Did you know anything about the Trenchcoat Mafia?
>
> IG: Oh, of course. Everybody called them the "Trenchcoat Mafia." It was a joke. They didn't even given themselves that name. … And it was just because everybody in that group wore a trench coat, they were black [meaning "dark"] for the most part, and they hung out together. It was just kind of, "Oh, here comes the Trenchcoat Mafia." It was just kind of a coined term, like "the jocks."
>
> RL: Well, according to Joe Stair, they kind of gathered together for self-protection. Did you see anything of that? Were these people who were continually picked on by other students or not?
>
> IG: They got their share, just like everybody else of that unpopular crowd, but again, they knew their place. If you don't want to be bothered, don't bother them. It's kind of like a bumblebee thing. But as far as getting together in order for self-protection, no more than any other group would.

RL: I see.

IG: At least I would think. Not being part of the group, I cannot really say what their mind-set was, but they hung out together because they had common interests, whatever those interests were. I didn't know. They were friends, and they happened to like trench coats and that was their thing. Just like my group of friends like Hawaiian shirts, but no one called us "the Hawaiian shirt mafia" or anything like that (Recorded May 1, 2003).

IG, like so many students at Columbine High School, could identify the Trenchcoat Mafia and its members but had no friends among them. His testimony is quite similar to that of EK above. The vast majority of students knew who they were but did not associate with them because of their strangeness and unpopularity. IG referred to them as "a joke." This attitude was prevalent among Columbine High School students; outcast students were subject to ridicule.

In some sectors of the student population, dark students were a source of unease. The concept of dark students or students being on the dark side generated suspicions of Satanism on the part of evangelical students. Some students did dabble in Satanism or Wicca, in the case of females (Brown and Merritt 2002), although there is no evidence that members of the Trenchcoat Mafia or Klebold and Harris did. In the heavily evangelical South Jefferson County, adolescent rebellion often took the form of witchcraft or Satanism, as in the case of Cassie Bernall, an evangelical student who was killed in the shootings, and who, prior to her reconversion to evangelical Christianity, practiced Satanism with a friend and fantasized about killing her parents (Bernall 1999). Students who considered themselves Satanists or witches were viewed by evangelical students as those who chose evil over good and in need of redirection into a life in Christ. This may be one reason why some evangelical students attempted to convert outcast students to evangelical Christianity.

The outcast students were something of a counterculture in the halls of Columbine High. The vast majority of students were school-oriented, conforming, and well-behaved. Where most students adopted the preppy mode of dress, maintained their physical appearance, did their homework for the most part, participated in athletics and after school activities, practiced for their SATs or their ACTs, and looked forward to college, the outcast kids ostensibly disliked school, did not attend to their outward appearances other than to be distinct from the larger population, hated the jocks and the stupidity they represented, and kept to themselves. Although many of the outcast students were quite bright, many of them received poor grades, especially in courses in which they had no particular interest. For example, Dylan Klebold was characterized by one of his teachers as a "slacker." He was unkempt, uninterested, made minimal efforts in the class, and was in danger of failing.

> He was one of those kids that didn't pay a lot of attention. He got a B in the [ninth grade] class, but he didn't work very hard. And he was just a normal student. But as a senior, he was one of those kids that just wore grubby clothes all the time, wore his hat backwards all the time. ... He was going to do the very least amount of work possible. That's basically what he did. He tried to talk me one time into letting him not have to come to class—just show up on the days of the tests. And I said, "No. You have a choice. You can come to class and stay awake, or you can drop the class." But he barely passed the first semester AP calculus. I'm not sure he would've passed second semester. He was borderline. 'Cause he just didn't work hard—he was a slacker. The kids had nothing to do with him, but when kids act and behave like that, the other kids that are in AP calculus, the really good kids, don't want anything to do with him (Recorded May 1, 2004).

For some students, the existence of the outcast students was a blight on the shining image of Columbine High. Because they were at the bottom of the social structure and such antipathy was directed toward them, the vast majority of students avoided them. Their isolation created a situation whereby the jocks could humiliate and harass them with virtual impunity. Looking at them from the outside, IG presumed that they received no more abuse than any other group on campus. However, IG was never stuffed into a locker, never had bottles thrown at him while walking home from school, was never gratuitously beaten up because it was a fun thing to do, although he could relate a story about being called a fag by one of his peers until he punched him, ending the harassment.

Simply put, the outcast students of Columbine High School suffered harassment on a daily basis. The rest of the student body either ignored or studiously avoided the predation, minimizing its prevalence in their own minds. The faculty and the administration were blissfully unaware of what was happening in the halls of the high school. In the next chapter, the issue of bullying and predation at Columbine High School will be examined in detail.

5

THE OTHER COLUMBINE

IN CHAPTER 2, I presented a view of Columbine High School as most people see it. The school has many virtues that are quite admirable: a strong academic program; a successful sports program; high student involvement in extracurricular activities; large, beautiful, and well equipped facilities; a highly qualified teaching faculty; and even a student body known for good sportsmanship and good manners. Yet on several occasions in my investigation, I heard former Columbine students say, "They [Harris and Klebold] killed the wrong students." The following came from an interview with a former Columbine student:

> After Columbine happened—this is one of the things that a lot of people don't really mention—no one at the school, and I mean no one, asked the question "why?" Not a single person who was in the school that day asked. … [Yet] everyone said the same thing, *"They got the wrong people." Everyone said that—cheerleaders, ballplayers, wrestlers, they all said the same thing* [Emphasis added] (Recorded May 13, 2003).

When probed about this comment, students said that Harris and Klebold did not point their guns at those students who harassed and intimidated their peers. As a matter of fact, students pointed out that their victims were nerdy kids or students who were kind to others, well-liked students such as Rachel Scott and Isaiah Sholes.

In a group interview with several former female Columbine students, the following transpired:

> FS1: One of the things, too, that always sticks out to me is that if you ask anyone, almost anyone, at Columbine, about the shooting, one thing you get a lot is "They killed all the wrong people." It's just that comment in general, that they killed all the wrong people, that's really saying something about our school.
>
> FS2: They're supposedly attacking all the popular people, but the people they killed were like, they were friendly to everybody, they weren't in major cliques, and I remember Richard Castaldo got shot and he's in a wheelchair, he's a paraplegic now. I remember going, "Why did they shoot him?" He used to hang out with them sometimes. I hung out with him. He was so … out of everybody, he was the least conformist, he hung out with nobody, he didn't care what people thought about him. He tried to be kind to everyone. … Out of everyone that I knew really really well, that was majorly effected by the shooting, that got shot or that died, he was a total loner. And Isaiah, why Isaiah [Sholes]? He was the only African American that got shot. And you know, there's lots of talk that's why he got shot, and he was nice to everyone he met. He was so nice [Crying] (Recorded May 13, 2003).

These comments revealed an underlying current of resentment against those who were the bullies and who harassed their fellow students. It also speaks to a tacit assumption that the main cause of the shootings was intimidation and harassment by students known to all. It also speaks to feelings of outrage and a sense of continuing injustice. In this chapter, the internal climate of Columbine High School will be explored.

In the previous chapter, the structure of peer group relationships was delineated. As was noted, the peer structure was highly polarized. Because this was a structural phenomenon, it was taken for granted. No interviewee stated that the peer group structure was polarized between the jocks and the outcasts. However, students did understand that anyone having the outcasts as friends was not going to have friends in the in-crowd and that having outcast friends meant sharing their stigma and being subjected to the same predatory victimization they experienced. It took a certain amount of bravery to befriend an outcast at Columbine.

This extreme polarization at Columbine between the jocks and the outcasts was quite different than contradictions reported elsewhere in the literature on high school cliques (Eckert 1989; Larkin 1979) in which the in-between students could have friends with both jocks and outcasts, and in Eckert's terms, function as "brokers" between the upper and lower ends of the student hierarchy.

In this chapter, the internal climate of Columbine High School is explored. As noted above, students' and community members' views of the internal climate of Columbine high school were strongly influenced by their positions. To illustrate the contradictory views, which, not surprisingly, reflect the polarization of the student environment, Brooks Brown (Brown and Merritt 2002) comments:

> By the end of my junior year, school shootings were making their way into the news. … When we talked in class about the shootings, kids would make jokes about "it was going to happen at Columbine next." They would say that Columbine was absolutely primed for because of the bullying and the hate that was so prevalent at our school (97–98).

However, in an interview with one of Brown's senior classmates who was near the top of the student peer hierarchy, the following transpired:

> I was on the Youth Advisory Council at Jefferson County my junior and senior year. What the Youth Advisory Council would do is we'd meet every month and they'd get together with students from each of the different schools in Jefferson County and they'd get together and talk about the problems that were going on, you know, if there were any, and highlight some of the positive things. And we just got to talk about making sure that everyone was having a positive experience within our high schools. And the April meeting of 1999 was a little strange. … April's discussion happened to be about school shootings, because of all the stuff that had happened in Springfield and Jonesboro and Paducah and all that kind of stuff, and they were asking us, seriously, if we thought what we would do or what we should do in case that happened. I was sitting in the back of the room laughing hysterically. These people were talking about sniper drills and all this other kind of stuff, and school shooting and exiting, and blah, blah, blah, and I thought it was hysterical. And I said, "Are you kidding me? We live in the middle of white suburbia, and if you really, really think that thing is going to happen at Columbine High School, you're crazy!" And fifteen days later, POP! It happened, and it's just kind of a weird, coincidental thing that happened to me.

> Wow! Looking back at myself in April 1999, sitting in back of that temporary building and laughing, whew! I was wrong. Just proof that it can happen anywhere (Recorded May 1, 2003).

In this chapter, several issues will be enumerated. First, to what extent did intimidation, bullying, and predatory relationships exist at Columbine High School? Second, how did students perceive the internal climate of Columbine High School, and how did they respond to it? Third, how did administration, faculty, and staff respond to conflicts among students?

BULLYING

Within days of the shootings, newspaper articles were reporting complaints by Columbine students about harassment and bullying in the school (Adams and Russakoff 1999; Greene 1999; Holtz 1999; Kurtz 1999). In response to allegations that not only did predatory relationships exist within Columbine High School, but that they were abetted by faculty members and ignored by the administration, the governor of Colorado established a commission to investigate bullying on a statewide basis (Sanko 2000). In addition, a researcher was dispatched to Columbine High School to study the internal climate, resulting in a nine page report (Huerter 2000). The report is scathing in its characterization of the internal climate of Columbine High School. Its observations are in accord with the data I have collected and with the journalistic representations. In at least two cases, data I collected independently matched the data collected by Huerter.

First, prior to April 20, 1999, students were routinely harassed by the group I named in the previous chapter as "The Predators." Second, only a small number of incidents were reported to faculty and administration. Third, the harassers, because of their status as leading athletes, received preferential treatment relative to the rest of the student population. Fourth, the tolerance of harassment by The Predators led others, including Eric Harris and Dylan Klebold, to harass students who were more vulnerable, younger, and weaker than themselves.

The Predators were led by members of the football and wrestling teams. One member was the state champion wrestler who had been expelled from his previous high school for fighting, enrolled in Columbine in 1997, and became Columbine's heavyweight wrestler and a member of the football team. His presence in the school intensified fears of being bullied by many students who tried to keep their distance from him. Another, a year younger than the wrestling champion, was the captain of the football team and played fullback, running for over 1000 yards in his senior season. Because of his physical and verbal harassment, his girlfriend was granted a restraining order against him (Kurtz 1999). One student suggested that students, including he himself, armed themselves in order to protect themselves from The Predators:

> SK: Kids bring pistols to school, knives, you name it. There were kids—not all of them, small groups—five or six who carried guns to school. They would carry pistols with them at all times. Knives were beyond common. I had a butterfly knife. Everyone did. Everyone carried knives with them.
>
> RL: Why did they do that?
>
> SK: Just in case. RH came after a friend of mine with a bat ... he's never gonna get me (Recorded April 30, 2004).

This same student, who described himself as an outcast, described two separate beatings he received at the hands of RH, plus a third that he witnessed when he was a freshman. In an interview with SK and CL, a female student who was a member of the leading crowd in 1999, the following transpired:

> SK: My friend D and I [went] to a drinking party, two houses up from [RH]. We were stupid freshman, didn't know that it was a jocks-only party, and someone [was] beating his girlfriend in the bathroom and she comes out and she's bloody. ... D makes a stupid comment because we're all about women's rights and liberation. I had to baby D [after RH beat him up] the rest of the night with a broken nose, and he was bleeding out of his ear. ... Did you see any beatings that bad?
>
> CL: Yes.
>
> SK: They [beatings] happened a lot more often than you saw (Recorded April 30, 2004).

As IG noted, one of the favorite activities of The Predators was to question the sexual orientation of other males. They were constantly calling other males "fags," "queers," and "homos." This is fairly standard and stereotypical behavior among jocks and has been documented by previous researchers (Garbarino and deLara 2002; Newman 2004). In an interview with six students, three who were on the football team, the male students stated that they called people "fags," "homos," and "queers." However, they defended themselves by stating that they only did it among friends and that it was all in fun. Dominant males attempt to humiliate their subordinates by questioning their masculinity. This practice has been a significant motivation for retaliatory violence in schools and has played a prominent role in several other rampage shootings, including Barry Loukaitis in Moses Lake, Washington, Michael Carneal in West Paducah Kentucky, and Charles Andrew Williams in Santee, California (Newman 2004). In the previous chapter, a student told how, when talking to a girl who dated football players, he was confronted by a member of the football team who threatened him with physical violence, called him a "fag," and told him that he should learn to "suck cock." After that, he kept his distance from her.

In January 1998, Harris and Klebold were surrounded by a large group of football players in the cafeteria and squirted with ketchup. According to interviews, RH suggested that because Harris and Klebold were always together they were a homosexual couple. Prendergast (2000) quoted Randy Brown, the father of Brooks Brown, as saying:

> People surrounded them [Harris and Klebold] in the commons and squirted ketchup packets all over them, laughing at them, calling them faggots. That happened while teachers watched. They couldn't fight back. They wore the ketchup all day and went home covered with it.

A food fight nearly erupted in the cafeteria between The Predators and the outcast students, described as follows (Adams and Russakoff 1999):

> Hoffschneider's circle—known as "the steroid poster boys"—had their cafeteria table. On the other side of the room, shy skinny boys—among them Harris and Klebold—claimed a table, too. The athletes threw Skittles candy at them, said senior John Savage. Once, athletes threw a bagel close to the table, and the cafeteria emptied for fear of a fight. In the boys' bathrooms, a graffiti war broke out—"Jocks rule!" Came the rejoinder: "Jocks suck!"

The Predators set the tone for the internal context of Columbine High School. Adams and Russakoff (1999) noted:

> In line at registration for new classes that year, football players pushed a 4-foot-9 freshman and called her dirty because she dressed like a hippie. On another occasion a boy called "Little Joey Stair," one of the wraith-like Trenchcoaters who was friends with Harris and Klebold, looked up in a hallway to see three football players shoving him into a locker,

saying, "Fag, what are you looking at?" remembered classmate Mikala Scrodin.

Last year there was a group of seniors who picked on everyone, not just the lowest people. Pretty much everyone was scared to take them on; if anyone said anything, they'd come after you, too. I don't think teachers realized it was serious, they just saw it as kids joking around," said Kevin Hofstra, a Yale-bound soccer team captain.

In the halls, body slams were common. Trenchcoat students got pushed more than most. "A football player reached out and stepped on the cord of one of these girls' Walkman and it ripped out and fell and broke," remembered Melissa Snow, who graduated in 1998. "She just didn't say anything. For those kinds of kids it's really hard to stand up to a bunch of football players, who are all standing around thinking it's really funny what this guy did to you.

Harris and Klebold absorbed it all. As the year went by, they drifted closer to the Trenchcoaters, but unlike most students, they seemed to take the taunting to heart. "They just let the jocks get to them," Colby said. "I think they were taunted to their limits."

Discussing his drugs of choice, Eric Harris, on his Trenchcoat Mafia web site, stated the following: "My recent OTC [over-the-counter] of choice is cough syrup. I recommend it highly. It's the best thing after a hard day of being called 'gay' by a schoolyard full of fashionable jocks and cheerleaders."

A member of the leading crowd related the following to the author:

RL: I want to ask you one more question. When the football guys walked down the hall, did you witness them walking down the hall together and harass people as they walked down the hall? What did they do?

CL: They walked in a line to cover up the hallway and pushed anybody else out of their way.

DL: And what was their reaction when they would confront people?

CL: What do you mean like reaction?

RL: If you didn't move?

CL: I'd feel sorry for you. You know what they did a lot was, as the kids were walking in the hallway, they'd grab their backpack and pull them to the floor, like real quick, if you pull someone's backpack, it's heavy enough, but if you pull them hard enough, they fall right to the floor. They did that a lot. They would walk down and just like, down the hallways and they filled up the whole hallway and just

> anybody who was in their way, you'd scoot out of the way and if you don't you're in trouble (Recorded April 30, 2004).

According to Brooks Brown, harassment was widespread. Below is an extensive description of his experience (Brown and Merritt 2002):

> Sometimes kids would just ignore us. But often, we were targets. We were freshman and computer-geek freshman at that. At lunchtime the jocks would kick our chairs, or push us down onto the table from behind. They would knock our food trays onto the floor, trip us or throw food as we were walking by. When we sat down, they would pelt us with candy from another table. In the hallways, they would push kids into lockers and call them names while their friends stood by and laughed at the show. In gym class, they would beat kids up in the locker room because the teachers weren't around.
>
> Seniors at Columbine would do things like pour baby oil on the floor, then literally "go bowling" with freshman; they would throw the kid across the floor, and since he couldn't stop, he crashed right into other kids while the jocks pointed and giggled. The administration finally put a stop to it after a freshman girl slipped and broke her arm.
>
> One guy, a wrestler who everyone knew to avoid, liked to make kids get down on the ground and push pennies along the floor with their noses. This is what happened during school hours, as kids were passing from one class to another. Teachers would see it and look the other way. "Boys will be boys," they'd say, and laugh (50).

Dylan Klebold actually videotaped an incident of harassment of himself and Eric. He was holding the camera and taping as he, Eric, and a boy named Mike were walking down a corridor in Columbine High School (Jefferson County Sheriff's Office 2003). As they walked down the hall, they would ask approaching students, mostly girls, to wave and say hello to the camera, which they did quite willingly. In the middle of the wide corridor down which they were walking was a double archway. The boys were headed toward the right archway. Approaching them from the opposite direction was a group of four boys; one was quite large, weighing well over 200 pounds, and wore a sweatshirt that said, "Columbine Football." Instead of keeping to the right, the four boys moved through the left archway just before Eric, Mike, and Dylan entered it. As the four boys walked by, the one with the football shirt walked to Dylan's left, and a taller, thinner boy walked to Dylan's right. In the split second before they passed Dylan,

FIGURE 5.1: *Hall scene videotaped by Dylan Klebold*

the boy on Dylan's left raised his left elbow, and the boy on the right raised his right elbow. The video camera spun to the right and Dylan yelled out, "Aagh." A short burst of laughter from the four boys resounded on the soundtrack as they walked away. As Klebold, Harris, and Mike proceeded through the archway, they muttered something to each other; however, voices were low and inaudible. The tape continued for another thirty seconds during which the boys continued walking down the hall as if nothing had happened.

Apparently such behavior was common enough to be accepted as normative. Figure 5.1 contains a sequence of six frames from the video. On the upper left, Mike, in a white shirt, is on the left, and Eric, in the black shirt, is on the right. Between them are the four male students as they approach through the arch to their left. In the frame on the upper right, the boys are passing each other, with the boy in the football shirt on the left, followed by the boy in the red shirt. Notice that as they pass, Eric has lowered his head and moved ahead of Mike. A third boy is on the extreme right. In the middle left frame, the right elbow of the boy on Dylan's left can be seen as can the right elbow of the boy on his right. Mike is in the middle. The camera begins swinging to the right. In the middle right frame, the camera is pointing down. Mike has turned to his right, and the upraised elbow of the boy on Dylan's right can be seen. On the bottom left is a blurred frame of the lockers to Dylan's right, as the camera has turned about sixty-five degrees to the right before swinging back. To the lower right, Eric and Mike walk toward the doors at the end of the corridor. Conversation continues as if nothing has happened. The boys turn left at the corner at the end of the hallway.

The abusive behavior by The Predators extended well beyond the grounds of Columbine High School. RH and several other athletes were convicted of trashing a home in April 1998 (Adams and Russakoff 1999; Kurtz 1999). A member of the Trenchcoat Mafia stated the following:

> RL: And what kind [of] experiences [did] you have in terms of harassment?
> SJ: Harassment and that sort, um, I personally suffered severe harassment.
> RL: Why don't you tell me about it.
> SJ: Almost on a daily basis, finding death threats in my locker. We're talking about going in detail. It was bad. People … who I never even met, never had a class with, don't know who they were to this day. I didn't drive at the time I was in high school; I always walked home. And every day when they'd drive by, they'd throw trash out their window at me, glass bottles. I'm sorry, you get hit with a glass bottle that's going forty miles an hour, that hurts pretty bad. Like I said, I never even knew these people, so didn't even know what their motivation was. But this is something I had to put up with nearly every day for four years.
> DL: Did they wear white hats?
> SJ: Sometimes they wore baseball caps. I could never really get a good look at them, too busy dodging stuff.
> RL: Why do you think that you were targeted?
> SJ: I would assume that it was just because I was an outcast, different; I didn't fit into any of the groups (Recorded April 10, 2003).

Eric Harris, in his journals, also complained of being the target of objects thrown from cars on his way home. Brooks Brown related the following experience to a reporter (Adams and Russakoff 1999): "This past year, they [Harris and Klebold] and friend Brooks Brown were outside school when a carload of athletes, wearing their trademark white caps, threw a bottle at them, which shattered at their feet. Brown recalled Klebold saying, 'Don't worry, man, it happens all the time'" (A1).

In the wake of the shootings, a reporter interviewed a member of the Trenchcoat Mafia who otherwise remained anonymous. He related the following incident (Greene 1999): "While the teen biked home from school, he said, jocks would 'speed past at 40, 50 mph' and toss pop cans or cups full of sticky soda at him. Sometimes they threw rocks or even sideswiped his bike with their cars.

Although The Predators were the major source of the bullying, they were not the only ones who attempted to intimidate their peers. IG retold the story of a fellow student who spread false rumors about his sexual orientation. Another student, who admitted that he had been harassed, seemed to accept such behavior as normal in high school:

RL: When you were at Columbine, were you harassed or bothered by other students in any way?

AM: Yeah. I think a lot of people were. It's just high school, I guess. I mean I wasn't in the popular crowd, but I had friends who were popular and stuff, but I think everybody got picked on at one point or another (Recorded May 20, 2003).

Another former student told a much darker, and in retrospect, scary, story about harassment and intimidation of her brother, a special-education student with learning disabilities:

EK: Harris and Klebold … would follow my brother around and threaten they were going to kill him. It got to the point where my brother didn't want to go to school at all, because he was very intimidated by them. And my parents got the administration involved, and said, "Hey, these two kids are threatening my son that they're going to kill him, and my son doesn't want to go to school or anything like that." Basically all the administration did was call Eric and Klebold into the office, have a talk with them, but nothing happened. Like they stopped threatening my brother, but nothing, you know, they didn't like punish them or anything like that.

RL: But they did get them to stop threatening your brother?

EK: Yes.

RL: And that Harris and Klebold spent the better part of a semester harassing and intimidating your brother?

EK: I'd say it was for a month or two. And my brother said that they'd be outside of a good majority of his classes; they'd follow him to the next one. He said it seemed like they were always there, and that he didn't want to go to school because he was outright scared of them, and he was in tears when he told my mom that he didn't want to go to school because of these kids (Recorded May 12, 2003).

THE VISIBILITY OF BULLYING

How visible was bullying at Columbine high school? According to many students, bullying was an everyday occurrence. Obviously, the recipients of bullying claimed that it was widespread and that it was highly visible. However, numerous students, faculty members, and Principal DeAngelis claimed that bullying was rare. Once the media began focusing on bullying and accusing the faculty and administration of tolerating it, many students and adults became highly defensive about the image of Columbine High, denying the existence of predatory relationships in the high school. Not surprisingly, such denial was most often found among students in the leading crowd and the administration. The following was reported in an interview with several students who were members of the leading group:

MS1: The whole thing about jocks is not true. Like jocks or football players run the school. We are the same as anybody else. It's the same in every other school I've been to. I've been to Chatfield, Heritage schools. It's the exact same everywhere else. There are cliques in high school no matter where you go. [Another student interjects "yes."] People say there is a lot of stereotyping, but there's not.

MS2: Kids don't get picked on in the halls.

MS1: Yeah.

MS2: Kids are treated the same. The administration does a great job.

MS3: I think Columbine is more accepting of people than most schools.

MS2: Yeah. They may call them "cliques" or whatever, but, like, this is my group of friends; it's not like I necessarily don't like other people, but these are my friends; they are the people I hang out with more often than anybody else. It has nothing to do with, like, tension between them being a skater and me being a jock. That's middle school stuff. That's out of the window.

RL: So there is no harassment that goes on?

MS2: No, there's harassment, but there's no more harassment [at Columbine] than any other high school.

MS1: Yeah. Probably less.

MS2: ...I've seen a lot worse at Chatfield [relative to] Columbine. I've seen at Chatfield, "You're a freshman," and they'll throw them up against the locker. Sometimes I've seen a kid break his arm because of it. At Columbine, it's not like that at all (Recorded May 9, 2003).

Another student, who, although not a member of the leading crowd, was a high-status inbetweener, stated the following:

RL: What was the climate like inside the school? Were there people who lorded over other people, and engaged in systematic harassment, or was it fairly copasetic?

IG: I wouldn't call it systematic harassment. I don't think anyone showed up on any particular day and said, "I'm going to make fun of or harass this person or this group of people today. Everybody kind of understood where the boundaries were, kind of "this clique doesn't talk to this clique" and the mechanics of it were very well understood. There was definitely resentment among the cliques. I mean I'm not a big fan of jocks. I'll tell you that right now.

RL: Okay. Did you ever see any physical intimidation?

IG: A little bit, but only from one individual. An individual by the name of RH. He ...

RL: He's the wrestler.

IG: He was a wrestler, but his little brother got more attention that he did. He was a much better wrestler. RH's a head case, to say the least. I mean, he got kicked out of the school he was in before for some violent act, and we landed him. I don't know how. But he was a jerk. And he would intimidate people physically. That was what he was all about. I mean, there were so many different stories about how RH did this, that, or the other. There were times that you could see him using his size and using his, I guess you could say "prowess," to intimidate people. He even tried it with me once, and he asked

> me why I had quit the football team. I just looked at him and said, "It's none of your business. I wanted to swim anyway." He went, "Okay." That's really the only individual I ever saw who really got violent. I mean, there were fights, but nothing of real merit, and there weren't any knock down, drag out brawls in the school. If anything started, a teacher was there to break up things. For the most part, everybody either knew their place, or they got along. There wasn't any real—I didn't see anything as far as clique wars, or anything like that. Like I said, everybody kind of knew their place (Recorded April 10, 2003).

This particular point of view was held by Principal DeAngelis, who said,

> DE: I've been here twenty-five years, and I'll bet you that I can count on the fingers of two hands, the number of fights we've had in school. Not that they don't occur off campus. But I'll tell you, some of the worst fights we've ever had in this school were between two females. Hair pulling, and biting, and scratching ... I never want to get in the way of a female fight. But usually, we're in a situation where if I walk up and say "knock it off," they stop. They're hoping someone will break it up. There wasn't a lot of violence in the school. Was there bullying going on? There was bullying going on. The kids that were bullying. ... The kids were going home and telling their parents, and their parents were calling me (Recorded April 28, 2004).

The dominant view about bullying and harassment was that it occurred, but it was relatively rare. The administration was aware of The Predators, but figured that they had the situation under control. However, Principal DeAngelis claimed, rightly, that students are not going to harass and intimidate their peers in front of adult authorities. Therefore, the vast majority of harassment and intimidation occurred outside the purview of faculty, staff, and administration. Because of this, many school officials radically underestimated the amount of violence that occurred in their school. This was in evidence in the investigation of the Colorado State Attorney General's Office into bullying in schools (Sanko 2000). The investigation included thirty high schools in Colorado. Students routinely reported dramatically more incidences of school violence and drug abuse than administrators. Garbarino and deLara (2002), in their study of bullying, reported that parents and professional educators were unaware of the level of violence experienced by adolescents:

> It is one thing for adults to determine that a school environment is safe based upon their experience of it or their perceptions of day-to-day life. It is quite another thing for the students to declare that same school to be safe. The adults may feel safe, for instance, because they have power. Students overwhelmingly reported teachers and other adults on the school grounds do not have any clue about how many actual incidents of physical and emotional violence and harassment occur in the course of a day (34–35).

This was certainly the case at Columbine High School. Not only were the adults unaware of the level of predation, but so were the majority of students. Recall the testimony of IG, who, when attending a Youth Advisory Council of Jefferson County School District days before the shooting, during discussions about rampage shootings, such as those in Jonesboro, Arkansas, and Paducah, Kentucky, thought that the idea of a rampage shooting at Columbine High School was "crazy." IG was not the only student who was deluded by the seeming pacifism of Columbine's halls. Because of the extreme polarization of the student peers structure at Columbine High School, literally two perspectives existed about bullying and harassment; those students who adopted the dominant perspective downplayed or, as in the case of IG, did not perceive the predation occurring routinely. Kurtz (1999) reported:

> At Brooke Gibson's high school, nasty nicknames were the norm. "Nigger lover" was what they called her when she listened to rap. "Dyke" when she cut her blond hair short.
>
> At the school her sister Layn attended, nicknames might poke fun at someone's shirt color, but never their skin color or sexual orientation.
>
> It was the same school.
>
> Columbine (4A).

As a matter of fact, students may have witnessed such intimidation but redefined it as kids having fun, as did Brooke Gibson's sister, Layn. This self-justification was asserted by members of the leading crowd and their hangers-on not as predatory behavior but as mutual friends kidding each other. Kurtz (1999) reported, "'They were kind of like bullies,' said Dave Deidel, a star athlete who graduated this year. 'But most of the "bullying" was aimed at fellow athletes, and it was all in fun,' Deidel said" (4A). Similarly this researcher recorded the following:

> RL: Why do you like [Columbine] so much?

MS1: Everybody gets along. I have never seen any bullying. In disagreements among people, I have never seen anybody go out of their way to make people uncomfortable or anything.

RL: Has anybody here been harassed?

MS2: The only harassment that occurs is harassment between your friends. ... It's not like, "Oh, that is a nerd, let's go pick on him." The media has a view on Columbine, they don't understand, because they hear some words. They don't know because they haven't been in the building to see what goes on between classes ... (Recorded May 9, 2003).

The dominant view of harassment literally defined it out of existence. It's not harassment at all, but just friends having a little fun among themselves. Yet, according to the outcast students, they were targeted for abuse by the jocks because they were at the bottom of the peer status structure. Although anyone who happened to be in the wrong place at the wrong time could be confronted by the jocks, the outcasts were the preferred targets of the jocks and were harassed mercilessly on a daily basis. The testimony above by SJ, Eric Harris's angry rantings on the Trenchcoat Mafia web site, Dylan Klebold's casual remarks to Brooks Brown that they were targets of objects thrown from cars all the time, indicate the ubiquity of the harassment. Another member of the Trenchcoat Mafia provided similar testimony:

RL: Did you ever experience any harassment or anything like that when you were [at Columbine]?

ED: Every day (Recorded May 10, 2003).

This kind of predatory behavior, although primarily the province of the jocks, was apparently widespread in Columbine. IG described above how he was harassed by another student, which led to a physical confrontation between himself and the smaller student that put a stop to the harassment.

ED transferred from Columbine to an alternative school because of the treatment he experienced there. When interviewed by the police in the investigation of the shootings because he was identified as a member of the Trenchcoat Mafia, even though he was not enrolled at Columbine High School at the time, he indicated that he had transferred because of harassment by students and faculty. This raises a serious question about the role of adults in the perpetuation of predatory relationships among the students at Columbine High School.

THE ROLE OF ADULTS IN HARASSMENT

Most adults were not only unaware of how much bullying and intimidation occurred in the halls of Columbine, but they were also ignorant of what constituted bullying and intimidation. Numerous statements by students indicated that faculty, especially teachers who were also coaches, either inadvertently or openly encouraged or participated in the harassment or humiliation of students. Principal DeAngelis has continually defended the school and the faculty against accusations of systematic harassment. He has maintained throughout that harassment was not a serious problem at Columbine High School. DeAngelis was most defensive about the putative role that faculty played in encouraging bullying. In an interview, he stated the following:

> [O]ne of the things that really bothered me [was] when they said bullying was going on and teachers would just turn their heads the other way. Oh, I'm not saying bullying wasn't happening, but as far as teachers turning the other way … letting a lot of kids get by with it; I'm sorry, that's not the case (Recorded April 28, 2004).

However, a staff member told this researcher the following:

> RL: So you have some insight into the internal climate of the school. What about the roles of the teacher in violence prevention, and things like that?
>
> L: I would say there were probably several staff members that would intervene, but I think there's a huge portion would not intervene and felt it was more administrative responsibility. [However,] the administration wasn't willing to tackle some of those things … (Recorded May 12, 2003).

Yet far more serious accusations about the faculty aiding and abetting student harassment were reported in the media and to this researcher by students who had been victimized in situations where faculty members were active participants. The following was related to me by ED after telling me that he was harassed on a daily basis:

> RL: Can you describe a typical instance for me?

ED: A typical instance would be one of the more popular people because for some reason they felt like it, like better people, just decided to insult me and my friends, and it was ... another of those things that really frustrated me. Because they would be there, obviously specifically picking on me, with teachers standing nearby or other faculty members, and if I did anything to stand up for myself, such as return the insult with repartee, I would be the one who would get in trouble if anybody did. Most of the time there was [a problem], the teachers just ignored it, probably the best thing they could have done. But every once in a while they would ignore it, or in one particular case, they kind of joined in.

RL: Can you describe it to me? What I need is specific instances. ...

ED: One time that I can recall, quite clearly, I was sitting in the lunchroom in my free hour, just talking with my friends, and the guy who was most popular at the time. ... He would came down ... it seemed like he was trying to pick a fight with me or just trying to belittle me, and one of the—he happened to be the star player on one of the wrestling teams—but I don't think it was his coach, but like an assistant coach or something, who also happened to be the vice principal at the time, came up and also joined in.

RL: What did the vice principal say?

ED: It wasn't really that he said anything. He was kind of in there, cheering him on. Basically the "attaboy" type of thing (Recorded May 10, 2003).

Similarly, a female member of the leading crowd told a story of her public humiliation by a coach. The interview was with two former Columbine students. As CL related the story, SK, who witnessed the incident, confirmed her version.

CL: Did you guys [NB: the interviewers] ever hear about the megaphone incident?

RL: Not that I can remember.

CL: One of the teachers was using the megaphone. [To SK] Tell me you remember that.

SK: I remember it. I'm starting to remember who. ...

CL: Coach T. You know the megaphones you use for police to call people?

SK: He'd walk down the fucking halls with it.

CL: And he would stand in the hallways during passing period and make fun of kids, like oh, you look like a fag, or like, cool backpack, or you guys are holding hands, just like pick on individual people. And my personal incident with that, which ended it for a little while; he let RH have that megaphone for a little while. So RH's picking on people until he sees me.
SK: This is [Coach] T who's now in charge of the Bible Club.
CL: Right.
DL: Bible Club in the school?
SK: Oh my God, yeah. …
CL: Well RH sees me in the hallway with LJ, and he doesn't like LJ. … So he decides to shout profanities over the megaphone about me, like CL's a slut, CL has sex with all the guys at Columbine, she's been passed around the football team.
SK: I remember this.
CL: And I was horrified, just like, 'cause everyone was staring at me and laughing, everybody. And Coach T, the look on his face was like, "Uh oh, I'm going to get in trouble for this one." So he takes the megaphone back from RH, and that's it. Nothing ever came of it. That was it. I was horrified. Over a loud speaker, saying those things about me.
DL: What did the other kids, general group of kids that heard it… ?
CL: Laughing. They were laughing.
DL: Nobody was as horrified as you.
SK: Some of us were. We couldn't act it. It was a bad school. It was not fun.
CL: *And those were like daily occurrences* (Recorded April 20, 2004, emphasis added).

Other investigators reported similar complaints by other students who attended Columbine high school. For example, Adams and Russakoff (1999) reported the following:

> The state wrestling champ was regularly permitted to park his $100,000 Hummer all day in a 15-minute space. A football player was allowed to tease a girl about her breasts in class without fear of retribution by his teacher, also the boy's coach. The sports trophies were showcased in the front hall—the artwork, down a back corridor.
>
> Columbine High School is a culture where initiation rituals meant upperclass wrestlers twisted the nipples of freshman wrestlers until they

> turned purple and tennis players sent hard volleys to younger teammates' backsides. Sports pages in the yearbook were in color, a national debating team and other clubs in black and white. The homecoming king was a football player on probation for burglary.
>
> All of it angered and oppressed Eric Harris and Dylan Klebold, leading to the April day when they staged their murderous rampage here, killing 13 and wounding 21.
>
> Columbine may be no different from thousands of high schools in glorifying athletes. But in the weeks since one of the worst school shootings in history, every aspect of what had seemed "normal" is now being re-examined. Increasingly, as parents and students replay images of life at Columbine, they are freeze-framing on injustices suffered at the hands of athletes, wondering aloud why almost no one—not teachers, not administrators, not coaches, not most students, not parents—took the problem seriously.
>
> No one thinks the high tolerance for athletic mischief explains away or excuses the two boys' horrific actions. But some parents and students believe a school wide indulgence of certain jocks—their criminal convictions, physical abuse, sexual and racial bullying—intensified the killers' feelings of powerlessness and galvanized their fantasies of revenge.
>
> In one episode, they saw state wrestling champion Rocky Wayne Hoffschneider shoving his girlfriend into a locker, in front of a teacher, who did nothing, according to a close friend. "We used to talk about Rocky a lot," said the friend, who asked not to be identified. "We'd say things like 'He should be in jail for the stuff he does.'" Another friend of Klebold's, Andrew Beard, remembers distinctly Klebold's rage at four football players' "getting off" after destroying a man's apartment last year (A1).

Kurtz (1999) also reported instances in which faculty and staff members seemed to be unresponsive to the complaints of students who were harassed by members of the football and wrestling teams:

> Being different at Columbine ... was difficult for Brooke Gibson. ... Gibson wore her blond hair long when short hair was the style in junior high. Before graduating in 1996, she cut her hair short like a boy's when other girls had long hair. For this she was called lesbian and dyke.
>
> She didn't bother to report it to an administrator or counselor. Nor did she report the boy who told her his injured ankle might feel better

> if Gibson gave him oral sex. She said she didn't see the point. She felt nothing would have come of it. She was a 100-pound girl. Her tormentors were star jocks. …
>
> Brooke Gibson still has questions about the 1994 weight lifting class where she tried to report harassment by athletes. It started with the radio. She told male athletes in the class she wanted to listen to rap. They wanted to listen to '70s rock. They called her a "nigger lover." Then, she said, they suggested she have sex with a black student in the class. She said she reported one boy to counselor Charles Shom. "He denied it, and nobody believed it happened," Gibson said. "They were like 'Oh, all right, whatever, some little mediocre girl'"(4A).

Garbarino and deLara (2002) pointed out that one of the most risky acts students can do is to inform an adult about the behaviors of their peers. There is no assurance that it will be handled properly by the adult authority. A student revealed the following:

> At Columbine, here's how [conflict resolution] worked. … It started off sophomore year, TS was one of RH's right hand men, and TS came up to the smokers one day, and he wanted to bum a cigarette from me, and I refused. I said "no," because I only had like three left—I don't remember why. I had a good reason, but it wasn't just because I didn't like him. So his friends grabbed me and threw me up against a chain link fence and pounded my stomach. I fell on the ground. A teacher saw this, and they pulled us in for conflict resolution with Mr. Collins, my school counselor. He then did this thing with TS and me where he had us talk through the whole thing. He had us go through all the problems we were having, blah, blah. Afterwards, [TS] and his friends found me outside behind the temporary [bungalow] at Columbine where they had first aid classes, oddly enough. They threw me into it, and they kicked me in the face a number of times. I never told anyone again about TS. He continued to beat me mercilessly up until my senior year (Recorded May 13, 2003).

Although the student did not alert the adult authorities, the situation came to the attention of the adults, who, although well-meaning, bungled the conflict resolution process, failed to report physical violence to the appropriate authorities, failed to inform parents, and failed to follow up on the incident. Ineptness or disregard by adult authorities often creates situations worse than those they attempt to solve. When authorities, such as Principal DeAngelis, ask why students do not inform them of their problems, the answer is that too many of them have had bad experiences in doing so.

Although The Predators denied their participation in harassing and humiliating their peers to the media (Adams and Russakoff 1999; Kurtz 1999), one member let down his guard and told a reporter for *Time Magazine* the following:

> Columbine is a clean, good place except for those rejects [NB: outcast students, including Klebold and Harris]. Most kids didn't want them here. They're into witchcraft. They were into voodoo dolls. Sure, we teased them. But what you expect with kids who come to school with weird hairdos and horns on their hats? It's not just jocks; the whole school's disgusted with them. They're a bunch of homos, grabbing each others' private parts. If you want to get rid of someone, usually you tease 'em. So the whole school would call them homos, and when they did something sick, we'd tell them, "You're sick and that's wrong." [Quoted in Garbarino and deLara (2002), 79].

The candor of this predator suggests that in addition to having fun at the expense of fellow students, the predators perceived themselves as defending the moral order of the school. They perceived themselves as acting with the will of the majority of the students. The mere presence of the outcast students was judged to be a blot on the pristine nature of Columbine High School, which gave them the right to harass and humiliate them. This astonishing admission raises serious questions about the unintended consequences of faculty members, who were also coaches, in tolerating and, in some cases, abetting the behavior of the predators. Not only does it create a climate in which interpersonal violence is tolerated, but it also justifies in the minds of those who engage in it the harassment of those persons who have been defined as outside the normative standard. That is, the tolerance of predation by adults is *corrupting* (Garbarino and deLara 2002). Not only does it encourage the repetition of such behaviors, but it teaches impressionable young minds that it is all right to treat with disdain and prejudice those who are different. This particular view had some support in the larger community. Adams and Russakoff (1999) quote a parent: "'They [those students who were outcasts] had no school spirit and they wanted to be different,' Randy Thurmon, parent of a wrestler and football player, said of the killers. 'Anyone who shows any kind of school spirit, any pride in the school, they're accepted.'"

As the evidence above has shown, this particular view of the openness of the internal climate of the school was counterfactual. Although the outcast students took the brunt of the abuse by the predators, numerous students testified that anybody could be violated if he/she happened to be at the wrong place at the wrong time. The student elites, both male and female, defended their status quite viciously.

A TOXIC ENVIRONMENT

These stories raise several issues about the internal context of Columbine High School that evoked numerous complaints from many students. First, male faculty members who were also coaches were perceived by students as encouraging predatory behavior by members of the football and wrestling teams. Several incidents were instigated by the same student who everyone in the school, including faculty and administration, knew engaged in predatory behavior. He had been expelled from his previous school because of his violent predilections. Yet some coaches encouraged his antisocial behavior. Second, many students complained about the hypocrisy of those people who called themselves "Christians" as a way of differentiating themselves as a moral elite from nonobservant Christians or members of mainline Protestant sects. These students engaged in such un-Christian acts as abetting or participating in the public humiliation of others and violence toward the weak, socially different, or those otherwise incapable of defending themselves. Third, many students, especially those at the bottom of the student status structure, perceived a hierarchy of privilege in which those at the top were given special treatment and exempted from punishment except when such behavior could no longer be ignored. Many students thought that such differential treatment was unjust.

RELIGIOUS INTOLERANCE

Brooks Brown (2002) was perhaps the most vociferous accuser of the evangelicals, citing their hypocrisy and aggression. In a personal interview, Brown indicated that the leadership of the predatory jocks was identified as part of the group of students who identified themselves as "deep Christians."

RL: Were there kids who were … evangelicals who also engaged in physical intimidation … , I mean other than saying you're going to hell?
BB: RH and his group, they were all Christians. Good little Christians.
RL: Were they practicing evangelicals?

BB: I don't know if they were evangelicals. I don't know what religion most of the kids were; I know that they were deep Christian. I think evangelicals were reborn or born-agains. Most of these were born-agains, New Age Christianity, whatever the hell it's called. None of them were actually Christian; they just said they were. There's a difference (Recorded in May 13, 2003).

Despite Brooks Brown's antagonism toward proselytizing evangelicals, this statement reveals a certain sympathy toward them. He identified those who call themselves "Christians," but who act toward others in unchristian ways as not truly Christian. Coach T., who was the faculty sponsor of the morning Bible study group called Young Life, had been implicated by at least two students in encouraging predatory behavior. In Chapter 3, the religious overtones of the shooting were discussed in detail; the antagonism toward evangelicals expressed by Klebold and Harris in the basement tapes was elaborated. They reviled deep Christian students for their self-perceptions as moral elite. In addition, the aggressiveness of evangelical community in attempting to define the killings as specifically an attack on them without consideration of alternative motivations, the hijacking by evangelicals of the nationally-televised memorial service on April 25, 1999, attempts by evangelical preachers to use the shootings to expand the movement and recruit new members, the beatification of Rachel Scott and Cassie Bernall as martyrs in the defense of their beliefs, and vilification of Lutheran minister, Don Marxhausen, who, as a consequence, lost his congregation and temporarily moved away from the area, indicate the aggressiveness and viciousness with which the evangelical community could act. In response to criticism of the takeover of the national memorial service, leaders of the evangelical community maintained, in effect, that this was their territory and those who did not like it could move away, a local version of "America, love it or leave it."

Also in Chapter 3, several young women who were former Columbine students complained about members of Young Life claiming piety, but who were heavy partiers, drinkers, dope-smokers, and sexual players. The fact that the worst predators on campus also identified themselves as deep Christians, who were also abetted by the coach who was the sponsor of Young Life, tended to make many Columbine students cynical about the religious commitment of their peers. It was not at all uncommon for students to make distinctions between those people, such as Rachel Scott, who seemed to embody the Christian ideal of acting out of love, and people such as RH and LJ, who also claimed to be deep Christians, but who bullied, harassed, and intimidated their peers.

Religious intolerance was also in evidence in the form of anti-Semitism. Very few Jewish students lived in the Columbine area and attended Columbine High School. The following incident was reported extensively (Adams and Russakoff 1999; Kurtz 1999). Several versions of the story exist. However, RH identified as a "deep Christian," and a fellow football player, early in the 1996–1997 school year, began harassing Jonathan Green in gym class, first by saying, "There's another Jew in the oven," every time they made a basket. The intimidation escalated. Adams and Russakoff (1999) wrote:

> "They pinned him [Green] on the ground and did 'body twisters,'" Greene said. "He got bruises all over his body. Then the threats began about setting him on fire and burning him."
>
> Stephen Green, Jonathan's father, went to Place [the gym coach], DeAngelis and his son's guidance counselor. "They said, 'This stuff can happen.' They looked at me like I was a problem," he said. Green called the school board, which notified the police. Hoffschneider and the other athlete were charged with harassment, kicking and striking, court records show, and sentenced to probation. But Hoffschneider was allowed to continue his football and wrestling (A1).

Kurtz (1999) noted that Stephen Green, Jonathan's father, claimed that the administration did nothing until he threatened a lawsuit, after which, the Jefferson County Board of Education called the police. In another version, Coach Place called the boys into his office and called the Jefferson County Sheriff's department, which cited the two boys for "ethnic intimidation." This story was retold to this researcher by several persons.

INJUSTICE

The most serious and corrosive result of adult sanctioning of predatory behavior was a sense among the students of powerlessness and a lack of justice. For example, ED, who was verbally harassed by RH in the presence of a vice principal, perceived himself as in a no-win situation: If he responded verbally to RH's taunts, he would get into trouble; if he did not respond, he would be publicly humiliated. He did not respond and eventually transferred to another school. Brooks Brown (Brown and Merritt 2002) summarized the feelings of injustice voiced by students at the bottom of the peer structure:

> If people wanted to know what Columbine was like, I'd tell them. I'd tell them about the bullies who shoved the kids they didn't like into lockers, called them "faggots" every time they walked past. I'd tell them about the jocks who picked relentlessly on anyone they considered to be below them. The teachers turned a blind eye to the brutalization of their pupils, because those pupils weren't the favorites.
>
> I told them about the way those who were "different" were crushed, and fights happened so regularly outside school that no one even paid attention. I told what it was like to live in constant fear of other kids who'd gone out of control, knowing full well that the teachers would turn a blind eye. After all, those kids were their favorites. We were the troublemakers.
>
> "Eric and Dylan are the ones responsible for creating this tragedy," I told them. "However, Columbine is responsible for creating Eric and Dylan" (163).

Perhaps one of the most serious sources of injustice was the perceived differential treatment of RH, who has been identified by numerous students as the prime source of predation on campus. Stories abound about personal confrontations and witnesses of violence to students, including female students, whom he physically and verbally abused. SK related a story about how he turned a corner in the hallway and bumped into RH and was beaten up. He and his crowd of wrestling and football teammates abused and humiliated fellow students at will. Every student that was interviewed by this researcher knew him either first-hand or by reputation. One student (IG), who identified himself as having relatively high peer status though not a member of the leading crowd, referred to RH as a "head case."

The students at the bottom of the social structure, including members of the Trenchcoat Mafia, could all relate a story in which they had been verbally or physically attacked by him. Although the moniker "Trenchcoat Mafia" was meant as a pejorative, the Trenchcoaters, in an act of cultural defiance, turned it into a badge of honor. Media reports told of RH and his friends stuffing a member of the Trenchcoat Mafia into a trash can (Adams and Russakoff 1999). Although the media did not mention names, the individual in the news report confirmed it in an interview with the researcher.

What bothered students the most, especially those at the bottom of the peer social structure, was the perception that, because RH and his posse, popularly known as the "Steroid Poster Boys," were star athletes, they received deferential treatment. Prendergast (1999) interviewed a female student who was a freshman and a goth, putting her at the bottom of the student status hierarchy, who, echoing students quoted above, indicated her sense of vulnerability and injustice at the hands of the jocks.

> There were a lot of things Melissa Sowder didn't like about Columbine High School. The bullies, for instance. They were football players, mostly. They shoved her friends in the halls and threw snowballs or bottles at them on the way home. Sometimes they shoved her, too. Who needed it? "Teachers would see them push someone into a locker, and they'd just ignore it," she says. "I think they were afraid of the students. They didn't stop half the fights in that school."

According to Prendergast (1999), Melissa Sowder was a student whom the administration identified as a problem:

> In her first few weeks at Columbine, Sowder ditched class several times, resulting in a parent conference and restrictions imposed on her ability to leave campus during the day. But when she tried to complain to teachers about harassment by jocks, she was told, "Deal with it," she says.

Prior to the attack on the school on April 19, 1999, Miss Sowder was interviewed by a counselor after being late to a class (Prendergast 1999). He asked her what she thought during the day when she was in school. She told him she thought about blowing up the school. She was given a one-day suspension, and her parents were called. The school authorities viewed her comment as a threat, and her behavior was closely monitored by faculty and staff.

Although such thoughts were anathema to the vast majority of students attending Columbine High School, students who were fiercely proud of its athletic and academic achievements, such sentiments were quite common among the outcasts. They felt that they were being unjustly treated. A well-known incident, reported above from a different perspective (Adams and Russakoff 1999) was recounted by Huerter (2000):

> I spoke with some … Trenchcoat Mafia [members]. They talked about not being picked on as a group, but about individuals being picked on when they were separated. Specifically, females remembered being called "sluts" and "Nazi lesbians" by jocks. Other times there were accounts of members being shoved, thrown into walls, pushed and on and least one occasion having a bag of ice water thrown onto a Trenchcoat Mafia member by a table of "jocks." On this particular occasion the

> jocks and the Trenchcoat Mafia were in the cafeteria, the bag was thrown, words were exchanged, and both groups got up to go outside and fight. "Sid," a security person, intervened and escorted those in the "Trenchcoat Mafia" to administration. The "Trenchcoat Mafia" members were suspended for 3 days while none of the "jocks" were taken to administration nor received any apparent disciplinary action (3–4).

The Huerter Report (2000) contains an enumeration of incidents where jocks were given preferential treatment or untoward leniency, or other students were punished in a given incident where the jocks were not. One of the more egregious examples was the way in which the administration dealt with a restraining order issued by a judge against the star fullback of the football team. His girlfriend found him to be extremely possessive and emotionally out-of-control. She told the researcher the following:

> The boyfriend I was with ... he was taking supplements, I guess you could say, to perform better in football. And some of those supplements caused you to have outrages and your emotions are heightened, and so I had to deal with that, and I had broken up with him, but he wouldn't take no for an answer, I guess you could say. And on a repeated basis, he would come to my house when I wasn't there. He would follow me to work, and he was always threatening to beat up people. He was stalking, basically, legally it was stalking. So I ended up getting a restraining order. And he violated the restraining order and he went to jail (Recorded April 30, 2004).

The parents met with Principal DeAngelis about enforcing the temporary restraining order. The male student continued to violate it, and DeAngelis stated that the school would have difficulty honoring the restraining order and suggested that they would have somebody follow her around at school, which was not acceptable to her and her family, because they perceived themselves as being victims and that if there was to be accommodation, it should be done on the part of the aggressor. This occurred just prior to the shootings on April 20, 1999. She told this researcher that while the assault was occurring in the school, she had gone home to lunch, had locked the doors to her house, and had pulled down the shades in an effort to hide from her former boyfriend. He came to the house, banged on the door, yelled that he knew she was there, and claimed that he could not live without her.

According to Huerter (2000), the male aggressor was allowed to stay in school. Because he was a junior and she was a senior, when classes reconvened at Chatfield High School following the shootings, she was allowed not to return to classes without penalty to her grades. Her former boyfriend took full advantage of the fact that he was in school and she was not by publicly disparaging her, claiming, as did RH, that she was sleeping around with the football team and that she was a slut.

The balance of the year at Chatfield High School was not devoted to academics but was directed toward counseling students and providing them a communal experience in which they could deal with their traumatic experiences. Many Columbine students reflected on that period in which the status hierarchy literally melted away and students who had never talked to each other experienced an incredible sense of collective identity and community. A student who was in the school during the shootings noted:

> You know, one thing that I noticed that really affected me about it afterwards, was that even the people that hated me before, after the shooting happened, when we saw each other, when we basically recognized, you just, all of those grudges went away. Everything went away. You just hugged that person. And you felt that they were really happy to see you (Recorded May 13, 2003).

Thus, the girlfriend ended up paying doubly for the transgressions of her boyfriend, who, by violating the terms of the restraining order, committed a felony. One must ask, as some students did, if this had happened between a member of the Trenchcoat Mafia and his girlfriend, whether such an outcome would have been adjudicated by the administration. Not only was she deprived of the healing forces of a community coming together in sharing their sorrow and pain, but her boyfriend was given the opportunity to besmirch her reputation without her having a chance to defend herself. Even more egregiously, this incident was carried over to the next year by members of the faculty. Huerter (2000) reported that a shop teacher, in front of the victim's brother declared the issue as "bullshit." The victim's mother was informed by another parent that Columbine staff members were repeating her boyfriend's accusation that she was being passed around by members of the football team. Huerter continued:

> The young male in question went on to play football at a university. The president, when challenged about having this young man playing on scholarship for that university, stated in a letter that his staff [had] received strong endorsement from Columbine staff about this young man. The university president's letter also stated that he was told from staff at

> Columbine that the young man "had never been charged with any wrongdoing, that the allegations filed [against] him were never substantiated and, while there was briefly an *ex parte* restraining order filed against him, it was dropped for lack of evidence to support it" (4).

An unnamed star member of the football team missed the team bus for a football game because he had been arrested and his release from jail was too late to make the bus (Huerter 2000). The coach of the football team had this person tell the rest of the team why he was late and told him that he could not play in the first half of the game. He was allowed in the game during the second quarter. Another player had forgotten his mouthpiece; without it, he was ineligible to play. Instead of having the latecomer provide his mouthpiece, another player was asked to supply his, making him ineligible to play in the game. Huerter noted that the incident left people with the belief that favoritism existed for some jocks; the lesson was that if you were valuable to the team, negative consequences did not flow from bad behavior.

The above story has a companion story that was related to this researcher by CL (Recorded May 13, 2004). Accordingly, one of the predators had rolled his expensive new car and was arrested by the county sheriff for driving under the influence of alcohol (DUI). According to CL, the wrestling coach, needing the arrested student to participate in the wrestling meet, bailed him out of jail, and drove him straight to the meet.

Several incidences were reported of students refusing to go to school or demanding a transfer because of intimidation by the jocks at Columbine. Huerter (2000) mentioned two such incidences. These incidents are probably just the tip of the iceberg, since one of the interviewees for this study, ED, transferred out specifically because of the harassment he experienced and the apparent toleration of such behavior by faculty members.

In addition to the toleration of sexist behavior in several cases described above, a female student wanted to talk to a girlfriend of one of the predator jocks. She called out her name; the predator came over, confronted her, and said if she wanted to know something, she should talk to him. He cornered her against the stairs, continuing to yell, clenching his fists, and calling her names. A male student who attempted to intervene was thrown off by the boyfriend. Finally, two buddies, also jocks, pulled him away from her. She recalled that two faculty members witnessed the incident but did nothing.

Another female student, a freshman, after talking with Dylan Klebold, was accosted by one of the predators who slammed her against the lockers, calling her a "fag lover" for talking with the likes of Dylan. This was quite similar to the experience of SK, described above, who was confronted by a jock when talking to the girlfriend of the football team captain.

According to Huerter (2000), the bullying by the members of the football team had become so bad that Columbine students started to boycott football games.

> In spring 1998, Coach Lowry called a meeting of the football team. He said he and received a letter from the district—they weren't bringing enough people to the games to use the larger Jeffco [NB: Jefferson County] Stadium—so they were going to have to use Trailblazer Stadium. Coach Lowry stated that he wanted all team members to treat everyone with respect *in order to increase attendance*. It was reported that several students had gone to Lowry questioning why they should attend the games when members of the football team were harassing students (7, emphasis added).

Columbine High School is surrounded by acres of play fields and practice fields, but it does not have its own football stadium. It plays its games, as do all Jefferson County high schools, in stadiums provided by the Jefferson County School District. It is remarkable that Coach Lowry demanded improved behavior of football team members for the purpose of increasing attendance at games. This kind of mixed message seems to indicate that harassment of students would be all right if it did not suppress attendance at football games, making it necessary for the Columbine Rebel football team to play their games in the less prestigious, smaller stadium.

Among those students who were subjected to predatory behavior on the part of the jocks, a pervasive sense of powerlessness and injustice was felt. Brooks Brown (Brown and Merritt 2002) articulated those feelings in relationship to Eric Harris and Dylan Klebold:

> Kids are raised on the playgrounds of their schools, where they learned that "might makes right" and that physical brawn is a far more important asset than intelligence and cunning. Yet they also learned that when they fight back, they're punished by the people [who] were supposed to protect them and dispense justice.
>
> Dylan [Klebold] was a smart kid who could see the injustices of the world as clearly as I could. He was frustrated by them, and, like many other kids he saw a bleak future for our generation.
>
> Eric [Harris] felt the same way. ... And like Dylan, Eric saw the injustices of the world quite clearly, even as he was getting beat up in

> the high school locker room or jumping to avoid the glass bottles thrown at him out of the passing cars of Columbine football players (20).

The student culture was rife with stories about the special treatment of the jocks, especially those who were members of The Predators. Huerter (2000) reported that there was a perception on the part of many students that the school was run by the jocks; if you were not a jock, you didn't fit in. There can be no denying that students perceived the campus as being run by The Predators. However, Huerter disputed that perception, noting that there were no posters in the hallways cheering on the football team. She stated, "While I believe there's a strong emphasis on sports, after reading three editions of 'Red Line,' the school's bulletin, all types of successes were noted" (7). However, she was looking in the wrong place. Her own data suggest that not only did jocks run the school, but they enforced their domination through violence or the threat of violence. It is not posters on the wall or official school news bulletins that determine who rules in adolescent peer culture. It is quite literally who rules the hallways. Without a doubt, the jocks did so without much interference by faculty or administration.

For the outcast students, who were as horrified as anybody at the shootings, empathy existed for Eric and Dylan because they knew how much they had to endure. Several of the outcasts who were interviewed for this study indicated that, in retrospect, they were not surprised by the shootings. They, too, experienced the towering rage generated by feelings of powerlessness in the face of continual humiliation and harassment (Garbarino and deLara 2002).

They were also very much aware of their own isolation as a consequence of the indifference and open hostility of their peers. In addition, as ED noted, many teachers felt similarly about them and did little to disguise it. When the jock, quoted above, said that the outcast students were a blot on the goodness and cleanliness of Columbine High School, he was reflecting the majority view. And that majority view was enforced by The Predators.

APPEARANCES AND REALITY

Entering Columbine High School on a lovely spring day in 2003, this researcher saw students going about their business, perhaps going to the library, a class, a rehearsal, the gym, the computer center, or out to lunch. The halls were clean and orderly. The students seemed happy and purposeful. Locker doors opened and slammed shut. Students walked around the spacious hallways alone or with peers or in small groups of three or four. Sometimes the talk is quiet; sometimes it is boisterous. Occasionally, students will be seen running down the halls because they are late for class or their errand is particularly urgent. These observations are expected in a well-run school.

The virtues of Columbine High School have been detailed earlier. It was the flagship high school of southern Jefferson County. It had a reputation for strong academics, a wonderful sports program, and fabulous offerings of extracurricular and enrichment activities. It had a campus a New York City high school teacher could only imagine. People moved into the area especially so their children could attend Columbine High School.

We have also examined the underbelly of Columbine. The student body had a three-tiered class system with the jocks at the top, most of the rest the students in the middle, and the outcasts at the bottom. Although many of the students in the middle resented the jocks/poms/cheerleaders for their snobbishness, viciousness, and willingness to defend their position with violence, they were acceded their role as the leading crowd in the school by virtue of their athletic prowess, physical beauty, personality, or socioeconomic status. The students at the bottom of the peer structure, if not openly vilified, were disparaged and disdained by nearly all students who were not members of that very small group. When they were bullied by the jocks, few students protested; many did what they accused teachers of doing, turning a blind eye to it. A good portion of the students thought that the outcasts invited and deserved the abuse they received.

Every adult this researcher talked to who was asked the question stated that the school was run by the coaches. But what did that mean? One teacher explained it this way:

> RL: I was told that coaches run Columbine High School. Do you have any idea what people mean by that?
>
> T: The coaches are the leaders in the school. They don't run the school. The school is run by the administration and the department chairmen—they're the ones who make the policies. The coaches don't run the school. But, like, if you look at the entire faculty, the top faculty members are people that coach. That's just their personality.
>
> RL: I see.
>
> T: But they don't run the school. They can't go to the principal and say, I want this, and this, and this (Recorded April 20, 2004).

A less favorable view of the same phenomenon was described by a parent:

> So we've got your bully teachers in that school. And there's a network of them, and they're new coaches. And it's disgusting. And the kids all know it, and the principal. ... The dynamic in the school makes me crazy. It truly does. There is nowhere to go if you are not an athlete in that school. There is nowhere to go for protection. It's sad. It just breaks my heart when you think about it. The problem is they're not helping these kids. These athletes who are getting away with stuff, you know, so that they have a good football team, and you've got to play because we've got to go to State, they're not teaching these kids because now these kids go out into the world and they have these behaviors that they're going to get away with, they're going to break the rules, break the law. They're not helping any of the kids. And there are kids that follow the rules on the football team that don't get to play. This school is not about the kids. This school is about a principal who is reliving his high school years knowing the cheerleaders and the football players. And the coaches that are there are doing the same thing: they want to win; they want to win at all costs. You have teachers there who are wonderful, who have no one to go to when they've got complaints, because Mr. DeAngelis will go in his office and close the door. He doesn't want to know what is going on. And that's the dynamic of that school (Recorded April 30, 2004).

A pastor whose children attended the school stated:

> So, our kids survived Columbine. My son went there as well [as my daughter]. He basically stayed on the periphery. The core of the school was jock. I think it still is, but I'm not sure. The core of the school was jock (Recorded April 29, 2004).

What people meant when they said that the school was run by coaches was that the coaches had both formal and informal power. Principal DeAngelis, although a social studies teacher, was also a coach, and a successful one at that, leading the baseball team to two state championships. He was formerly an assistant football coach. In addition, coaches were overrepresented in the administration. The following were excerpted from my field notes:

> The first thing I noticed in Mr. DeAngelis's office was a blooming columbine plant on his desk. On the walls were plaques honoring him, the school, and memorializing the victims of the shooting. One small

> plaque honored him as "Mr. Baseball," for his baseball coaching. Several years before, he coached a team that won the state championship. On the wall was a picture of two championship baseball teams. There was a crocheted tapestry that was dedicated to the thirteen victims of the shooting; right under that was a drawing of Dave Sanders with a columbine flower in the background. On my way out of the office, which was cluttered with trophies garnered by the soccer and football teams, I walked over to a hanging trophy case that had more awards by the football, soccer, baseball, and volleyball teams. I think that the football team won the state championship four out of the last five years (Field notes, May 12, 2003).
>
> Across the hall [from Mr. DeAngelis's office] was a dean's office that had an entire wall papered with pictures of sports figures (Field notes, April 28, 2004).

It is true, as several reporters (Adams and Russakoff 1999; Greene 1999; Kurtz 1999) have noted, that Columbine puts its athletic contributions on public display more prominently than its academic successes. This researcher's experience is similar to others who have visited the school. The office was filled with trophies celebrating state championships won by various teams. The hanging trophy case in the middle of the foyer contains some of the most important championship trophies along with footballs signed by members of the victorious teams. Also at the end of the foyer near a hall leading to the athletic facilities is a huge trophy case celebrating athletic victories of the various teams. Next to the gymnasium is a display case that contains sports memorabilia sent to the school in the wake of the shootings, such as signed jerseys from basketball and football stars and a football helmet from the 2000 National Football League champion St. Louis Rams with signatures from the members of the victorious team. In addition, in the hallway leading to the gymnasium is Columbine's Wall of Fame, celebrating outstanding athletes in the history of Columbine High School.

Mr. DeAngelis

Mr. DeAngelis, the principal of Columbine High School, is a modest man of unremarkable appearance. After first meeting with him, I described him as follows:

Mr. DeAngelis is about 5' 5" tall, about 190 lbs. He has a shock of black hair with small amounts of silver on the sides. He was dressed in a plaid sports jacket, beige slacks, and a beige shirt that buttoned at the top. It did not have a collar;

it was meant to be worn without a tie. The shirt was well-worn, pilling around his ample waist. He was short, overweight, but had a muscular build (Field notes, May 12, 2003).

In my second meeting with him, he was more relaxed, less stressed, and had lost a few pounds. His entire career in education with the exception of a single year has been at Columbine High School. He graduated from Metropolitan State College in Denver in 1978 with a bachelor's degree in social studies and started teaching at Columbine in 1979. He served as a social studies teacher through 1991, in 1992–1993 he was dean of students for two years, then assistant principal for two years, and was selected principal in 1996. He received a master's degree in secondary education and social studies from the University of Colorado in 1994 and received his administrative certification in the same year. Between 1986 and 1994, he was the coach of the baseball team and assistant coach of the football team. He also supervised basketball and wrestling matches and was the announcer and scorer in those sports. Principal DeAngelis is a sincere and earnest man. He has also developed skills in handling the media and interviewers, such as this author. In my interviews, he focused on the academic aspects of Columbine. Although he acknowledged that sports were important at the high school, he celebrated its academic achievements and the superior extracurricular activities offered by the school. I have heard detractors refer to him as "evil," and "pathetic," not so much because of his inherent qualities, but because it was under his leadership that bullying was allowed to occur and that athletics took precedence over all other aspects of high school life, including academics and morality. Principal DeAngelis perceives himself as a fair person, claiming that all students were treated equally and that he even turned his own son in because of an off-the-field escapade (Prendergast 1999). A pastor described him as a wonderfully compassionate man as exemplified by his behavior in a family tragedy:

> A lot of people criticize DeAngelis. … Be that as it may, when the youth worker from the Catholic Church and I were trying to get the family through their kid's suicide—I mean you've got to pick a funeral home, you've got to get clothes picked out, you've got to pick a cemetery—you've got to move people along. A funeral is a wedding in three days. You know all the craziness with a wedding? Well, you've got to do that in three days with a funeral. … So, our job is to move that along. DeAngelis came in and did the pastoring on the brother, sitting on the bed with him and holding him and all that kind of stuff (Recorded April 30, 2004).

Yet, DeAngelis was a principal who had been a very successful coach in a school where coaches were overrepresented in the administration, and in which athletics were strongly emphasized. Teachers demand that principals defend them from outsiders. Principals who side with parents against the teaching staff do so at their own peril. Even when a faculty member may have done something egregious, the usual response to the parent is to defend the teacher and deal with the problem directly with the teacher, reporting back to the parent what was done. When Principal DeAngelis stated that teachers never abetted or participated in the harassment of students, he was defending his faculty.

Although DeAngelis has certainly had his judgment questioned in the national and local media (Adams and Russakoff 1999; Brown and Merritt 2002; Garbarino and deLara 2002; Von Drehle 1999), only a small minority of parents and community members called for his resignation. Instead of questioning his regime and demanding his immediate resignation in the face of serious allegations of allowing predatory violence in the halls of his school, the community rallied around him and defended him. Any attempts to force him out of the position of principal of Columbine High School were met with strong resistance. As a matter of fact, DeAngelis came out of the shootings more popular then he was prior to them. DeAngelis became a symbol of Columbine's pain, indomitable spirit, and will to recover from the tragedy.

Although numerous parents were unhappy with the way they and their children were treated by Principal DeAngelis, their difficulties were private and individualized. If they did not like Columbine High School, they could attend one of the neighboring schools. To them, as well as to DeAngelis, Klebold and Harris were an aberration; they were a visitation of pure evil in an otherwise model community. The major reason that, in the face of accusations of incompetence and malfeasance, the community stood behind DeAngelis was because he was providing them the kind of high school that they wanted. Certainly, the parents of Columbine High School students did not want academics sacrificed to athletics; however, the fact that Columbine had emerged as a multi-sport state power provided them a sense of collective identity and pride.

DRUGS

This and the previous chapter have alluded to the various forms of drug use at Columbine. Although drug usage was not the focus of this investigation, it crept into the data in a variety of ways. Students testified that to party, get drunk, and smoke marijuana was normal, especially among the jocks. I emphasize the word "normal." That is, within the peer group, this kind of behavior was routine and accepted. Most students that I interviewed who were in attendance at Columbine in 1997 and 1998 knew about the arrest of RH for DUI. Eric Harris, in his Trenchcoat Mafia web site, admitted to dosing on cough syrup. Both he and Dylan Klebold (whose moniker was "VoDKa") were swigging from a Jack Daniels bottle when they made the basement tapes. Students testified that liquor was easy to get and that the jocks obtained their marijuana from their pals who were "stoners." In this most conservative community, drugs, especially alcohol, were easy to come by.

Perhaps what was most alarming was the unsubstantiated rumors that members of the football and wrestling teams were taking steroids. The testimony of CL indicated that her boyfriend was on steroids; he would fly into a jealous rage at the slightest provocation. Rumors abounded about the use of steroids by athletes; rumors also indicated that the family of a football team member was supplying steroids and other drugs within the community. With all the rumors, one would think that the administration would investigate steroid usage because it is a serious health problem, especially among adolescents. In addition to "roid rage," it can generate depression and has been attributed to suicides of several adolescent athletes across the country (Longman 2003). If the administration has looked into the issue, it is not public knowledge.

Much has been made about the possible influence of Luvox on the behavior of Eric Harris (Bergin 1999; Murphy 2001; O'Meara 2001). Luvox is a serotonin-specific reuptake inhibitor (SSRI) in the Prozac family. Eric had first been prescribed Zoloft, another SSRI, when he was diagnosed with obsessive compulsive disorder following his arrest for the theft of equipment from a truck the previous fall. Subsequently, Zoloft was replaced by Luvox. As noted by the medical community, SSRIs can produce psychotic responses, especially mania and paranoia. However, it is as senseless to suggest that Luvox caused the Columbine shootings as it is to blame it on psychopathology. It may be that Luvox paradoxically intensified Harris's manic state and sense of persecution. However, planning and preparing for the massacre began long before Eric Harris started taking Zoloft and Luvox. Dylan Klebold had no drugs in his system according to the autopsy (Columbine Research Site 2003). The effects of Luvox on the Columbine shootings are unknown, as the effect of steroids on the behavior of members of the football and wrestling teams is unknown.

MORAL LESSONS

Social theorist Robert Merton (1957) talked about manifest and latent functions when examining institutions. He noted that institutions may be structured for some overt purpose but takes on other functions that may be covert and unarticulated but, when subjected to sociological analysis, can be unearthed. He also noted that latent functions can often undermine or corrupt manifest functions. There is little dispute that the manifest functions of education are to provide the younger generation with the skills, attitudes, and understandings necessary for positive social participation in a technological society and as a citizen in a democratic society, although citizen education has atrophied over the last two decades. It is undeniable that a major function of the institution of education is moral; over a century ago, sociologist Emile Durkheim (1956) identified the major function of education as providing attitudinal, behavioral, and moral continuity between older and younger generations.

In high schools across the United States, the latent function is to provide the community an identity through sports participation, primarily football. In Columbine, the efforts to have a dominating sports program and to have a nationally ranked football team undermined its ability to provide students with an environment that promoted democratic civic values, that is, an environment where the will of the majority is tempered by the protection of the weak. In this chapter, overwhelming evidence has been presented that indicated that a small minority was able to rule the halls of the school. The vast majority acquiesced and allowed that minority to engage in violence toward a small minority of nonconforming and generally despised students because of their nonconformity. The civic lesson that Columbine High School taught its students was that might makes right, that some citizens are more worthy than others, and that those who express dissent with the dominant perspective or who, for whatever reason, would not or could not conform to the dominant mode, deserve predation, get what they deserve, and have no claim to dignity.

Columbine is, as has been shown, an upper-middle-class, predominantly white Christian community, with a handful of blacks and a small minority of Chicanos, many of whom can only be distinguished by their Hispanic surnames. Residents of southern Jefferson County view themselves racially tolerant and free from discrimination. Ethic and racial minorities were represented in the student elites. However, as demonstrated above, the jocks were overtly racist (as were Klebold and Harris), sexist, homophobic, and anti-Semitic. They were not afraid of calling other students "nigger lovers"; female students "Nazi-lesbians," "sluts," or "skags" or publicly commenting on their bodies or putative sexual lives; intimidating other males by calling them "homos," "fags," or "queers" or telling them to "suck cock"; or to harass Jewish students.

By allowing the predators free reign in the hallways and public spaces and by bending the rules so that bad behavior did not interfere too much with sports participation, the faculty and administration inadvertently created a climate that was rife with discrimination, intimidation, and humiliation. The lack of consistency in the enforcement of rules at Columbine led students, especially those at the bottom, to feel that the school was a dangerous place and that they could not expect justice when appealing to adult authorities. Those at the top of the peer structure adamantly claimed that Columbine was a place where people were respected, regardless of their differences, and that when rules were broken, justice was done. This researcher does not know whether those students really believed this attractive picture of their school to be true or were attempting to fool an outsider. Students at the bottom of the peer structure became cynical about Columbine's image as the ideal school. Eric Harris and Dylan Klebold came to the conclusion that the best way to solve the problem was to blow up the school and kill as many as they could.

6

ERIC AND DYLAN

TO THIS POINT, the focus has been on school and community contexts of the shootings. The perpetrators of the shooting, Eric Harris and Dylan Klebold, will be examined in depth in this chapter. Several issues will be explored: their family backgrounds, relationships with peers, schooling, psychological issues, their life together in Columbine, and their behavior prior to the assault on the school.

ERIC HARRIS, INSTIGATOR AND THEORIST

Eric Harris's Background

Relatively little is known about Eric's background, especially prior to his living in Columbine. He was born in Wichita, Kansas, on April 9, 1981, to Wayne and Kathy Harris (West 1999). His brother, Kevin, was three years older than Eric. Their father, Wayne, spent the majority of his adult life as a pilot of United States Air Force transport planes (Shepard 1999). Throughout his career, he was stationed at eight different bases in Kansas, Ohio, Michigan, and New York State. Before he was forced into retirement because of cutbacks in the military budget, he was stationed at Plattsburgh Air Force Base in upstate New York. In 1993, after Wayne served twenty years in the military, the family moved into southern Jefferson County where he obtained a job with Flight Safety Services Corporation in nearby Englewood. Kathy was employed part-time as a caterer.

The move to Columbine was a return home. Wayne had grown up in Englewood, which is just a few miles north of Columbine, and had graduated from Englewood High School. His father had been employed as a valet at the Brown Palace Hotel in downtown Denver. Kathy was also a local girl; she was raised in southeast Denver, where her father, a retired military officer, owned and operated a hardware store (Bartels and Crowder 1999).

Media inquiries into the background of the Harris family and Eric in particular uncovered no indications of pathology. The Harrises were characterized as good neighbors, reserved but friendly, and their children seemed to be perfectly normal. When her children were young, Kathy was a stay-at-home mom, tending to the needs of her family. The family was described by acquaintances as an ideal, loving family. According to one media source, former military friends described Eric as smart and cute (Bartels and Crowder 1999). One of Eric's former friends, from Plattsburgh, said in *USA Today* ("Massacre Foreshadowed by Gunmen's Videos" 1999) in the wake of the shootings, "My mouth just dropped," former classmate Kyle Ross said. "He was a typical kid. He didn't seem anything like what is portrayed on TV" (1).

Eric the Adolescent

Eric and Dylan videotaped themselves on numerous occasions. Dylan seemed to be the cameraman most of the time. Therefore, Eric was the subject in numerous scenes. Visually, he seemed like a typical teenager. His hair was cut short. He wore jeans and T-shirts, like most of his peers. Again, like many of his peers, some of his T-shirts were bought at rock-and-roll concerts, such as the one he wore on the morning the boys videotaped themselves in the hallways of Columbine High School where they were accosted by other students, at least one whose sweatshirt suggests he was a member of the football team. This particular T-shirt was black and advertised one of Harris's and Klebold's favorite industrial rock bands, KMFDM. As is the custom, the back of the T-shirt listed the venues for the band's recent tour. In the videotapes, Eric gave every impression of being a normal teenager, talking about school, girls, and cars. His eyes were bright; he had an engaging smile. His facial expressions belied a quick intelligence. In his conversations, he engaged other students and interacted with them in a positive manner. Even after being pushed aside in the hallway by other students, he showed no particular anger. The incident seemed to be forgotten soon after it occurred. The only indication that Eric Harris had a dark side was his KMFDM T-shirt.

Heavy metal music has its greatest popularity among suburban white males, as does rap (now hip-hop) (Berry 1994; Gaines 1993; Kotarba 1994; Weinstein 1994). Eric Harris was a great fan of German industrial music. His favorite bands were KMFDM and Rammstein. Industrial music is a subset of heavy metal and tends to be harsh, loud, and violent. It also has a techno quality to it that gives it movement and drive. The lyrics of the music express anger, violence, nihilism, and an apocalyptical vision. The title of one of KMFDM albums is "World War III." Other titles from KMFDM include "Megalomaniac," "Jihad," "Spit Sperm," "Bullets, Bombs, and Bigotry," and "Anarchy." Rammstein titles are in German.

Eric had taken some German in school but apparently was somewhat self-taught. His journals are interlaced with German phrases, and he was known for reciting Rammstein's German lyrics among people who knew him. Based upon his web site in which Adolf Hitler was adulated, Eric was apparently a Naziophile and planned the attack on Columbine to coincide with Hitler's birthday on April 20 in celebration of his "contributions to white culture" (Shepard 1999).

In the basement tapes, Eric Harris complained about moving to a new community every two or three years (Gibbs and Roche 1999). His school records (Shepard 1999) indicate that by the seventh grade, he had attended five schools. He was unhappy about attending a new school and starting at the bottom of the social structure each time, having to make new friends and being an outsider. Ironically, his arrival in Columbine meant the end of his career as an Air Force brat, moving from base to base every two or three years, having to jettison old friends and make new ones. In Columbine he had a new start in which his life would assume stability.

However, he arrived at Ken Caryl Middle School in the middle of the seventh grade. According to several informants, the peer group structure at Ken Caryl had pretty much solidified, with students associated with the Columbine Sports Association, which sponsored football, baseball, and soccer leagues, given elite status. Eric played sports along with Brooks Brown and other students in the YMCA League, a community-based sports league that had less status than the Columbine Sports Association. The Columbine Sports Association functioned as a conduit to Columbine High School sports teams. Members of the high school coaching staff were involved in the Association and oversaw the development of players in that league. For example, the Association sponsored Pop Warner style football leagues for various age groups from seven to seventeen years old. The Association provided training and experience for youngsters who aspired to play on Columbine High School sports teams. The high school coaches knew and communicated with the Association coaches. By the time an Association athlete got to high school, he had been thoroughly evaluated and the high school coaching staff had a substantial idea of his capabilities.

Students participating in the less prestigious YMCA League, which deemphasized competition and focused on enjoying the game, according to students and parents whose children were in that league, tended to be overlooked when trying out for Columbine High School sports teams. Because, as noted in Chapter 4, the core of the Columbine elite is sports stars, competition for elite positions in the adolescent peer structure begins quite early. By the seventh grade, it is fairly well consolidated.

As a consequence, Eric gravitated toward the outcast students. His friends would be other students at the low end of the peer status structure, what Brooks Brown referred to as the "loser students," such as Brooks, Nate Dykeman, Chris Morris, and, of course, Dylan Klebold.

Eric fit the masculine prototype: he was bright, athletic, and gave the appearance of self-assurance. According to people who knew him, he was a good soccer player and accounted for himself well on the baseball field. However, he had two disadvantages: first, he was below average in height, measuring about 5'8" in his senior year of high school. Second, he had a slight concavity of his chest, which gave the appearance of a pushed-in sternum. In the hyper-competitive world of adolescent peer groups, any difference or deviation from the norm invites ridicule. In actuality, in adolescent subcultures, those of low status are ridiculed and harassed by their upper status peers because they are of low status. Higher status peers find and latch on to any personal quirk, physical difference, or behavioral oddity. With Eric, it was his concave chest. This slight physical deformity had no apparent health or physical consequences related to athleticism. He was apparently agile enough and had enough body control to be invited to try out for the Columbine High School soccer team by the coach in the tenth grade. He declined the offer.

"I'm full of hate and I love it": The Mind of Eric Harris

Soon after Eric Harris's life assumed stability, he began to show signs of psychological problems. Eric was apparently a very bright and sensitive child. His Little League coach in Plattsburgh, New York, remembered him as a timid player who would not swing his bat for fear of striking out and letting his teammates down (Bartels and Crowder 1999). What little evidence exists suggests that Eric Harris was highly sensitive about his status among his peers. He was keenly aware of what others thought about him.

It did not take long for Eric to figure out that although his family life was going to be stable, his peer status would be at the bottom of the heap. Because of his physical stature and his status as a newcomer in a peer structure organized around football heroes and their hangers-on in middle school, he did not stand much of a chance for wide social acceptance. He was new, he was shy, he did not belong to a church youth organization, and he was not a football player. He was on the outside of a peer structure that was well formed and had few doors of entry. He found himself at the bottom, yet again, through no fault of his own.

In addition to his low peer status, Eric was experiencing psychological problems. After his arrest for breaking into a van in the fall prior to the attack on Columbine, the court recommended that he receive psychological services. He was diagnosed by local psychologist with obsessive-compulsive disorder for which Luvox was prescribed (Bartels and Crowder 1999). However, that diagnosis was disputed by FBI profiler Supervisory Special Agent Dwayne Fuselier, the FBI's lead Columbine investigator and a clinical psychologist, who diagnosed Harris as a psychopath, which is a behavioral disorder. Dr. Frank Ochberg, a psychiatrist who helped the FBI profile Eric Dylan, told me he that he thought that the mental health professional who diagnosed Eric as obsessive-compulsive would be embarrassed by that diagnosis. Whether Eric was a psychopath or not will be discussed below; however, what interested parties, whether professional or lay, have indicated was that Eric, by the time he arrived at Columbine High School, was out of control. Given his writing, Eric was probably aware of his lack of psychological stability.

Although Eric's psychological problems remained largely undetected, clearly his behavior was disturbing to Randy and Judy Brown, the parents of Brooks Brown, who had a volatile and on-again, off-again relationship with Eric, which tended to be based upon how angry Eric was with them. The Browns filed two complaints against Eric with the Jefferson County Sheriff's Department, one in 1997 and the other the following year. In a personal conversation this researcher had with Judy Brown (March 1, 2004), she said that she had forgotten that she had filed a complaint in 1997 and was informed by the Department that they had recently uncovered the earlier complaint. The *Rocky Mountain News* reported the incident as follows:

> In August 1997 and again in March 1998, Jefferson County sheriff's officials received allegations of criminal activity by teenagers Eric Harris and

> Dylan Klebold, including charges that they had authored violent rants and a death threat on the Internet and were building pipe bombs and vandalizing property.
>
> The 1997 report was apparently never followed up on, but the 1998 allegations sparked an investigation involving several deputies, one of whom drafted an affidavit to support a warrant to search Harris' home more than a year before he and Klebold opened fire at Columbine High School. But that warrant was never taken to a judge, and it was withheld from the public for nearly two years after the April 20, 1999, attack on the school (Vaughan 2004).

According to Brooks Brown, the precipitating incident for the complaint in March 1998 occurred when he was approached by Dylan in the hallway of Columbine High School. Dylan and told Brooks to look at Eric's web site and handed him a paper with Eric's Web address (Brown and Merritt 2002). That evening, Brooks logged on to the web site and found the following:

> I will rig up explosives all over town and detonate each one of them after I mow down a whole fucking area full of you snotty ass rich motherfucking high strung godlike attitude worthless pieces of shit whores [*sic*]. I don't care if I live or die in the shoot out, all I want to do is to kill and injure as many of you pricks as I can, especially a few people. Like Brooks Brown (Columbine Research Site 2003, 10, 417; an earlier part of the quote can be found on 189).

In addition, Eric had posted Brooks's phone number, a list of reasons why he hated Brooks, and a promise of a reward to the person who killed him. Brooks told his parents about the web site. They printed the pages, called the Sheriff's Department, and handed the pages over to a deputy. They also described to the deputy prior problems they had with Eric, the fact that Eric had been making pipe bombs, and his desire to kill people.

The discovery of the web site by Brooks Brown occurred a full year prior to the shootings. Clearly, at this time, Eric was already seething with hatred and homicidal thoughts. It was about this time that he started compiling his "S-hit List," which contained the names of fellow students who had slighted him in some way. Police interviews with list members indicated that some indicated that they barely knew Eric and could not explain why he had a grudge against them; other males on the list indicated that they may have had a confrontation with him. The female students on the list were almost exclusively girls that Eric had asked out on a date and who had refused him (Columbine Research Site 2003, 10,276–10,296). Eric had special enmity for girls who would string him along before refusing.

Eric's rage was all-consuming. His web site ended with the following warning:

> I live in Denver and I would love to kill all its residents. Well all you people out there can just kiss my ass and die. From now on, I don't give a fuck what almost any of you mutha fuckas have to say, unless I respect you which is highly unlikely, but for those of you who happen to know me and know that I respect you, may peace be with you and don't be in my line of fire. For the rest of you, you all better fucking hide in your house because I'm comin' for EVERYONE soon, and I WILL be armed to the fuckin teeth and I WILL shoot and kill and I WILL fucking KILL EVERYTHING! No I am not crazy, crazy is just a word, to me it has no meaning, everyone is different, but most of you fuckheads out there in society, going to your everyday fucking jobs and doing your everyday routine shitty things, I say fuck you and die. You got a problem with my thoughts, come tell me and I'll kill you, because … god damn it, DEAD PEOPLE DON'T ARGUE! (Brown and Merritt 2002, 86–87, emphasis in original).

Eric's written rants were accompanied by an eerie behavioral coolness. Other students did not perceive Eric's anger. Although judging by the comments made by girls on his hit list to police officers, they sensed something unnerving about him when they were in his presence. Upon completion of an interview with one girl on his list, the officer wrote, "There was just something about him she didn't like, she didn't know what it was, but he seemed a little evil" (Columbine Research Site 2003, 10,280). Another girl stated that he was not her type, that he was "nice, but weird" (Columbine Research Site, 2003, 10,277). The girls were wary of Eric, but did not know exactly why. They intuited something dark and deep. On his web site, Eric stated that he was kind of a goth and was "dark"; despite his ranting and his overwhelming hatred, he was able to keep that dark side hidden from other people with the exception of the Browns and Dylan Klebold, although in the last semester of his senior year, more people became aware of his negativity.

In the videotapes that Eric and Dylan made for classroom projects, Eric appears decidedly normal. He is clear eyed, relaxed, seemingly open, and, well, a typical teenage boy. In school, he was not a troublemaker. He was a bright student who was quite articulate. He apparently did not cause trouble in the classrooms. Both publicly and in an interview with this researcher, Principal DeAngelis claimed that he had no interactions with Eric and did not know him (Scanlon 1999). In a school of 1800 students, Eric did not stand out. Dylan's videotape of his own harassment, described in Chapter 5, barely fazed Eric. The boy in the videotape seems to have no relationship to the boy who spewed out his hate on his web site.

That is not to mean that Eric did not allow his dark side free play. In his midnight missions, he vandalized homes of people he did not like and then wrote about his exploits on his web site. He made pipe bombs and exploded them. He illegally bought semiautomatic rifles; he also illegally sawed off the ends of shotguns. He and Dylan broke into a van and stole its contents. He played first-person killer games, Doom, and Quake, for hours on end. He devised levels in Doom in which the protagonist was overwhelmed by the enemy, leading other Doom players to complain that he gave them no chance to defeat them (Prendergast 1999). And, of course, he planned the destruction of his high school.

On the one hand, he covered up his dark side very well; on the other hand, he was foolhardy and lucky that he was not discovered. He was quite stealthy in hiding his activities. In the basement tapes, he provided a tour of his bedroom, showing where his weaponry and his pipe bombs were hidden (Gibbs and Roche 1999). He and Dylan were able to keep their plans concealed from their closest associates. There is some justification for accusations of the Harris's turning a blind eye to Eric's nefarious activities. Eric's father, Wayne, picked up the telephone, and on the other end was a gun shop owner who said that the ammunition that was ordered was ready to be picked up. Mr. Harris just said that he had not ordered any ammunition and hung up. No questions were asked about who ordered the ammunition or whether the clerk had dialed the correct number.

Eric documented his midnight exploits on his web site, which was a public venue that anybody could have accessed. He also vented his anger, hate, homophobia, racism, pet peeves, and plans for the destruction of Columbine High School on his web site. He took a pipe bomb to work when he was employed by Blackjack Pizza and showed it around (Johnson 1999). As early as 1997, he was talking about collecting bombs and blowing up the school in the very cafeteria in which he and Dylan dragged two twenty-pound propane tanks on April 19, 1999 (Vaughan, Washington, and Carnahan 1999):

> "Every once in a while, Eric would talk about blowing up the school—but we all talked about blowing up the school, or 'going postal' and shooting someone you're mad at," said Justin Preziodi, 20, who graduated from

> Columbine in 1997. "But you would never think someone would actually do it."... Harris' obsession with explosives was a frequent topic of his conversations with fellow students.

In chapter 5, several students admitted to fantasizing about blowing up Columbine High School. It was a fairly common fantasy, especially among outcast students for whom attendance at Columbine seemed to be an invitation to harassment, humiliation, and abuse. Given that nobody had ever bombed their high school before, such talk was dismissed as fantasy.

Eric Harris had sensibilities that are rarely seen in an eighteen-year-old. First, he was extremely well-accomplished in the design of computer games, especially his favorite, Doom. Prendergast (1999) described his skill this way:

> You master Doom and its even more violent successor, Doom 2. You engage in "deathmatch" versions of the game involving two or more players, vying on a single computer or over the Internet. It isn't enough.
>
> You spend long hours in your room designing new levels to the game, called wads, and posting them online for other fanatics to play. You alter the noises that the weapons make, the screams of your victims [NB: like having his victims cry out "Lord, why is this happening to me?"]. Eventually you will design fields of combat that resemble your neighborhood—and, it's rumored, your school.
>
> It's still not enough. You hunger for recognition. You slap a plea on the side of a building in one of the wads, urging players to send comments to your e-mail address. "This one took a damn long time to do," you write in the text file attached to another wad, "so send me some bloody credit, man!"
>
> By the middle of your sophomore year, you've completed your most sophisticated wad yet, a tricky, brutal, two-level shootout that's many times the size of your previous efforts. It climaxes in an orgy of killing, the screen flooded with hundreds of demons. The player has only two options: engage in a tedious, mechanical ritual of slaughter, or end things quickly by using a cheat command to go into "God mode," in which the player is invincible.

Prendergast points out Eric Harris's desperate need for recognition. He had an inflated sense of himself as a person to be reckoned with but who was ignored by his audience and brutalized by his more physically endowed peers. He felt unappreciated. What he could not achieve in life, he achieved in death. Alive, he was just another miserable square peg in the world of round holes. Only through death would he gain notoriety.

Second, he was able to plan and execute the most destructive act against an educational institution in the history of United States. Although Dylan was his trusty sidekick, Eric was the planner. Eric was the one who actually went into the cafeteria and conducted an analysis of when it was most populated. The boys planted two diversionary bombs to explode a few minutes before their assault on the school. They kept their plans hidden from their families and closest friends for over a year. They even booby-trapped their cars so that they would explode when students ran into the parking lot. They bought weaponry, made bombs, and stashed them in preparation for the assault. For eighteen-year-olds, this is pretty sophisticated planning.

Third, Eric wrote voluminously. He paraphrased Shakespeare's "Good wombs have born bad sons," from *The Tempest*, as an entry in his 1999 journal for Mother's Day (Shepard 1999). Most of his writings are rants, such as several pages describing his pet peeves and hates. At other times, he wrote his opinions about various aspects of his life, listed under such categories as "philosophy," "America," and "society." Other writing included notes to himself, to-do lists, and descriptions of his so-called midnight missions in which he vandalized houses in the area. Much of his writing was cited earlier.

Eric's writings, suffused as they are with anger, hate, and desires to kill, are laced with humor, social criticism, double (or hidden) meanings, and intentional contradictions. The humor is a mix of typical adolescent humor and Eric's own sardonic sense of what is funny. An example of the former comes from his web site on a page titled, "Jo Mamma," which is a white kids version of African American verbal insults known as, "the dozens" (Abrahams 1962). The dozens is a verbal sparring game of insults oftentimes about one's mother, which usually begins, "Yo momma. …" According to Brooks Brown (Brown and Merritt 2002), friends would sit around and tell Jo Mamma jokes. The intention was to make them deliberately insipid. Eric compiled about seventy-five such jokes on his web site (Shepard 1999). They are deliberately silly:

> JO mamma has so many bag clips her neighbors ask to use some occasionally!
>
> JO mamma has so much salad every day that she buys salad at Sam's Club and saves her money! (from Harris's defunct website).

Of greater interest is what Eric thinks is funny. It provides insight into Eric's mind. Some examples come from Eric's "DO YOU KNOW WHAT I HATE!!!?" rant:

> DO YOU KNOW WHAT I LOVE!!!?
>
> —When some rich ass stuck up piece of shit white trash person gets in a car wreck with their brand new car!
>
> DO YOU KNOW WHAT I LOVE!!!?
>
> —when some stupid ass kid blows his fucking handoff [*sic*] because he couldn't figure out that the lit fuse means that the firecracker is going to go off soon! HAHAHA… "DUMBASS." (Columbine Research Site 2003, JC-001-010424).

The first entry is a reference to Rocky Hoffschneider, whose parents apparently bought him a Dodge Viper, which he totaled within days of receiving it. The second reference is apparently to a news item. In both cases, Eric is engaging in *schadenfreude*, gleefully enjoying the misfortunes of others. In the first case, he is elated at the fact that one of his tormentors gets his comeuppance. In the second case, Eric is gloating over the stupidity of some kid playing with firecrackers, whose misfortune it is to lose a hand. Throughout his writings, Eric is disdainful of people who are "stupid." For example:

> DO YOU KNOW WHAT I HATE!!!?"
>
> —STUPID PEOPLE!!! Why must so many people be so stupid!!?
>
> DO YOU KNOW WHAT I LOVE!!!?"
>
> —Making fun of stupid people doing stupid things! Like one time when I was watching this freshman to try to get on a computer that needed a password. … He typed in the password and waited. The retard didn't press enter or anything. He just waited. Then he started cussing at the computer saying it was screwed up. Then the freshman went and got a teacher and the fucking teacher could not figure out why it wasn't going anywhere!!! Jesus!!! Personally, I think they should be shot. (Columbine Research Site 2003, JC-001-010424).

Throughout this rant, in which he outlines pet peeves ranging from people who drive slowly in the left lane, Star Wars fans, telephone solicitors for charities, people who don't believe in personal hygiene, people who overuse or mispronounce words, slow walkers, television commercials, country music, R-rated movies on cable, liars, braggarts, young smokers, and people who cut in line. In a Dante-like quality, Eric metes out imaginary punishments. For stupid people, in an earlier version of his web site, he suggested they should be "smacked across the face a couple million times or so ... give or take 1" (Columbine Research Site 2003, JC-001-010411). For people who think professional wrestling is real, he suggests bombing their house and breaking their arms. For racists, he suggests that he will come in and break their legs with a plastic spoon, not caring how long it takes. Slow drivers should be sent to every driving class every day for a year. People who are mean to animals should be severely hurt.

One of the ideas that Eric Harris gets caught up in is natural selection, which in his mind evolved into social Darwinism. During the assault on Columbine, he wore a shirt that had "Natural Selection" emblazoned across the front. By natural selection, it is quite obvious that Eric understands it as the survival of the fittest in a social Darwinian sense. In his web site rant, he stated:

> YOU KNOW WHAT I LOVE!!!?
>
> —Natural SELECTION!!!!!!!!! God damn it's the best thing that ever happened to the earth. Getting rid of all the stupid and weak organisms ... but it's all natural!!! YES! I wish the government would just take off every warning label so that all the dumbasses would severely hurt themselves or DIE! And boom, no more dumbasses. Heh. (Columbine Research Site 2003, JC-001-10411).

Eric's belief in natural selection as a mechanism for removing weak and stupid people from the face of the earth is ironic. Whether the irony is intentional or not, given the fact that Eric is homicidal and suicidal, is unknown. However, much of Eric's writing is suffused with irony. Take for example his moniker, "Reb," short for rebel. On as AOL site, he had several profiles over time, all with screen names that began with REB: REBDOOMER, Rebldomakr, and REB DoMiNe. The mascot of Columbine High was the Rebels. In his writings, he calls his peers "trendy punk little smart asses," "self-centered, selfish, lazy, impatient, rude, and ... damn, I've run out of adjectives," and slaves to trends (Columbine Research Site 2003, JC-001-10411). Eric sees himself as a rebel against the Rebels, who are not rebels at all, but unthinking conformists.

Eric's sense of irony leads him to generate numerous cryptic references. Obviously, some of these references escape this writer. However, in reading over the available materials, I discovered the following:

In his profile under the screen name, REBDOOMER, for location, he entered Littleton, CO USA. *Nil sine numine* (Shepard 1999). The Latin translates as "Nothing without Providence," which is the Colorado State motto. Under hobbies, he entered, "Semper Fidelis" ("always faithful"), the motto of the United States Marines. Eric wanted to join the Marines upon graduation from high school, but was rejected for mental health reasons. For his personal quote, he wrote, "Si vis pacem, para bellum," or "if you want peace, prepare for war." This last quote seems to conform to Eric's Hobbsian view of nature and human relationships as an anarchic struggle of all against all, and Eric's view that the predators are the big winners in the struggle for survival. His desire to become a Marine apparently would have been the actualization of his desire to become a predator.

Of greatest interest to this investigator is apparently his last screen name, "REB DoMiNe." I do not know why the "m" and "n" in "Domine" are capitalized. However, "Domine" is Latin for "God," and Eric combined "REB" with God. The rebel God is, of course, Satan. In their writings, there is little evidence of the boys being Satanists. However, in some of Eric's drawings are images that could be interpreted as Satanic. These images were posted on the Trenchcoat Mafia web site. Eric viewed himself as a goth and considered himself "dark" (Shepard 1999). One would expect that in a predominantly Christian community that dissidence would cloak itself in Satanism. This was the case in Columbine, but it seemed to be primarily a practice among disaffected female students (Prendergast 1999).

In the profile for REB DoMiNe, Eric's personal quote was, "It's fun being a schizophrenic" (Shepard 1999). This cryptic entry seems to signify two things: first, Eric seems to view himself as a schizophrenic in the subjective sense R. D. Laing (1999) described in *The Divided Self*, in that his "inner self" is hidden from view and is divorced from his public persona. His writing seems to be venting from his hidden dark side. His description of himself as a schizophrenic suggests his awareness that he was living a double life; that he inhabited a persona that hid his "true self." He seemed to understand that his "true self" was dark, evil, and abhorrent. Even though he was successful for the most part in keeping his dark side hidden from adult authorities and from many of his peers, his lack of success with girls seemed to stem from their sensing the violence seething within. Second, it suggests that Eric viewed his social interactions as inauthentic and part of a façade. Third, it suggests that Eric, at some level of understanding, knew there was something desperately wrong inside. He had been diagnosed with obsessive-compulsive disorder and was taking Luvox. He admitted to self-medicating on cough medicine on his Trenchcoat Mafia web site. On the one hand, he seemed to revel in his anger and hatred; on the other hand, he wanted to destroy himself. However, if he was going to destroy himself, he was going to do it in a way that would send the world a message.

Those who knew Eric with any level of intimacy were aware of his volatility. The Brown family, who knew him fairly well through his relationship with Brooks, had experienced his violence. When they read the threats to Brooks's life, they did not think that it was merely verbal venting; they feared that he was capable of homicide. Eric's moods were mercurial. When Brooks encountered Eric in the parking lot of Columbine High School on that fateful day of April 20, 1999, Eric could have just as well pulled a gun and shot Brooks rather than warn him off.

The schizophrenic metaphor applies to the many contradictions in Eric's life: a cool persona covering roiling anger and hatred, on-campus wimp with a computer identity as a tough guy, victim and homicidal maniac, and good kid versus incorrigible villain. Eric was overwhelmed with hatred. The expression of that hatred was what gave him pleasure. In his journal he noted,

> HATE! *I'm full of hate and I love it*. I hate people and they better fucking fear me if they know what's good for them. Yes I hate and I guess I want others to know it. … (Harris 1998, emphasis mine).

Eric, with his feelings of grandiosity, had come to perceive himself as an avenging angel sworn not so much to right the wrongs of humanity but to terrorize lesser humans and demonstrate his own superiority. He perceived himself as devalued and unappreciated by others and hated them for that.

Perhaps the most chilling evidence of how engulfed Eric was in his hatred was revealed in a diary entry dated November 17, 1998, five months before the assault on Columbine (Harris 1998):

> [What I] want is [to] be surrounded by the flesh of a woman, someone like [name blacked out] who I wanted to just fuck like hell, she made me practically come when she wore those shorts to work—instant hard on. I couldn't stop staring at her and others like [names blacked out], and others who I want to overpower and engulf myself in them. Mmmm. I can taste the sweet flesh now—the salty sweet, the animalistic movement. *Iccchhh liebe fleisccchhhhh*. … Who can I trick into my room first? I can sweep someone off their feet, tell them what they want to hear, be all nice and sweet, and then "fuck 'em like an animal, feel them from the inside" as Reznor [NB: an apparent reference to Trent Reznor, vocalist for the rock group Nine Inch Nails] said. Oh—that's something else, that one. [Describes a video where] a guy is kidnapped and tortured like hell—total hell. I want to do that, too. I want to tear a throat out with

> my own teeth like a pop can. I want to gut somebody with my hands, to tear a head off and rip out the heart and lungs from the neck, to stab someone in the gut, shove it up to the heart, and yank the fucking blade out of their rib cage! I want to grab some weak freshman and just to tear them apart like a fucking wolf. Show them who is God, strangle them, squish their head, bite their temples into the skull, rip off their jaw. Rip off their collar bones, break their arms in half and twist them around, the lovely sounds of bones cracking and flesh ripping, ahh... so much to do and so little chances [*sic*].

Eric begins with a sexual fantasy, naming girls to whom he was attracted. He begins with the desire to touch, to feel the flesh of a woman. However, the sexual fantasy changes into reverie of rape, torture, and savagery. In this journal entry, the sexual merges into the homicidal. Even in the sexual fantasy, power plays an important part. No sense of mutuality exists; the other is victimized. The sexual act is construed as tricking and overpowering. As long as Eric is fantasizing about his ability to overpower someone else, he might as well do what he really wants, and that is to maim, torture, and kill. Eric Harris had a monster inside of him that wanted to be let out. That's what happened on April 20, 1999.

One subtext of all of Eric's writing is about power: the power to influence, the power to punish, the power to determine life and death, the power to control the world. Eric's adulation of Adolf Hitler seems to derive from Hitler's ability to exterminate anyone who did not conform to his image of the world. Repeatedly, Eric fantasizes about killing anyone who causes him the slightest inconvenience, people who are snobs, or just anyone: "[We] will hijack a hell of a lot of bombs and crash a plane into NYC with us inside firing away as we go down. Just something to cause more devastation" (Harris 1998). In that same journal entry Eric states, "I want to leave a lasting impression on the world."

Eric's friends, such as Brooks Brown, stated that Eric had a very strong sense of justice. That sense was violated on a daily basis, which increased his anger and frustration. However, Eric's writings betray a disdain for justice. He was too obsessed with power to be concerned about justice. His rant that anybody who disagreed with him should be killed contravenes the notion of any concept of distributive justice. What Eric was concerned about was lack of justice for himself and not for others. In light of his subsequent behavior of randomly killing convenient targets and his megalomaniacal notion that he was somehow superior by dint of an elevated state of consciousness and, therefore, could arbitrarily make decisions about who lived and who died, it can hardly be claimed that he had a highly developed sense of justice. What he did have was a very strong sense of his own victimization.

A second subtext is Eric's need for recognition. Eric wanted to be a somebody. Alas, in the life of material reality, he was a nobody. Although he was bright and had a critical vision, those virtues were pretty far down the list of attributes admired by his peers, and it was peer recognition that Eric desperately desired. He wanted to be a person to be reckoned with; the last thing he wanted to be was a low status outcast who was not worthy of being taken seriously. He was going to be taken seriously if, quite literally, it was the last thing he did. Eric Harris, the unappreciated short kid at the bottom of the Columbine High School peer structure reconstituted himself as a Superman. In his journal, he rhetorically asked what made him and Dylan Klebold different from other people. He answered his own question:

> Because I have something only me and V [NB: his nickname for Klebold, derived from Dylan's screen name "VoDKa"] have, SELF-AWARENESS, call it exoctenstiolism [existentialism] or what ever the fuck u want. We know what we are to this world and what everyone else is we learn more than what caused the Civil War and how to simplify quadratics in school we have been watching you people we know what you think and how you act [*sic*] (Harris 1998).

In the basement tapes, Dylan repeated what Eric had earlier written when he claimed that they were godlike because they had self-awareness. But from where did this self-awareness come? It apparently derived from a consciousness generated by their positions as despised members at the bottom of the social structure. Unlike other students who had a vested interest in the peer structure and who accepted it uncritically, Eric and Dylan, who were oppressed by it, viewed it critically. They viewed themselves as having a special consciousness that rejected conventional interpretations of reality and substituted their own opposition ideology. They were observing, taking notes, and planning revenge. Together, they were a force to be reckoned with.

DYLAN KLEBOLD, WILLING FOLLOWER

In many ways, Dylan Klebold is more difficult to understand than Eric Harris. Eric vented his hatred through his writings. Because of the intensity of his hatred, writing constituted a release for Eric; it was as if he was compelled to write.

Dylan was outwardly shy and reserved. Although he kept a journal, he did not write nearly as much as Eric. Therefore, it is more difficult to get a sense of Dylan's consciousness. Because Eric was the "theorist" and wrote treatises, one does not know the scope of Dylan's input into the process. What evidence that does exist seems to indicate that Eric did the conceptualizing and Dylan accepted it as his own.

Dylan, the Early Years

Dylan was born on September 11, 1981, in Englewood, Colorado, the second son of Tom and Sue Klebold. His brother, Byron, was three years older than Dylan. His entire life was spent as a resident of Southern Jefferson County. His parents, however, were both from Ohio. They met when they were students at Ohio State University, married, and moved to Southern Jefferson County where they put down roots and started a family.

It was a mixed marriage; Tom came from a Protestant background and Sue came from a wealthy, prestigious Jewish family. She was the granddaughter of Leo Yassinoff, a construction magnate and philanthropist in Columbus (Shepard 1999). His philanthropic works included a foundation that provided grants to educational institutions and social organizations and a Jewish community center in Columbus that bears his name. She was raised as a Jew; however, after marrying a Protestant, she led a mostly secular existence, and the family celebrated major Jewish and Christian holidays together (Culver 1999). However, an interviewee suggested that Tom Klebold was not particularly happy about celebrating Jewish holidays, but Sue insisted.

Religion was a problem for the Klebolds. Apparently, Tom Klebold had problems with organized religion. Reverend Marxhausen said that the Klebolds had attended services at St. Philip Lutheran Church for a few months five or six years before the shooting, but they stopped attending. They apparently never dealt with the issue of Judaism, other than celebrating Passover and Hanukah, two religious holidays that could be celebrated at home. They did not belong to a temple, and they apparently did not celebrate High Holy Days of Rosh Hashanah and Yom Kippur.

The Klebold family, according to confidential sources, was not a particularly happy one. Dylan and his older brother fought continuously. Relationships within the family were not particularly nurturing. This does not mean that the parents were not caring; they were. Tom Klebold, who worked at home, said that he treasured the afternoons when Dylan would come home from school early and spend time with him. In the wake of the shootings, Kate Battan, the chief investigator of the Jefferson County Sheriff's Department, stated, "I sat down and I've spent a lot of time with the Klebolds, and they're nice people. It's not like they're these monsters that raised a monster" (Cullen 1999b).

However, Sue and Tom were not particularly demonstrative, nor were relationships with their children characterized by warmth or touching. Although relationships were filled with conflict, they were not physically violent. Tom and Sue Klebold attempted to raise their children with a strong sense of morality and adhesion to personal values. Both boys knew right from wrong. However, there was not much joy in the house.

In a strange way, Dylan tended to be isolated from other kids. The Klebold's house was in a canyon, and there were not many neighbors in the vicinity. Therefore, as a young child, when Dylan wanted to play with another peer, he was dependent upon a parent to take him to a play date. He attended first and second grades at Normandy Elementary School. In the third grade, Dylan passed the CHIPS (Challenging High Intellectual Potential Students) entrance examination and was entered into the program for gifted and talented children. The program was separated from regular students. This tended to limit the number of peers from which Dylan could choose friends.

Based upon interviews with adults and peers who knew Dylan, he was described consistently as insecure, shy, and immature. Although he had friends, such as Brooks Brown, and he participated actively in sports leagues sponsored by the recreation department in tee-ball, baseball, and soccer, he had trouble making friends. When he moved from the relative security of elementary school into middle school, there was a shakedown in the peer group as children from several elementary schools were collected into a single middle school. A new peer elite emerged. Dylan, because he was shy and immature, experienced adjustment problems. As mentioned earlier, the prime source for the stratification of the peer group in Ken Caryl Middle School was whether or not a child participated in the Columbine Sports Association. Dylan did not. Given that he was structurally underprivileged by virtue of his playing sports in the recreation league and he was devoid of the requisite social skills for upper mobility in the peer structure, Dylan found himself near the bottom of the newly evolving peer hierarchy.

Dylan apparently met and became friends with Eric Harris at Ken Caryl Middle School in the seventh or eighth grade. Because Eric was new to the area and was forced to enter a peer structure that had already crystallized, he had to pick his friends from those among whom he had access. Although Eric and Dylan were decent athletes, they did not have the quality of athletic prowess that would gain them entry into the elite group. Because of Eric's alien status and Dylan's apparent lack of social skills, it was a friendship that was made at the bottom of the peer structure of Ken Caryl Middle School.

Identity Problems

Dylan had identity problems. He came from a mixed marriage, in which the Jewish part was only begrudgingly acknowledged. Although his mother did not deny her Judaism and celebrated major Jewish holidays in the home, Dylan's Jewish background was not easily acknowledged. Evidence from the basement tapes indicate that not only did Dylan's best friend idolize Adolf Hitler specifically because of his final solution to exterminate the Jews, but Dylan apparently hid his Jewish background from his closest friend until he accidentally revealed it while making the basement tapes in the weeks before the shooting. In one of the basement tapes while the boys were declaiming religion, Dylan exclaimed that his parents were going to a "fucking" seder, which took Eric by surprise. Eric then asked Dylan if he was Jewish, to which Dylan shamefacedly responded, "Yes." Eric responded, "I'm sorry, man" (Jefferson County Sheriff's Office 1999, 10,374).

It is likely that Dylan experienced a fair amount of identity confusion. Was he a Jew, a Protestant, or neither? Clearly, he did not identify himself as a Jew or associate with Jewish kids, who were rare in southern Jefferson County. Until his revelation to Eric on the eve of the shootings, no one in Columbine High School, with the possible exception of Brooks Brown, knew Dylan had a Jewish background.

Was he ashamed of his background, or did he hide it because its revelation would have provided more ammunition to his tormentors? In Columbine, racism and anti-Semitism are muted to the point that the adults can deny their existence. As noted earlier, adults in southern Jefferson County regard themselves as tolerant of religious, racial, and ethnic differences. However, it is easy to maintain such a collective image in a community that is overwhelmingly white, Christian, and upper-middle-class. In Columbine, racism and anti-Semitism exist as unspoken assumptions that underlie the ethnocentrism of the community.

However, younger, less socialized members of the community have tended to be more vocal and outspoken about their biases. For example, Wayne and Kathy Harris were not only unaware of their son's racism and anti-Semitism, but when the racist and anti-Semitic content of the Trenchcoat Mafia web site was revealed, Mr. Harris responded by saying that he did not know where his son got that "Nazi stuff" (Culver 1999).

During the rampage, Dylan unabashedly called Isaiah Sholes a "nigger" and singled him out for death. Dylan, apparently imitating Eric, would shout "Heil

Hitler" in bowling class when he rolled a strike (Culver 1999). A Jewish kid, even one who is "half Jewish," whose closest friend is an anti-Semitic Naziophile, who shouts "Heil Hitler" when he bowls a strike, who modifies the word "seder" with "fucking" and identifies himself in an Internet chat room as an admirer of Adolf Hitler, seems to have internalized hatred of Jews. Dylan seems to have adopted Eric's reality system as his own.

In addition, Dylan may have been confused about his sexual identity. Dylan presented himself as a bisexual in an online chat room (Columbine Research Site 2003). Given the homophobic nature of American male culture (Kimmel 1996), even in the anonymity of Internet chat rooms, it would be extremely rare for a heterosexual male to claim bisexuality if there was no question about his sexual identity. There is no evidence that Dylan was sexually active; however, this may have actually added to his confusion.

So who was Dylan Klebold? At Columbine High School, he was a cipher. In the early reports following the shootings, he was identified as a member of the Trenchcoat Mafia. Trenchcoat Mafia members knew him as a friend of a member, not one of their own. He and Eric were primarily identified by other students by their social position at the bottom of the student hierarchy. They were viewed alternatively as dark, or Gothic, and as such, mildly threatening, or as ridiculous posers who were, in the words of IG, "a joke." Whereas, girls may have found Eric "cute," that term was not used to describe Dylan.

A former teacher described him as unattractive to his peers. The bright shy normal ninth grader, according to this teacher, changed into what the teacher clearly saw as a repugnant character. He had become a slacker, unmotivated to learn, trying to get by with as little work as possible. Not only was Dylan Klebold unlikable to the teacher, the teacher perceived him as rejected by his peers. Dylan had changed from being a nobody to one who was recognized for his negativity.

Out of the detritus of his life, with the help of Eric Harris, Dylan began to construct an identity as a badass outlaw. His anger and his hatred were used as the basis of a constructed identity. In videotapes he made with his friends, he played the role of enforcer, threatening, beating, and killing various and sundry enemies, especially bullies and preppies. In a paper that he wrote in English class, it is clear that he is both witness and protagonist:

> What was most recognized about the man was the sound of his footsteps. Behind the conversations [and] noises of the town, not a sound was to be heard from him, except the dark, monotonous footsteps combined with the jingling of his belt chains striking not only the two visible guns, in their holsters, but the large Bowie knife, slung in anticipation of use. …

> This man walked, fueled by some untold purpose, what Christians would call evil. … He stood about 6 feet and 4 inches, and was strongly built. His face was entirely in shadow, yet even though I was unable to see his expressions, I could feel his anger, cutting thru [*sic*] the air like a razor. He seemed to know where he was walking, and he noticed my presence, but paid no attention, as he kept walking toward a popular bar, The Watering Hole. He stopped about 30 feet from the door, and waited. "For whom?" I wondered, as I saw them step out. He must've known their habits well, as they appeared less than a minute after he stopped walking. A group of college-preps, about nine of them, stopped in their tracks. … The street light illuminating the bar [and] the sidewalk showed me a clear view of their stare, full of paralysis [and] fear. They knew who he was, [and] why he was there. (Jefferson County Sheriff's Office 1999C-001-016016).

"The Man," who had apparently been confronted earlier by the preppies and had been challenged to a fight, coolly dispatched the nine preppies, using handguns, a knife, and a metal truncheon. The slaying is explained in graphic detail with the preppies alternatively manifesting fear, denial of culpability, and bravado before getting their just deserts. Just before executing his last victim, who was seriously wounded, "the man" set off two remote diversionary explosions, foreshadowing the boys' attempt to do the same during the Columbine shootings. The story ended,

> The town was utterly still, except for the wail of police sirens. The man picked up the bag and his clips, and proceeded to walk back the way he came. I was still, as he came my way again. He stopped, and gave me a look I will never forget. If I could face an emotion of God, it would have looked like the man. I not only saw his face, but also felt emanating from him power, complacence, closure, and godliness. The man smiled, and in that instant, thru [sic] no endeavor of my own, I understood his actions. (Jefferson County Sheriff's Office 1999, JC-001-016017).

"The man" can be viewed as Dylan Klebold's ego ideal: two inches taller than he, muscular, smart, self-assured, resolute, in control, and coldly murderous. "The man" was, quite literally, an avenging angel. For a child raised in a predominantly secular household, the story has numerous religious references. The man is both evil and godly. In the story, the man laughs at one of the preppies' attempt at bravado. Klebold described the laugh as one that "would have made Satan cringe in hell." Klebold places himself in the story as the lone witness to the event. He is not horrified by the slaughter; rather, he is awed by the power and self-composure of the man.

Dylan Klebold's writings and videotapes seem to be obsessively concerned with avenging wrongs. In the videotapes the boys made for class, they hired themselves out to avenge bullies. In another story written for his creative writing class, based upon this scenario of the Doom videogame, he portrayed himself as the last Marine alive to defend the earth from an alien invasion. In this particular story, the protagonist is overwhelmed by the death and destruction and becomes psychologically paralyzed.

In his senior year, Dylan wrote a twelve-page paper entitled "The Mind and Motives of Charles Manson," which was not so much about the mind and motives of Manson as a description of the lethal activities of the Manson family drawn primarily from the work of Vincent Bugliosi (Bugliosi and Gentry 1974). Manson, who was idolized by the characters in Oliver Stone's movie, "Natural Born Killers," of which Klebold and Harris were enamored, was characterized by Bugliosi as a revenge killer. He was a serial killer who murdered people who crossed or slighted him. The killings of Sharon Tate and her friends and the LaBiancas in August of 1969 were supposed to set off a racial war between whites and blacks that would lead to social revolution; Harris and Klebold thought that their actions would start a revolution in which oppressed kids would rise up against bullies.

In the paper, Dylan wrote about Manson:

> Helter Skelter, revenge was part of his beliefs. Humans had corrupted the Earth and ATWA [Air, Trees, Water, Animals], and were ignorant about it. Manson had felt that society dumped him and he felt great rage for society, and people, and later found an anthem for his rage. When asked about his actions, many years after the murders, he had said that he is part of everyone, that he mirrors people, because they shaped him. The Beatles' *White Album* included songs ("Helter-Skelter," "Revolution #9," "Piggies," and others) that Manson felt documented his rage toward society. (Jefferson County Sheriff's Office 1999, JC-001016026-27).

Dylan's fascination with Charles Manson was probably stimulated not only by the violence he perpetrated but also by his position as social outcast. The actions of Klebold and Harris were similar to those of Manson and his family in an earlier era. According to Bugliosi (1974), Charles Manson was literally raised by the State of California, alternating between foster care, institutionalized care, and the criminal justice system; he had a towering hatred for society. In a period of a social movement among young people, he managed to legitimate that hate by incorporating movement interpretations of reality into a pseudo-theory he called "Helter-Skelter." He thought that by engaging in high profile murders of celebrities, white society would blame blacks for the murders, instigating a war between the races that would eventuate in a revolution. However, by the time of the Tate-LaBianca murders, Manson had already killed several dozen victims.

Although the paper reads like a term paper based upon a single source, which it is, it betrays an affinity Dylan Klebold had with Charles Manson. He empathized with his outcast status, viewed his actions as an attack on an unjust society, and apparently adopted his theory that high profile violence would start a revolution, even though, in Manson's case, it did not. Rather, it signaled the beginning of the end of the middle-class youth movement (Foss and Larkin 1976).

The man, the Marine from Doom, Charles Manson, the persona adopted in the basement tapes, and the fantasy role of avenger in the videotape made with Eric, all emphasize the desire to exact revenge for injustices. Dylan Klebold, in the world of his peers, was perceived by others as clumsy, oafish, unkempt, immature, and nerdish. He was subject to ostracism and harassment. He was less than a nobody. Many of his peers thought he was "an asshole." The young man who was negatively perceived by others probably did not like himself. Being "half" Jewish did not help, and the revelation of his Jewish ancestry probably created more problems. Dylan Klebold was a jumble of psychological contradictions: Jew/Gentile, nerd/avenging hero, heterosexual/homosexual. In the flinty, competitive, gun-crazed, moralistically rigid environment of southern Jefferson County, these contradictions were transcended through violence.

THE BOYS TOGETHER

In this section, I will attempt to answer the following questions: What attracted the boys to each other? What were the internal dynamics of the relationship? What did they do together?

Nobody was quite sure about how or when Eric and Dylan met (Bartels and Crowder 1999). The best guess is that they met and became friends sometime during the seventh or eighth grade. That friendship, made at the bottom of the peer structure of Ken Caryl Middle School, lasted until April 20, 1999.

In overwhelmingly white middle-class high schools, kids at the bottom of the social structure form a cultural opposition to the dominant elite (Eckert 1989). In part, outcast students are those who either cannot or will not conform to the norms of the dominant elite. They may not have the physical attributes, athletic abilities, socioeconomic status, social skills, or interests required by the elites. On the other hand, their cultural sensibilities, musical tastes, intellectual capabilities, and world views also set them apart. However, as the peer structure solidifies, elites and outcasts define themselves dialectically such that what is associated with the other is anathema within the peer subculture. If the elite is homophobic, then the outcasts may engage in gender bending and flirt with homosexuality. If the elite dresses in Abercrombie and Fitch, outcasts will dress in black, adopt a Gothic image, and wear Doc Martens. If elites are highly Christianized, outcasts will dabble in Satanism and Wicca. While elites presume their dominance to be part of the natural order of things, outcast students are cynical about the nature of existing social arrangements. For some outcast students, pariah status can be a source of great psychological pain; for others, it becomes a badge of honor. For most, it is probably a combination. Humans are social animals and rejection is a blow to the self.

Eric and Dylan found themselves at the bottom of the peer structure for different reasons. Dylan did not fit in apparently because of insufficient social skills, lack of athletic prowess, and his own confusion about his identity. Eric's complaints about always having to start over at the bottom of the peer structure in each new community he lived in was visited upon him in Columbine even though this was going to be his permanent residence and there would be no more moving around as an Air Force brat. Had he arrived in southern Jefferson County a year or two earlier, things may have been different for him. Although, in many ways he was a "typical boy," he had neither the physical prowess nor interest in sports that would have elevated him in the peer structure. Unfortunately for him, he was short and slightly built, making him a target for bullies. His feelings of injustice were related to the fact that he never had a chance for acceptance given the structure of the peer group system.

In a school of 1,800 students, outcast students occupying a visible oppositional culture were estimated to be fewer than twenty, including the Trenchcoat Mafia. Although Dylan and Eric dressed in the oppositional mode and had friends who were TCM members, they were not themselves members. They tended to split themselves off from others, although they maintained relationships with other students such as Robyn Anderson, Mark Manes, Chris Morris, Cory Friesen, and Nick Baumgart. Chris Morris and Cory Friesen appeared in a picture of the Trenchcoat Mafia in the 1998 Columbine High School annual yearbook. Of the numerous students interviewed for this study, none who were in the middle of the peer group structure knew Eric Harris or Dylan Klebold. Some noted that they had seen them around campus. Because they dressed similarly and had friends who were members of the TCM, many students mistakenly identified them as TCM members (Cullen 1999d).

Dylan was apparently attracted to Eric because he was open and personable. Eric was physically attractive, bright, and articulate. What was perhaps most attractive about Eric to Dylan was his sense of irony, strong sense of himself, and the fact that he could articulate a vision of reality that legitimated his own anger at and hatred for his social degradation. In addition, they shared interests in computer games. What apparently attracted Dylan to Eric was that Eric gave his life a spark that had not been there before. In many ways, Dylan worshiped Eric. Dylan began adopting Eric's ideas as his own even though they would be anathema to his parents' views. With Eric, he could swagger and cultivate a "badass" identity on the Internet under his moniker, "VoDKa." The relationship with Eric allowed him to fantasize himself as a person to be reckoned with.

For Eric, Dylan was a disciple. Dylan's acceptance of Eric's worldview tended to validate it. Long hours of playing Doom together reinforced their notion of themselves against the world. In the basement tapes, they claimed that they had arrived at a point of higher consciousness than mere mortals (Gibbs and Roche 1999). This idea was also reinforced through the Doom videogame, in which the lone Marine attempts to vanquish subhuman monsters in order to save the human race. Most likely, they saw themselves as the personification of the Marine in Doom and saw their predatory peers as the subhuman monsters that threatened the Marine.

Eric was obsessed with his anger, hatred, and feelings that he had been treated unjustly and that others did not appreciate his talents and qualities. Although physically attractive, girls initially attracted to Eric were put on guard by what they sensed as violent emotions beneath the surface. Dylan bought into those feelings and validated them. Eric's friendship with Dylan allowed him to express those feelings and have them reciprocated. Revenge for real and imagined slights propelled their relationship to the point of mass murder and mutual suicide.

Numerous writers, especially in chat rooms on the Internet, have speculated that the relationship between Eric Harris and Dylan Klebold was homoerotic. Writers have speculated about the sexual orientation of the boys on several occasions (Chase 2001; Cullen 2004). However, Eric's writings reveal him as heterosexual and homophobic. In his senior year, he maintained a relationship for a few weeks with a girl several years his senior who lived miles away from him. Logistics and age differences made the relationship difficult and eventually impossible to maintain. One should recall, too, that his sexual fantasy that transformed into gore and violence began with his attraction to girls. In addition, in one of his rants, he stated:

> YOU KNOW WHAT I HATE!!!?
> HOMOSEXUALS!! It is just plain WRONG. (Columbine Research Site 2003, JC-001-010414)

Even though Dylan had a date to the senior prom and Eric did not, no evidence exists indicating that Dylan had a romantic or sexual relationship with a girl. His date to the prom was his friend Robyn Anderson, with whom he had a platonic relationship. The evidence gathered seems to indicate that Dylan had not yet become sexually active; because of his lack of social skills and emotional immaturity, he was probably incapable of maintaining a sexual relationship. A reporter named Mike Connors told investigators that he had encountered Dylan Klebold in an Internet chat room. According to the police report, Klebold spoke at length with Connors about his relationship with Eric Harris and that he, Klebold, described himself as bisexual. It is possible that Dylan's feelings toward Eric may have been erotic. However, it is likely that any attempt to approach Eric sexually by Dylan would have threatened their relationship on which Dylan was highly dependent. Therefore, it is highly improbable that Eric and Dylan engaged in any homosexual behavior, and that any erotic feelings that Dylan may have felt toward Eric were kept to himself.

Several informants, including Frank Ochsberg, a psychiatrist at Michigan State University who helped the FBI develop psychological profiles on Klebold and Harris, suggested that without the other, neither boy could have carried out the attack alone; that they tended to reinforce each other; and that the presence of the other prevented them from backing out of their plans. Evidence from the boy's writings and the videotapes seems to indicate that once they committed themselves to their plan and began to collect weaponry and draw up a strategy, if there were thoughts about abandoning the plan, they were not expressed openly.

Clearly, each boy desperately needed the other. Eric gave Dylan's life momentum, purpose, and direction. Prior to his relationship with Eric, Dylan's life was drifting downward. He seemed not to know who he was or where he was going. Eric changed all that. Although Eric's life would be short, it would be significant, and he would die a celebrity. For Eric, Dylan was a willing accomplice and validated a worldview in which he was unjustly treated and victimized by his moral inferiors. Together, they were a force to be reckoned with. Separately, they were just a couple of nerds at the very bottom of the social structure of Columbine High School.

Together, Eric and Dylan constructed a reality parallel to conventional society in which they were heroic, like the Marine in the Doom videogame. In their alternative world, they were the arbiters of morality. They were like gods who would avenge themselves on their moral inferiors who were their social superiors and who defended that superiority by harassing and humiliating anybody, especially those who opposed or rejected the social order at Columbine High. Therefore, online they constructed their own identities as hard ass "natural born killers." The contradiction between their social identities in the lived-in world of Columbine High School and those constructed on the Internet was resolved through the attack on their high school on April 20, 1999, and their subsequent suicides.

THE DEPRESSIVE AND THE PSYCHOPATH?

In the wake of the Columbine massacre, the FBI convened a conference of mental health specialists and forensic psychologists in Leesburg, Virginia, for the purpose of developing psychological profiles of Eric Harris and Dylan Klebold (Cullen 2004). Two of the attendees of this conference, psychiatrist Frank Ochberg and Special Agent Dwayne Fuselier, revealed the findings of that conference to free-lance journalist Dave Cullen, who had been writing numerous articles about the Columbine shootings. The apparent conclusions of the conference were that Dylan Klebold was "a depressive" and Eric Harris was "a psychopath." According to Cullen, Dylan Klebold was easier to diagnose because he was a garden-variety depressed teenager:

> Fuselier and Ochberg say that if you want to understand "the killers," quit asking what drove *them*. Eric Harris and Dylan Klebold were radically different individuals, with vastly different motives and opposite mental conditions. Klebold is easier to comprehend, a more familiar type. He was hotheaded, but depressive and suicidal. He blamed himself for his problems.
>
> Harris is the challenge. He was sweet-faced and well-spoken. Adults, and even some other kids, described him as "nice." But Harris was cold, calculating, and homicidal. "Klebold was hurting inside while Harris wanted to hurt people," Fuselier says. Harris was not merely a troubled kid, the psychiatrists say, he was a psychopath. (Cullen 2004).

Whether or not Dylan Klebold blamed himself for his problems is an open question. It may be that the profilers had data unavailable to others. However, the Klebolds were not interviewed by this researcher, although the lead investigator of the Jefferson County Sheriff's Department, Kate Battan, spent considerable time with them, concluding that they were good, concerned parents. My interviews with Dylan's friends suggested that he did not blame himself for his problems, but blamed others, especially football players and bullies. According to Cullen, Ochberg, and Fusillier, Dylan internalized and Eric externalized their personal problems. The evidence from this study suggests that both externalized their problems.

Was Dylan Klebold depressed? A great deal of evidence exists to indicate that he was. Life at home was not particularly pleasant although his parents were certainly concerned and well-meaning. Life at Columbine High School was miserable and humiliating. He was struggling with several identity issues: Was he a Jew or a Naziophile? Was he gay or straight? Was he a nerd or a natural born killer? In each case, the contradictions were irresolvable. His Jewishness was a deep dark secret to be covered over by a public identity as a neo-Nazi. What ever homosexual urges he had were suppressed because their expression would destroy his relationship with Eric. He would avenge his nerd status on April 20, 1999. A Jew, a homosexual, a nerd: These aspects of his identity in deeply Christian, homophobic, red-blooded American southern Jefferson County had to be the source of tremendous fear, anxiety, and self-loathing for Dylan Klebold.

Was Eric Harris a psychopath? The terms "psychopath" and "sociopath" are not used by the psychological profession anymore. The term listed in the DSM-IV manual is "antisocial personality disorder" (AllPsych online 2004). The symptoms of antisocial personality disorder include difficulty with and hostility toward authority, illegal behavior, cruelty to animals, and pyromania. The psychological components are a depressed ability to feel empathy and the lack of remorse for wrongdoings. Psychopaths lie for sport; they obtain pleasure from deceiving others. According to Cullen (2004), "Harris'[s] pattern of grandiosity, glibness, contempt, lack of empathy, and superiority read like the bullet points on [psychologist Dr. Robert] Hare's (1999) Psychopathy Checklist and convinced Fuselier and the other leading psychiatrists close to the case that Harris was a psychopath."

In a personal communication with Dr. Ochberg, I was told that the prime evidence of Eric's psychopathology was his ability to use the language of emotion in a manipulative fashion. Ochberg's case was presented in the Cullen (2004) article:

> Harris married his deceitfulness with a total lack of remorse or empathy—another distinctive quality of the psychopath. Fuselier was finally convinced of his diagnosis when he read Harris'[s] response to being punished after being caught breaking into a van. Klebold and Harris had avoided prosecution for the robbery by participating in a "diversion program" that involved counseling and community service. Both killers feigned regret to obtain an early release, but Harris had relished the opportunity to perform. He wrote an ingratiating letter to his victim offering empathy, rather than just apologies. Fuselier remembers that it was packed with statements like "Jeez, I understand now how you feel and I understand what this did to you."

"But he wrote that strictly for effect," Fuselier said. "That was complete manipulation. At almost the exact same time, he wrote down his real feelings in his journal":

> Isn't America supposed to be the land of the free? How come, if I'm free, I can't deprive a stupid fucking dumbshit from his possessions if he leaves them sitting in the front seat of his fucking van out in plain sight and in the middle of fucking nowhere on a Frifuckingday night. NATURAL SELECTION. Fucker should be shot.

Both boys took pleasure in duping others and being able to hide their plot from their parents and friends. The diversion class was a charade. Yet it is clear from Eric's response (Harris 1998), he understood the content of the program in great detail.

In my view, the evidence for Eric's psychopathology is, at best, mixed. Could he be cold and calculating? Yes, he could be. However, he could also be volatile and violent in his interaction with others, such as the incident in which he threw a rock and cracked the windshield of Brooks Brown's car. Paradoxically, although Eric took pleasure in duping adult authorities, he was also highly respectful of them, including his own father. In the windshield incident, Judy Brown confronted him. According to her observations, he was fearful of the reactions of his parents. He was remembered in Plattsburgh, New York, as shy and respectful. He never constituted a behavior problem in class; Principal DeAngelis did not know him because apparently there were never any problems with Eric in school, although one of the students interviewed (EK) indicated that her brother was bullied by Harris and Klebold, which was adjudicated by Mr. DeAngelis. He apparently forgot about the incident. At work at Blackjack Pizza, when it was discovered the boys were exploding firecrackers and making ice bombs behind the store and their boss told them to stop it, Eric did so. In one of his final diary entries (Harris 1998), Eric stated, "[Just] because we went on a killing spree doesn't mean everyone else will and hardly ever do people bring bombs or guns to school anyway, *the admin. is doing a fine job as it is*, I don't know who will be left after we kill but damnit don't change any policies just because of us" (Emphasis mine).

Yet this same administration that Eric is praising is the one that stands accused by many observers, including this writer, of tolerating the conditions that led to predatory behavior on the part of the jocks in the school that angered Eric. Clearly, Eric did not display empathy on April 20, 1999. But in talking with people who knew Eric, a quite different picture emerged: Eric had a pet dog that he loved and cared for. He was described as a good friend who could give emotional support to people he liked; he empathized with those like himself who were victimized by the jocks. I doubt whether the profilers talked to any of his friends.

Was Eric a psychopath? Was Dylan a depressive? Obviously, both boys manifested characteristics of these psychological categories. The problem with such characterizations, especially used by a nonprofessional such as Cullen, is that it tends to engulf the boy's identities and reduce them to labels. Once the boys were labeled, then it became easy to engage in crude psychological reductionism. "Most Americans have reached one of two wrong conclusions about why they did it. The first conclusion is that the pair of supposed 'Trenchcoat Mafia outcasts' were taking revenge against the bullies who had made school miserable for them. The second conclusion is that the massacre was inexplicable: We can never understand what drove them to such horrific violence" (Cullen 2004).

Aside from the simplistic notions of causality, Cullen (2004), drawing on the information from FBI profilers, concluded that the shootings were the consequence of the psychological pathologies of Harris and Klebold. He decided that the shootings were a result of Klebold's depression and Harris's psychopathology. The problem with Cullen's conclusion is that depression and psychopathology are insufficient factors in determining any given behavior. Depression can evince itself in any number of behaviors ranging from inability to get out of bed in the morning and function to homicide. Psychopathology can be present in any number of people, from clever and manipulative politicians and CEOs to serial killers. Environmental influences give direction to psychopathology. For Cullen to attribute the Columbine shootings to the psychological states of the killers is to deny environmental influences in the generation of those psychological states and tacitly to absolve others of any culpability. It is the equivalent of Columbine High School Principal Frank DeAngelis attributing the killings to the fact that the boys were "evil." It is a case of labeling and throwing away the label. Nothing is explained; however, it gives the labeler a false sense of certainty of a *deus ex machina*, or more precisely, *diabolus ex machina* explanation.

In this chapter, I have reconstructed the mental states of Eric and Dylan based upon their behavior, writings, and videotapes. I have also derived information from friends and adults who knew them and from media reports. In addition, I also talked to an FBI profiler. I have also attempted to explore the nature of their relationship and how it led them to try to blow up their school and kill as many of their peers as they could.

Central to Freudian and social interaction psychological theories is the belief that the human mind is generated and shaped from the interactions of individuals with their environment, especially their human environment. This insight was codified at the beginning of the nineteenth century with Freud's (1952) essay, "The Ego and the Id"; George Herbert Mead's (1964) work on mind, self, and society; and Charles Horton Cooley's (1902) description of the "looking glass self." The self, or what we perceive ourselves to be, is an amalgam of attitudes, orientations, and social categories that have been internalized through the socialization process and is influenced by our reference groups (Berger and Luckmann 1966; Sherif and Sherif 1964). As children grow, the family declines in importance as a reference group relative to the peer group, which emerges into primacy during adolescence (Harris 1999). Both theoretically and practically, it makes sense that the family provides the basis for early childhood psychological development, which is taken over by other agencies as the child grows, including the school, the peer group, and the media. In many cases, the family competes with other socialization agencies for the attention and adhesion of their children. Norms and values of the school, peer group, and mass media may conflict with those of the family, creating intergenerational conflict as the children become independent from their parents.

Of familial influences on Eric and Dylan, little is known; however, prior to adolescence, both boys and both families were described as normal. Although friends and neighbors may have little insight into the internal workings of the family, they do see the consequences in the attitudes and behaviors of the children. What we do know for sure is that prior to adolescence, no alarm bells rang for either boy or either family. As far as we can tell, for both boys, the spiral downward into hatred and violence began in middle school. As I noted above, middle school is the point in time where the peer group assumes ascendancy in a child's life and can be a terrorizing force. In southern Jefferson County, middle school children faced an unusual situation in which a single middle school fed into the local high school. In addition, the peer group structure in middle school was influenced by community sports leagues, one of the very few organizations that spanned the entire area. For preadolescents, sports leagues, church clubs, and shopping malls are the main venues that bring them into contact with children outside their own elementary school catchment areas. Sports leagues, more than the other two venues, integrated children from all over southern Jefferson County into organized interaction. Because of their size and popularity, they provided the basis for the structure of the adolescent peer culture.

In urban contexts, adolescent peer groups or gangs, are organized around ethnicity (Jankowski 1991). Because of the makeup of urban peer groups, acceptance is premised on ethnic group membership, which constitutes the basis of solidarity. In most suburban contexts, the peer group is not fractionated by ethnicity, and, furthermore, it assumes a unitary structure with athletes at the top (Eckert 1989; Wooden and Blazak 2001). This unitary structure tends to create an environment in which interpersonal competitiveness takes precedence over intergroup conflict. Eric and Dylan found themselves at the very bottom of a nasty pecking order.

Some aspects of identity are chosen, and others are thrust upon us. Identities have both personal and social components. The major social categories that form identity— such as gender, race, social class, and age—are those over which people have little control. Eric and Dylan were stigmitized as losers, which subjected them to predatory treatment that they "deserved" because of their degraded status. The predatory treatment they received was legitimated within the peer culture because in American society, people at the bottom of the social structure are perceived as being there because of the choices they made, which reflect their own degraded morality. The conflation of the moral with the social justifies the predatory behavior directed toward outcast students. The fact that Eric and Dylan, who were preyed upon by student athletes, also bullied those who were weaker than they demonstrates the normative structure of the peer group in terms of violence. Even though their degraded status in the peer group system was a fact, they rejected it, and constructed alternative identities on the Internet and in their videotapes.

A tremendous amount of thought, to the point of obsession, was spent by Eric and Dylan in avenging themselves on their peers. Their desire for revenge permeated practically everything they did from video games to English assignments. They cultivated their anger, developing a plot to destroy their school and kill as many of their peers as they could. Even though Eric drew up a hit list, their primary target was the peer structure, the secondary target was the community at large, and the tertiary target was American society. In an interview on National Public Radio on the fifth anniversary of the shootings, Brooks Brown stated that Eric and Dylan were crazy, but it was Columbine that made them that way (Brand 2004).

7

FROM OKLAHOMA CITY TO COLUMBINE

THE ASSAULT ON Columbine High School was a unique event in the history of American education. Prior to the attack, school shootings involved a lone and deranged student or former student bringing a gun to school and shooting at teachers and peers for real or imagined humiliations. Although the shooter may have obsessed over the actions prior to the shootings, the actual act tended to be either a rampage or a targeting of a specific individual or small group. The exception to this is Jonesboro, where two boys ransacked their fathers' gun cabinet, took weapons to their middle school, set off a fire alarm, and as the school was evacuated, began shooting at girls and female teachers in an apparent retaliation by the older shooter, Mitchell Johnson, for being rejected by a girl (Domestic Violence Project 1998). In none of these cases, did the assailants plan to blow up their school. None engaged in long-term planning, collected explosives and weaponry, employed diversionary tactics, reconnoitered their school, tested their weaponry, or thought about killing hundreds of students, devising ways that would maximize the destruction.

The Columbine attack was planned over a period of at least eight months. Even though the actual attack ended up as a rampage with Harris and Klebold shooting wildly and randomly killing peers, they conducted what they planned as a "strategic military assault" (Gibbs and Roche 1999). Although puny by the standards of *Soldier of Fortune* magazine, the boys were heavily armed for an assault on a school: Each had a sawed off shotgun; Klebold had a TEC-9 semiautomatic handgun; Harris carried a Hi-Point 9 mm carbine rifle. Between the two of them, they had four knives, described in Chapter 1. They carried shotgun shells in utility belts, ammunition and CO_2 bombs in their cargo pants pockets. They also carried bombs in a duffel bag. They hauled two twenty-gallon propane tank bombs into the school cafeteria that were timed to explode at 11:17 A.M., when the lunch area was most crowded (Jefferson County Sheriff's Office 1999). Why did Harris and Klebold want to create so much destruction? Where did they get the idea to blow up their school? What social and cultural forces influenced their ideas and behaviors? Why did they adopt paramilitary tactics in their assault on Columbine? What were the roles of each young man in the planning and the assault?

ERIC HARRIS AND NAZI SKINHEADS

On April 20, 1999, Eric Harris, the putative leader of the two boys, was dressed in classical paramilitary style: he wore black cargo pants held up with suspenders, combat boots, short-cropped hair, and his own personal twist, a T-shirt with the words, "Natural Selection." Such an outfit would have made him feel right at home in a gang of Nazis skinheads (Finnigan 1998; Ridgeway 1995). Moore (1993) described skinhead attire as characterized by the wearing of red tag Levi pants and jackets, flight jackets, and braces (suspenders). They also wore Doc Marten boots and T-shirts with the phrase, "No Remorse."

Eric Harris was not a member of a skinhead gang, nor is there any evidence that he had friends who were skinheads. He did, however, identify himself as a "Goth" on his web site and adopted many aspects of skinhead culture. Although both goth and skinhead youth subcultures are outcast groups, they are derived from quite different constituencies and have quite different norms, values, and behaviors. Goth is a vague and generic term that can refer to such ephemera as dressing styles and musical tastes (Hodkinson 2002). Goth youth subcultures tend to be found in middle-class high schools and contain students who may be artsy or intellectual but are alienated from the dominant student culture inhabited by jocks and their hangers-on. The mode of dress is black; clothes are often obtained from secondhand stores and further individualized by cutting holes, sewing on rock band insignia, or splashing with bleach or dye. Although there is truly no such thing as goth music, a number of rock bands, such as The Sisters of Mercy, Christian Death, Switchblade Symphony, Cruxshadows, and Marilyn Manson seemed to be associated with goth culture. Because goths are so individualized and their subcultures are localized, there is little agreement on what constitutes goth subcultures.

Skinhead subculture is an entirely different phenomenon. Skinhead subculture might be called "in-your-face." Skinheads are aggressive and hypermasculine where goths are ethereal and androgynous. Eric Harris did not use makeup and eyeliner or eye shadow, nor did he always wear black to school, although the trench coat he wore was apparently black. The politics of goth is that of cultural disaffection without an overtly political view. Although skinheads are culturally disaffected, their politics are openly right wing, nativist, and authoritarian (Moore 1993; Ridgeway 1995).

Other than an anomalous link to a web site entitled "Why Skinheads Suck," Eric Harris's website seems to be strongly influenced by Nazi skinhead ideology. Because of their antirationalism, skinheads do not have what would be considered a coherent ideology. However, skinheads share certain core beliefs (Moore 1993): anti-Semitism, racism, nativism, white supremacy, homophobia, working-class identity, nihilism, and glorification of violence. Skinheads have been closely aligned with the Ku Klux Klan and Tom Metzger's White Aryan Resistance (WAR) organization, a virulent racist and anti-Semitic neo-Nazi organization that has ties to the Klan. With the exception of working-class identity, middle-class Eric Harris's writings fit quite easily into the skinhead belief system.

The term "Natural Selection," which was written across the T-shirt that Harris wore on the day of the massacre, refers to the white supremacist belief that those of Nordic background are superior not only to persons of color (mud people) but also to what racists referred to as "mixed breeds" such as Hispanics and southern Italians. Although other people, such as jocks and cheerleaders, are vilified in his web site, anti-Semitic and racist sentiments are laced throughout his web pages. For example:

- The holocaust never happened, but it would have been cool if it had.
- Negroes need to put down their forties [a reference to forty-ounce bottles of malt liquor supposedly popular in African American urban ghettos] and head back to Africa.
- Four "Hiel [*sic*] Hitlers"
- Hitler was an old school goth! He did not die in vain! Neither shall I!
- Littleton, Colorado, isn't a great place to grow up as a white boy. If I had my druthers, I'd be anywhere else at all, even in some place with lots of malt-liquor-drinking, rhyme-busting, ass-capping Negroes and perhaps a few squinty-eyed, dog-eating Chinese people!

- [If] you're not a jock, jew or jiggaboo, not a wop, spic or country hick, not a jap, slant or my old gypsy aunt and want to get with the program, send me an email[.]

So where does a middle-class white teenager obtain such ideas? Clearly, Eric Harris adulated Adolf Hitler, a person who ranks high in the American pantheon of evildoers. His racism extends beyond mere denigration of blacks to Asians, Hispanics, and southern Italians. He is virulently anti-Semitic, adhering to the counterfactual claim that the Holocaust never occurred. He identifies himself as a goth on his web site: "By nature, I'm fairly depressed most of the time. It pretty much goes with the territory when you're a middle-American suburban goth with a penchant for computer gaming and bomb making." He then identifies affinities between himself and Adolf Hitler and "Goths," as noted above.

Skinheads have been responsible for numerous unprovoked attacks on gays. Moore (1993) quotes a 1987 skinhead publication: "[S]kinheads worldwide are warriors. We never run away, back down, or sellout. We despise the traitors, the cowards, the apathetic and limp wristed queers. We will fight forever to defend our people and our land. Our heads are shaved for battle" (84).

Moore suggests that skinheads tended to be less obsessed with the sexual behavior of gays than with their political liberalism. He noted that skinheads seem to be angry with gays for more political than sexual reasons. (Eric's homophobia was discussed in the previous chapter.)

Evidence of Eric's anti-Semitism has been presented above. In comparison to skinhead anti-Semitism, with the exception of the adulation of Adolf Hitler, Eric Harris seems quite muted. Although he expresses anti-Semitic sentiments, he is not obsessed with Jewish conspiracies, proclaiming the validity of *The Protocols of the Elders of Zion*, or reading from *The Turner Diaries*, both of which are staples of right-wing anti-Semitism.

No doubt both Eric and Dylan had racist tendencies. Ironically, when Eric tended to portray himself as not racist, he came up with a racist rant:

> YOU KNOW WHAT I HATE!!!?– RACISM!!! Anyone who hate [*sic*] blacks, asians, mexicans, or people from any other country or race just because they arent [*sic*] from here or are a different color ... whoopie freakin doo man. And that goes for black people too. I've seen people on Ricki Lake or Opra or whatever saying things like "white boy, whitey, you say dat cuz you be white, yea. You white people all du same. She be white. So she baaad, I bet he did dat stuff cuz he a white boy" allll that stuff just pisses me off to no end. It is possible for BLACKS to be RACIST to [*sic*]

> ya KNOW ... people who think that should be dragged out onto the street. Have their arms ripped off. Then burnt shut at the stumps, and have every person of the race that YOU hate come out and beat the crap out of you. You people are the scum of society and arent [*sic*] worth a damn piece of worm crap. You are all trash. And don't let me catch you making fun of someone just because they are a different color because I will come in and break your f*ck*ng legs with a plastic spoon. i dont [*sic*] care how long it takes! And that's both legs mind you (Harris 1999; emphasis in the original).

While condemning the very racism that is in evidence in other parts of his web site, Eric Harris focuses in on black racism rather than the racism of whites against blacks of which he is obviously guilty.

Perhaps the most grisly evidence of the boys' racism occurred in the library, when they confronted Isaiah Sholes, one of the very few black students attending Columbine High School. When Dylan saw him, he said, "Hey look, there's that little nigger," and took him from beneath the table where he was hiding. Eric walked over and shot Isaiah point blank, killing him instantly. Dylan stated, "Man, I didn't know black brains could fly that far." Isaiah Sholes was selected for death by Klebold and Harris because he was black.

Perhaps the greatest affinity with skinhead culture exists in Eric Harris's nihilism and penchant for violence. In Eric's writings, these two characteristics were merged. Eric Harris and Dylan Klebold, in the basement tapes, stated that they had achieved a higher level of consciousness than mere mortals; they were God-like and had taken upon themselves to determine who would live and who would die (Gibbs and Roche 1999). On his web site, under the heading "philosophy," he wrote the following:

> My belief is that if I say something, it goes. I am the law, if you don't like it, you die. If I don't like you or I don't like what you want me to do, you die. If I do something incorrect, oh fucking well, you die. Dead people cant[*sic*] do many things, like argue, whine, bitch, complain, narc, rat out, criticize, or even fucking talk. So that's the only way to solve arguments with all you fuckheads out there, I just kill! God I can't wait till I can kill you people. I'll just go to some downtown area in some big ass city and blow up and shoot everything I can. Feel no remorse, no sense of shame. Ich sage FICT DU! [N.B.: German for "I say fuck you."] I will rig up explosives all over a town and detonate each one of them after I mow down a whole fucking area full of you snotty ass rich motherfucking

> high strung godlike attitude having worthless pieces of shit whores [*sic*]. I don't care if I live or die in the shoot out, all I want to do is to kill and injure as many of you pricks as I can. … (Columbine Research Site 2003, 10,417).

Eric Harris and skinheads maintained a wide-ranging hatred against those who were not like themselves, and neither was apparently hesitant to act upon that hatred. The literature on skinheads is replete with examples of precipitate and vicious violence against others, such as beating, stomping, knifing, and shooting putative enemies, including former members who dropped out of the organization and thus became "turncoats," members of minority groups, and leftists (Finnigan 1998; Moore 1993; Ridgeway 1995).

Eric Harris appears to be the theorist of the shootings; he wrote extensively on his web site about his hatred and his experiences in school. Dylan did not express himself as openly as Eric, but apparently he was every bit as angry. According to a mutual friend,

> Dylan was just as upset [as Eric] about the way the school was. Easily just as upset. He was possibly more angry than Eric was; he just had no outlet for it. Eric let his anger out. Whether it was his website, whether it was threatening people, … whatever it was. Whereas Eric constantly let his anger out, Dylan didn't really have that. So I actually think he was angrier about the situation than Eric was because he had no outlet (Recorded December 3, 2003).

Prior to the Columbine attack, Eric and Dylan acted upon their anger by vandalizing homes of people whom they regarded as enemies or people who had slighted them in some way. Eric chronicled their exploits on his web site under the title "Mission Logs." The acts of vandalism described in the web site were validated by a Columbine resident whose house was vandalized in ways similar to Eric Harris's descriptions. As part of their personas as members of a paramilitary terrorist group, they adopted *noms de guerre*. Eric was known as "REB," short for "rebel." Dylan's alias was "VoDKa," which was the name of his favorite drink with his initials capitalized (Gibbs and Roche 1999).

Harris and Klebold formed an underground collective. It included the two boys plus an unknown person, possibly their friend, Chris Morris. Harris described the group:

> Ok people, I'm gonna let you in on the big secret of our clan. We ain't no god damn stupid ass quake clan! [NB: a reference to an organization

> called, "Godz like us," which is apparently a group of people who play the video game, "Quake," and maintain a web site.] We are more of a gang. We plan and execute missions. Anyone who pisses us off, we do a little deed to their house. Eggs, teepee [toilet paper] superglue, busy boxes, large amounts of fireworks, you name it and we will probably or already have done it. We have many enemies in our school, therefore we make many missions. It is sort of a nighttime tradition for us (Columbine Research Site 2003, JC-001-010421).

On his web site, he described Mission no. 6 in great detail. Below is an edited version:

> Awwww yeya. This mission was so fuckin fun man. ... Beforehand we watched as some lights in the target's house went on ... then off. Maybe the bastard heard something. But when the strip [of firecrackers] started, he turned his bedroom lights off. The strip lasted for about 30 seconds. ... It was very fucking long. Almost all of it went off. Loud and bright. Everything worked exactly how we wanted it to ... the first target's lights were on-again in the bedroom, but we think we got away undetected. While we were walking to the next target, we shot some stuff. Heh, VoDKa brought his sawed off BB gun and a few BB's too. So we loaded, pumped, and fired off a few shots at some houses and trees and stuff. We probably didn't do any damage to any houses, but we arent [*sic*] sure. The gun was not loud at all, which was very good. At the next target, we set up the Saturn missile battery and the rockets. These both have fuses about 2–3 feet long. I lit them as VoDKa and KiBBz were over hiding in the shadows.

In addition to these exploits, Harris and Klebold were suspected of other acts of vandalism, such as putting a hose through a mail slot, turning on the water, and flooding the house. They also squirted superglue into house locks, rendering them inoperable. They vandalized property, victimized other people, and wrote about it gleefully.

Although Eric Harris and Dylan Klebold shared the towering rage that motivates skinheads to violence, prior to the Columbine shootings, violence was expressed in the form of making and setting off bombs, theft, vandalism, death threats, and fantasies. Skinheads tend to express their violence directly in the form of beatings, knifings, and shootings, emphasizing direct physical violence. Skinheads have a reputation for stomping their antagonists. Eric and Dylan expressed their violence in more indirect and devious ways, doing everything they could to avoid being caught.

So how does a middle-class suburban teenager figure that he can carry out a paramilitary attack on his high school, bomb it, burn it to the ground, and kill as many of his fellow students as he possibly could? As Eric stated in his web site:

> We of the Trenchcoat Mafia still march around, military-style in our trenchcoats, [*sic*] especially in the school hallways, honing and developing our master plan. We will conquer the entire world once we get a few things straight and make our bombs! ... Our master plan is to kill at least 500 people at our high school, besiege the local neighborhood, seize the airport, and then crash a plane full of jocks and cheerleaders into the Pentagon.

Although Eric Harris mixes purposeful plans with fantasy, he was deadly serious about wanting to kill five hundred students. He carefully created a plan with Dylan Klebold that could have killed hundreds. His flight of imagination was prescient, prefiguring the attacks of 9/11. No high school student in American history had attempted to carry out such a deadly plot.

YOUTH AND HISTORY

The normative view is that youths live outside history. Their behavior is not perceived as being influenced by national events. The factors that impress upon their lives pretty much end at the boundaries of the local community, although city, county, and state budgets may influence the educational, recreational, and social services they receive. James Garbarino is probably the leading researcher in the field of youth violence and victimization. With Ellen deLara, he wrote the definitive book on the emotional costs of bullying (Garbarino and deLara 2002). Central to his theme is that school bullying is institutional violence for which the institution must, but seldom does, take responsibility. He applies a systems approach to the analysis of school violence; according to Garbarino, "In a system, all people in all parts of the system are interconnected" (11). Although he mentions national trends in this analysis, he focuses on the institutional level. Talcott Parsons (1951) has suggested that the same integrative forces operate at the societal level of social organization as at the institutional level and that institutional processes are influenced by what occurs at the societal level of organization. Therefore, school violence is part of a larger issue of societal violence.

It is mentally facile to view youth as being merely acted upon by history as opposed to learning from history and acting on those lessons. For example, the vanguard of most social movements tend to be the young (Gillis 1974), whether peasants revolting against the depredations of the landlord, soldiers fighting for land and a way of life, or workers striking against capital. The 1960s witnessed a unique occurrence. Instead of young people identifying with the commune, the ethnic group, the country, or a socioeconomic class, they struggled together *as youth* against the "establishment." Those old enough may remember the youth movement aphorism, "Don't trust anybody over 30" (Rubin 1970), and the so-called generation gap. Between 1964 and 1969, an international youth movement began in United States, spread to Europe, including Eastern Europe, and Japan. "Youth," no longer a convenient social category, was a cohesive social collectivity that was struggling for its own interests, politically and culturally. The 1960s witnessed a middle-class youth movement, variously called the "student movement," the "antiwar movement," "the counterculture," or the "hippie movement" (Foss and Larkin 1976).

The movements of the 1960s began on February 1, 1960, when four African American students from North Carolina Agricultural and Technical College, an all-black school, sat in a segregated lunch counter at F. W. Woolworth in Greensboro, North Carolina (Newhouse 1966). From that sit-in emerged the Civil Rights Movement, led by the more adult Southern Christian Leadership Conference (SCLC) and the younger, more radical, Student Nonviolent Coordinating Committee (SNCC, pronounced "Snick"). After the voter registration drive in the summer of 1964, the black members of SNCC told the white members that the problem of racism was located in the white community and white students' responsibility was to organize their own community against racism.

The middle-class youth movement began in 1964 in the San Francisco Bay area. Two phenomena were happening simultaneously: teenagers were dropping out of their suburban high schools to live with no visible means of support in the Haight-Ashbury district of San Francisco. These young cultural dissidents became known as "hippies" (Cavan 1972). Meanwhile, across the bay at the University of California, student activists, returning from their experiences of racism and oppression while trying to register black voters in Mississippi, set up recruiting tables along Telegraph Avenue. The university administration told them that they could not engage in political activities on campus; when they refused to move, they were arrested by campus police. Using the nonviolent techniques they learned in the South, student activists convened a sit-in at the administration building, effectively shutting the school down. This was called the "Berkeley Free Speech Movement" (FSM); student discontents dramatically expanded from the exclusion of political activism on campus to *en loco parentis* regulations, lack of access to professors, and the dehumanized way in which students were treated (Mehnert 1976). The middle-class youth movement was at its most radical when cultural and political wings merged in 1968, creating the freak radical, who smoked dope, lived in a commune, took LSD and other psychedelic drugs, engaged in promiscuous sex, and protested everything from local vagrancy regulations to the prosecution of the war in Vietnam (Foss 1972).

By early 1970, the middle-class youth movement was in visible decline. Between the mythical Woodstock festival in mid-August 1969, and the disaster at the Rolling Stones concert at Altamont in January of 1970, the movement began to come apart at the seams. The counterculture was shaken by the vicious murders of the pregnant Sharon Tate, Abigail Folger, and Voytek Frykowski at the home of Roman Polanski, Sharon Tate's husband, committed by members of the Charles Manson family. Although the murders occurred a few days prior to Woodstock, it was not until shortly after that people realized that the murders occurred within the counterculture. By the spring of 1970, the major organization of the political arm of the youth movement, Students for Democratic Society (SDS), had split into two bizarre organizations: Progressive Labor, a Marxist-Leninist sect that had plotted to take over SDS for several years (when it did, there was nothing left); and the Weather Underground, popularly known as the "Weathermen," who named themselves after Bob Dylan's "Subterranean Homesick Blues," a song that had the lyrics, "You don't have to be a weatherman to know which way the wind blows." The Weathermen was a terrorist underground organization that engaged in acts of sabotage, robberies, and, ultimately, murder (Sale 1974). Hard rock gave way to softer, folk rock. The Beatles disbanded, singing to their disillusioned audiences, "Let It Be." The function of the Beatles since the early sixties was to express the current movement interpretation of reality in its most artful forms. Their movie *Yellow Submarine* was literally an allegory of the youth movement of the sixties, although unlike the sixties, it had a happy ending.

Yet, as the middle-class youth movement was declining, the dissidence it had addressed was spreading to women, gays, young workers, the military, and to high schools. The sexism of the New Left of the middle-class youth movement led to a schism in the 1970s with the rise of the Women's Liberation Movement (WLM) (Evans 1979; Freeman 1975; Morgan 1970). The WLM became increasingly radical until about 1973, when the radical wing was superseded by corporate feminism, and the critique of sexism and patriarchy was overtaken by demands for equal access to positions in the labor force. Radical feminism, with its politicization of lesbianism, raised the issue of sexual orientation. In 1969, the

Gay Liberation Movement began with the Stonewall riots in Greenwich Village of New York City (Duberman 1993).

As important, but less chronicled, was the rising dissidence of working-class youth. Young workers, to the horror of management and the disdain of older workers, were demonstrating their alienation by excessive tardiness and absenteeism, willful production of shoddy merchandise, and participation in wildcat strikes (Aronowitz 1973). Emblematic of working-class dissidence were the strikes of the General Motors plants in Lordstown, Ohio, in 1972 (Weller 1973). Younger workers did not have the work ethic of the older generation; they listened to rock music and smoked marijuana. Although they did not take pride in the objects they produced, they did take pride in the way they could challenge management and disrupt the productive process.

Of course, another sector of the working-class was the "grunts" who were being sent to Vietnam, ostensibly to make the world safe for democracy. By 1973, the world's greatest fighting force had been paralyzed to the point of being incapable of prosecuting the war. This situation forced President Nixon to engage in a policy of Vietnamization, that is, getting the South Vietnamese to carry on a war that American soldiers were unwilling and unable to conduct. Indiscipline among the troops had risen to an all-time high (*United States Army MPs in Vietnam, 1962–1975*). Between 1969 and 1973, approximately 2000 commissioned officers were either murdered or killed under suspicious circumstances by members of the troops they were leading. In many cases, officers in fear for their lives refused to order troops into the field. At other times, the troops themselves refused direct orders to fight. This period witnessed a new phenomenon called "fragging." Disgruntled soldiers rolled live grenades into tents of targeted victims, usually officers they hated. Between 1969 and 1972, more than 1,000 fragging incidences were officially recorded. Between 1967 and 1973, AWOLs nearly doubled from 46.9 per 1,000 to 77 per 1,000; in 1968, the rate was 138.5 per 1,000. Desertions doubled as well; drug prosecutions skyrocketed.

In the early 1970s, in upper-middle-class high schools across the country, many principals were confronting student activists who were demanding greater student participation in the decision-making process of the schools. They wanted more course options, relaxation of dress codes, and so forth. In addition, upper-middle-class high school students were adopting the trappings of the counterculture: more kids were using marijuana and psychedelics; their motivation to achieve was declining and alienation was increasing (Larkin 1979). High school students were increasingly viewing education as absurd and meaningless. They perceived themselves as on an assembly line that was leading them to be just like their parents, which, to many, was anathema.

The points to be made are thus: The dissidence of one group can stimulate dissidence of other, strategically located groups, and young people, more than older people, are vulnerable to such social processes. It is my belief that Eric Harris, a bright, sensitive, psychologically unstable eighteen-year-old, was swimming in the tide of history. His idea to destroy his own school and kill fellow students was a logical, if irrational, outcome of the social history of the 1990s.

THE REVOLT OF THE ANGRY WHITE MALE, 1992–1996

The revolt of the angry white male began with the standoff between federal marshals and right wing anti-Semite Randy Weaver and his family at Ruby Ridge, Idaho. It culminated with the bombing of the Murrah Federal Building in Oklahoma City in 1996. The movement involved a constituency that consisted primarily of marginalized males from working-class and lower middle-class backgrounds, and small farm families who had either been dispossessed or had been threatened with dispossession of their farms.

Although ostensibly about the defense of the Second Amendment to the Constitution, the revolt of the angry white male embraced white supremacy, anti-Semitism, fundamentalist Christianity, patriarchy, and hostility to the Federal government. The government was perceived as attempting to take away rights to gun ownership, promoting the interests of minorities and feminists, and secularizing public life (Dyer 1998; Niewart 1999; Stern 1997). The major events of the movement, besides the shootout at Ruby Ridge, included the destruction of the Branch Davidian compound, the rise of unorganized militias, the bombing of the Murrah Building in Oklahoma City, the derailing of an Amtrak train in the Arizona desert, and, finally, the holdout of the Montana Freemen, which ended in June 1996.

The movement was organized in the form of a funnel. At the wide end of the funnel were such conservative organizations as the Republican Party, the National Rifle Association, and various evangelical Christian churches. As the funnel narrowed, organizations existed that claimed they were legitimate and law-abiding, but either had a clandestine element or functioned, at least in part, as a conduit to underground terrorist organizations. One such organization was the Gun Owners of America, a Second Amendment defense organization to the right of the National Rifle Association (NRA). Perhaps most representative of such organizations were the private militias, which maintained a front of a legitimate organization of law-abiding members exercising their Second Amendment rights, but having a darker, hidden face of sponsoring illegal activities. Several militias, such as the Arizona Militia and the Washington State Militia, were successfully infiltrated, and members were prosecuted for a variety of terror-related activities, such as stockpiling illegal weapons, possession of bombs, and conspiracy to commit murder (Dyer 1998; Niewart 1999). Finally, at the narrow end of the funnel existed right-wing hate groups such as the Church of Jesus Christ Christian, Aryan Nations, the American Nazi Party, Posse Comitatus, the National Alliance (a neo-Nazi group), the Order, the Freemen, and the Phineas Priests, all of which engaged in illegal activities such as bank robberies, intimidation, fraud, theft, and murder.

Dissidence was expressed in right-wing ideology: its major fomenters were males who were economically and socially marginal. They advocated for an America that was white and Christian, who they thought had superior rights to immigrant populations, minorities, and Jews. They conceived of the American Northwest as territory that should be ceded to white Christians as a homeland, free from federal government interference. They were involved in cultural wars against urban hipness, multiculturalism, feminism, and homosexuality. They advocated for a muscular Christianity based upon men as the undisputed authority in the household, as promulgated by such organizations as the Promise Keepers.

Although there is no direct link between Harris and Klebold and the movement of the angry white male, there is a cultural affinity between them. As the angry white males were marginalized in the larger American society, Klebold and Harris were marginalized in their own school and community. Their hostility and anger at their humiliation and degradation by their peers was expressed in right-wing ideology. In Eric Harris's mind, student athletes were included with Jews, African Americans, immigrants, and people with dark skin. Angry white males hated the federal government and blamed it for their degradation and marginalization; Harris and Klebold hated their school for similar reasons. Finally, and most important, the movement of the angry white male took the form of paramilitary organizations.

ANGRY WHITE TEENAGERS

For adolescents, the most important governmental influence in their lives is the schools they attend. The question that is central to this chapter is, How do two adolescent boys not only come up with the idea for a paramilitary attack on their high school but also maintain interest, plot a strategy, field-test their weaponry, and carry out the attack with a precision not usually associated with teenagers?

Although numerous school shootings led up to the Columbine massacre, nobody had ever attempted to blow up a school. Up to that time, bombing one's high school was unthinkable.

Ideas do not come from nowhere. It is my opinion that Harris and Klebold were inspired, whether they knew it or not, by the actions of Timothy McVeigh, Terry Nichols, and their unindicted helpers (Dyer 1998). According to testimony by a reporter who corresponded with Dylan Klebold in a chat room, when the reporter identified himself as someone who had investigated the bombing in Oklahoma City, Klebold evinced a great deal of interest, asking questions especially about how the media responded to the event and how the bombing affected people (Columbine Research Site 2003). According to a friend of Klebold and Harris, when the Murrah Building was bombed in 1996, they were shocked because it was bombed by a white American; because of the media coverage, they probably thought that it was by Middle Eastern terrorists. They discussed the bombing in their philosophy class. Although they were repelled by the bombing, they thought that it was not completely unjustified. They were of the opinion that the bombing should make Americans think about the nature of their society, but they came to the conclusion that it did not.

Harris and Klebold constituted themselves as a self-defined paramilitary cell of two. They plotted in secrecy, keeping their plans hidden from their families and friends. The boys had a hidden life as members of their own two-man underground terrorist organization. They attempted to destroy their school within a month of their own graduations. Dylan attended the senior prom, and both boys attended the party after the prom with full knowledge that the following Tuesday they were going to bomb their school and kill their fellow students. Harris and Klebold documented their activities, explained their reasons for the assault, and bid farewell to their families in the basement tapes.

Earlier in this chapter, Eric Harris was compared to skinheads, which is a youth subculture tied in with right wing neo-Nazi organizations. Whereas skinheads are attempting to resurrect white-skin privilege in the face of lives that have no futures, Eric Harris was ostensibly living a life of white-skin privilege. However, that materially privileged life was a living hell because he was taunted, harassed, and humiliated on a daily basis by peers of his own race. So why did Eric Harris feel it necessary to hate Jews and people of color? He lived in a white suburb in which Jews and minorities were not only rare but had nothing to do with his degradation. To the best of anybody's knowledge, neither the Klebold nor the Harris family espoused intolerance or were racist. In Columbine the only time one might have to confront issues of race or ethnicity would be on TV, as evidenced by Harris's characterizations of blacks from midday exploitation shows such as Jerry Springer and Sally Jessy Raphael, although he attributes them to Oprah and Ricki Lake-type talk shows. In this investigator's experience visiting the school, eating in restaurants, visiting libraries, driving through neighborhoods, and shopping, the presence of a black or a Chicano was extremely rare; so much so that minorities stood out.

Dylan Klebold lived in Columbine virtually all his life. Eric Harris, an Air Force brat, lived there for about five years. His previous residence was in Plattsburg, New York, near the Canadian border and about as far as you can get from an urban ghetto in that state. African Americans that he would meet as peers on Air Force bases would certainly not be the "malt-liquor-drinking, rhyme-busting, ass-capping Negroes" he wrote about on his web site. Yet, Isaiah Sholes was singled out, degraded, and killed because he was an African American.

The murder of Isaiah Sholes suggests that the boys' racism was not merely rhetorical. Apparently neither was their anti-Semitism. Dylan Klebold, while not being a member of the Jewish community, would certainly have been put into the death camps by Hitler on the basis of his Jewish ancestry. In the basement tapes, Klebold said, "My parents are going to fucking Passover" (Jefferson County Sheriff's Office 1999, 10,374), apparently joining in with Eric Harris's anti-Semitism.

So where do two suburban-raised boys develop racism and anti-Semitism, even though one of them is technically Jewish? Of course, racism and anti-Semitism are staples of right-wing extremist groups. In middle-class white communities such as Columbine, racism and anti-Semitism are not expressed openly or virulently, but rather they are embedded in the subtexts of discourse. However, Colorado is a conservative state and has more than its share of right-wing activists and organizations that were part of the funnel into the movement of the angry white males. The boys were enamored of paramilitarism and apparently adopted the perspective of right-wing paramilitary groups. But how? We know that they attended gun shows, that Eric read *Guns & Ammo* magazine, that they downloaded the *Anarchist's Cookbook*, once a staple of the left but apparently now available from numerous web sites of right wing organizations, and that they were aware of the impact of the Oklahoma City bombings on America.

In the early to mid-1990s, a great deal of media attention was focused on the newly energized extreme right. To what extent Harris and Klebold read or saw on TV about these organizations and their ideologies is unknown. However, an alternative mode may have influenced them.

On his website, Harris lauded the video game Doom and claimed that he played it whenever he could. Doom is a combat game in which the player is a Marine on Mars whose buddies have been killed by strange life forms and whose mission is to rid the planet of these evil life forms by picking up weaponry and killing them as he progresses through labyrinths inhabited by humanoid beings. The art form is Gothic, reminiscent of comic book superheroes with an Aryan cast; the evil monsters are portrayed as sub-humans, while the heroes wear combat fatigues. Apparently Harris and Klebold took the subtext of Doom seriously, viewing themselves as superior beings whose mission it was to destroy beings less worthy than themselves.

Games such as Doom and Quake have no explicit politics. They are first-person attack games, that is, the player looking at the screen sees what is in front of him. A creature can jump out at any time and attack him. The viewer uses his weaponry to kill off the attackers and achieve his goal, which is to defeat the other side, whatever that is, and win the game. There is, however, an implicit political message. Obviously, the world out there is dangerous; if one is to survive, he must accumulate firepower. The problems confronting the player are monsters standing in the way of the achievement of the goals of the game. They are to be dispensed with as quickly and efficiently as possible with the weaponry one has collected. Because the characters of the game are visual images and take the form of subhuman monsters, there is an implicit message that the player is a superior being to those that he is killing.

Eric Harris was quite skilled at playing the video games. The games themselves can be reprogrammed by players. Harris apparently reconfigured Doom so that when victims were killed, they cried out, "Lord, why is this happening to me" (Hubbard 1999), an apparent allusion to evangelical Christians, toward whom both Klebold and Harris evinced a great deal of animus. This practice suggests that Eric used the game as a form of surrogate killing. He also used it to desensitize himself to the pain of others. According to Brooks Brown, a close friend of Dylan Klebold and an off-again, on-again friend of Eric, Eric reprogrammed Doom to be even more violent than originally conceived (Brown and Merritt 2002). He developed new levels to the game in which the protagonist was overwhelmed by the enemy. Brown stated that Doom players criticized it because there was no way the protagonist could deal with so many enemies.

Video games such as Doom and Quake glorify combat and paramilitary action. Although one can take many personas in Doom, the main protagonist is a United States Marine. Eric Harris wanted to enlist in the Marines but was rejected because he was taking Luvox for a psychiatric disorder. However, because the Marine is stranded on Mars, he is not subject to military discipline. Therefore, he is kind of a Rambo-like character who has military training but does not have to adhere to military discipline. It is fairly clear that in Harris's case, the characters in the video games were stand-ins for people he wanted to kill in real life.

Paramilitary culture is based upon revenge for past wrongs. Central to the mythology of paramilitary culture is the loss of the war in Vietnam (Gibson 1994). The iconic figure is John Rambo, the character brought to life by Sylvester Stallone. The Rambo movies were very popular in the mid-to-late 1980s; the original, "First Blood," was followed by two sequels. The character of Rambo was modeled after Bo Gritz, a former colonel in the Green Berets who ran for the presidency in 1992 on the Populist Party ticket, which promulgated a racist and anti-Semitic campaign, and who was a leading light of the movement of the angry white male in the mid-1990s (Stern 1997).

The mythos of paramilitary culture is that the primordial male role is that of warrior, which must be distinguished from that of a soldier. Warriors, unlike soldiers, are not subject to control by military bureaucracy. They either operate alone or in small teams or squads outside the command structure. They view themselves as autonomous beings beyond the control of conventional society. Klebold and Harris viewed themselves in precisely the same way. Ostensibly they were normal high school students, although they associated themselves with a small group of students who were nonconformists. Yet they led a secret life in which they made and exploded bombs, collected weaponry, and planned an attack on their school. They engaged in clandestine attacks on neighbor houses and were caught by the Jefferson County Sheriff's Department stealing equipment from a truck. They even thought of themselves as morally and intellectually superior to everyone else.

Second, paramilitaries are hyper-masculine (Gibson 1994). In high school, for males to be publicly humiliated by other male students who have greater physical prowess is a way by which the dominant males strip away the masculinity of those they humiliate. It is a matter of record that Harris and Klebold were publicly taunted with epithets questioning that masculinity; they were called "pussies," "queers," and "fags." Their tormentors consistently questioned their masculinity. The attack on Columbine was a way of reasserting their masculinity, taking power into their own hands, and making decisions over who lives and who dies. Certainly the long hours playing Doom and Quake allowed Harris and Klebold fantasy outlets in which their masculine prowess was unchallenged.

Third, paramilitary culture has as its fundamental ethic, "death before dishonor" (Gibson 1994). Paramilitary culture subsumes a survivalist strain that contains a paranoid notion of the righteous individual or team against a polluted and compromised world. Central to the paramilitary ethic is the concept of dying in a blaze of glory. Fourth, paramilitary culture is xenophobic, racist, and anti-Semitic; paramilitaries often view themselves as defending white culture against the pollution of alien cultures (Ridgeway 1995). Paramilitaries have a special affinity for semiautomatic and automatic weaponry, such as Tech-9s, Uzis, M16s, and AK-47s and heavy-duty handguns such as Smith and Wesson .44 magnum, Colt .45, and .357 magnum (Gibson 1994). Harris and Klebold were armed with a Springfield 9 mm carbine rifle, a Tech-9 semiautomatic pistol, two sawed-off shotguns—one double-barreled and the other a single-barreled pump gun that fired five rounds before having to be reloaded—several knives, CO_2 cartridges, and pipe bombs.

Harris and Klebold were particularly enamored of paramilitary culture, especially the notion of dying in a blaze of glory and taking as many persons with them as possible. The Trenchcoat Mafia website is replete with allusions to paramilitary culture. The security videotapes of the cafeteria of Columbine High School clearly show Harris and Klebold. Harris was wearing combat boots and pants with suspenders. Although not military fatigues, he was dressed in paramilitary style. Klebold was dressed in black. Both were carrying weapons. The assault on Columbine High School clearly aped a paramilitary mission. The boys claimed that they had been planning the attack for over a year. They developed a plan of execution and carried it out in a coordinated effort. They had the foresight to plant their large bombs in the cafeteria prior to the armed attack. They even successfully set off a bomb a few minutes before the attack in a park about two miles away from the school to divert police attention. It was simply luck that the bombs in the cafeteria did not explode, which would have increased the death toll into the hundreds.

RAMBO GOES TO SCHOOL

Where do two boys get the idea and the wherewithal to carry out a paramilitary assault on their high school? The evidence suggests that even those who purchased guns for them or sold them weapons were unaware of their purposes. Their closest friends did not know what they were plotting. Siblings and parents were totally in the dark. They were secretive, and they were dedicated to carrying out their deadly plot within days of their own graduation. Eric Harris, in a video he made of himself just prior to the shootings, stated that it was hard to believe that he would be dead in 2 1/2 weeks.

Harris and Klebold armed themselves to the teeth, dressed like paramilitaries, plotted their action, and when the plot went awry, went on the deadly shooting spree, killing twelve peers and a teacher and then committed suicide. From their writings, such as school papers that were preserved by the Jefferson County Sheriff's Department, and from their statements recorded in the basement tapes, it is clear that Eric Harris viewed himself as a righteous paramilitary fighter. Dylan Klebold did not have as coherent a political ideology as did Eric. Dylan was simply angry and wanted to exact revenge.

The evidence suggests that Eric Harris was the moving force behind the shootings; however, Dylan Klebold was more than a willing accomplice. He was with Eric every step of the way. He had a thirst for blood and revenge. However, unlike Eric, his politics were inchoate and unformed. In addition to rock lyrics, Eric quoted Shakespeare and Nietzsche in his writing. He actually theorized about what he was doing, a sophisticated intellectual process for a teenager. As far as I can tell, the sources for Eric's justification of his actions come from his own military background, television, video games, and informal and casual contacts with the far right, primarily at gun shows.

When Eric made lists, it was not of his favorite television shows, movies, or books, but of people he would like to kill. Therefore, ascertaining the sources of his ideological position is very difficult. As noted above, he apparently spent his time playing and programming video games, especially Doom and Quake. He apparently did not read very much and was not acquainted with the literature of the extreme right, such as *The Turner Diaries* or *The Protocols of the Elders of Zion*. Despite that, he managed to cobble together an implicit ideology that coincided with skinhead neo-Nazism and paramilitary sensibilities. Both he and Klebold had come to the conclusion that they had achieved a higher level of consciousness than average human beings and that made them supermen, which accorded them the right to determine life and death.

Although the data are sketchy, they lead to the conclusion that Klebold and Harris were in tune with the times and the cultural milieu of the West. Neither boy was afraid of being overtly racist. Although it has been said that they hated everybody equally (Gibbs and Roche 1999), that simply is not true. They did not hate adults, but they hated their peers for the humiliations they heaped upon them. They hated minorities; however, they were not overtly sexist. Eric Harris, in his hate list, described people who would be on a lot of people's pet peeve list: people who walk slowly in malls, O.J. Simpson, people who cut classes, liars, R-rated movies, people who try to predict the weather, country music, people who believe that progress is real, cigarette smokers, and so forth.

Somehow, Klebold and Harris tapped into some of the central tenets of paramilitary culture: Don't get mad, get even; if you're going to die, do it in a blaze of glory; defend yourself with a gun—and the more guns you have the better off you will be; don't let the enemy take you alive; a man is not a man without a weapon. The basement tapes open with Eric Harris sitting in a chair with a bottle of Jack Daniels and his sawed-off shotgun across his lap. The rifle is named "Arlene" after a character in the Doom video game. During the assault, they dressed the part: cargo pants filled with ammunition, T-shirts with messages ("Wrath," for Klebold; "Natural Selection," for Harris), and combat boots. The only deviation was the use of trench coats to hide their weaponry. The trench coats were taken off during the assault.

The boys borrowed from contemporary American cultural trends: They were angry at their harassment and rejection by their peers in the same way that marginalized white males were angry at what they perceived as their degradation by a hostile government that promoted the interests of minorities and women. In each case, masculinity was threatened: in the case of the angry white male, masculinity was threatened by downward mobility or relative deprivation by the putative increase in the social mobility of women and minorities. In the case of Harris and Klebold, their masculinity was threatened by the alpha males at Columbine High School who routinely and publicly humiliated them.

To be a male in America is to be able to deal with violence, especially against one's person. Dominant males, especially in high school, where sexual competition is extremely high, will seek to establish their status by humiliating their lower status peers and render them socially impotent. For Harris and Klebold, guns were not merely sexual symbols but instruments by which they reasserted their masculinity by visiting violence on their peers. Eric Harris compiled a hit list that consisted primarily of people who had harassed him and girls who had refused to go out with him. The boys, after repeatedly being harassed, humiliated, and degraded by jocks who pushed them in the halls, threw objects at them, and publicly questioned their sexuality, and by evangelicals who told them that if they did not take Christ into their hearts, they would burn in hell for eternity, asserted their masculinity, assumed their own moral superiority, and attempted to destroy their school and kill as many of their peers as possible. During their rampage, they enjoyed themselves immensely. They were thrilled with the power they exerted. They determined who lived and who died. In the last forty-five minutes of their lives, they exercised control over others. They were the ones who were meting out humiliation, making others pay with their lives, killing at will. They sacrificed their lives to avenge themselves and send a message to America that they and others like them had had enough.

8

DEAD CELEBRITIES

DYLAN KLEBOLD AND ERIC HARRIS engaged in their rampage in order to gain notoriety. Gibbs and Roche (1999) noted:

> Why, if their motive was rage at the athletes who taunted them, didn't they take their guns and bombs to the locker room? Because retaliation against specific people was not the point. Because this may have been about celebrity as much as cruelty. "They wanted to be famous," concludes FBI agent Mark Holstlaw. "And they are. They're infamous." It used to be said that living well is the best revenge; for these two, it was to kill and die in spectacular fashion (1).

Police investigators were in consensus with the FBI about the celebrity motive. Kate Battan, the lead investigator for the Jefferson County Sheriff's Department, fully concurred with the conclusion of the FBI. In the videotapes that Harris and Klebold made in the weeks leading up to the shootings, they revealed that they understood that the acts they were about to commit would simultaneously avenge their humiliations and elevate them to celebrity status. According to Gibbs and Roche (1999), two of the few members of the media who viewed the videotapes:

> Because they were steeped in violence and drained of mercy, they could accomplish everything at once: payback to those who hurt them, and glory, the creation of a cult, for all those who have suffered and been cast out. They wanted movies made of their story, which they had carefully laced with "a lot of foreshadowing and dramatic irony," as Harris put it. There was that poem he wrote, imagining himself as a bullet. "Directors will be fighting over this story," Klebold said–and the boys chewed over which could be trusted with the script: Steven Spielberg or Quentin Tarantino. "You have two individuals who wanted to immortalize themselves," says Holstlaw. "They wanted to be martyrs and to document everything they were doing (2).

This raises the question of why two teenage boys would choose to engage in mass murder in order to become celebrities even though they knew ahead of time that they would not be alive to enjoy it. What is it in American culture that would lead two adolescents to believe that by creating an atrocity, they would become cultural heroes to an underclass of young people and anathema to their social superiors? It also raises the question, To what extent were they successful?

In Chapter 3, I described the political and cultural conservatism of Southern Jefferson County and delineated the role of the evangelical community in defining the meaning of the Columbine shootings. Columbine became a battleground in the American culture wars as the religious and cultural right defined the massacre as the outcome of a liberal, crime-tolerating, secular, anti-Christian society that fails to teach children right from wrong, prevents children from praying in school, and refuses to display the Ten Commandments in public schools (Epperhart 2002; Porter 1999; Scott and Rabey 2001; Zoba 2000). Neither the crime nor the public reaction to it can be understood without an explication of the recent cultural history of the country.

Therefore, much of the rest of this chapter will be devoted to outlining the emergence of postmodern culture from the cultural revolution of the 1960s, which set into motion a concerted reaction against those changes that split the polity several ways. Some people on the left viewed the cultural revolution of the 1960s as a new chapter in the developing freedom of humanity and fought to extend newly gained rights and privileges;[1] others, especially those in the corporate sector, initially horrified by the changes, especially such radical changes as gender equality, communal living, sexual openness, the use of consciousness-expanding drugs, and acceptance of alternative cultures, realized that countercultural artifacts and sensibilities could be packaged and sold to middle-class consumers, be used in advertising copy as motivators, or constitute new forms of entertainment. Still others who were perhaps indifferent to the social moments of the 1960s found their lives changed despite their indifference because the world around them had changed (Faludi 1999). Finally, there were the resistors. Even though there was no returning to the *status quo ante*, they have done everything they can to return America to the halcyon days of the 1950s where men were men, women stayed home taking care of domestic chores, homosexuals were in the closet, teenage sex was deviant, the Cold War provided social discipline and an excuse to persecute Communists, the capitalist economy would lift all boats, and Americans could live in hypocrisy without others questioning them.

Southern Jefferson County is home to a significant fraction of the resistors. As noted in Chapter 2, if it were not for the high-tech trappings of the area and, of course, the newness of the community, Columbine is culturally pre-1964. It has a lower divorce rate, more stay-at-home moms, and is politically very conservative, with the main community influences being local religious institutions. The most visible indication it was the 1990s was the presence of goth students in the high school. Such students were reviled and were regarded as a blot on the purity and reputation of the school and community.

One consequence of the social movements of the 1960s was to reinvigorate the hard right, especially over cultural issues. The political right, always having more power than their numbers, fought the expansion of new cultural sensibilities through political activism. Although they have not made many inroads into the new cultural sensibilities, they have created an impressive political machine that wields an incredible amount of power. The emergence of the new right has changed the face of American politics. Ironically, the cultural changes initiated by the 1960s and the struggle against them created a climate where two boys from Colorado who were mercilessly bullied by members of the football and wrestling teams came to the conclusion that, in one fell swoop, they could wreak revenge on the bullies and all those who tacitly accepted that bullying, spectacularly blow up their school, and enter the pantheon of celebrityhood.

POSTMODERN CULTURE AND THE CULT OF CELEBRITY

The movements of the 1960s, in one way or another, all undermined the emotional constraints of bourgeois culture. The Great Depression era was a distant memory of the older generation. The baby boom generation lived in a time of an expanding economy and rising material wealth for the vast majority. The subjectivism of the 1960s ("If it feels good, do it.") that used feeling upon which to base decisions tended to subvert rational calculation that was the hallmark of bourgeois culture.

In the early part of the twentieth century, marketing visionaries understood that bourgeois culture with its emphasis on thrift, sobriety, rationality, impulse repression, the intrinsic value of work, and frugality constituted a brake on consumption and had negative consequences for expanding the economy. The demand for higher wages and shorter hours, while vehemently opposed by industrial corporations, was viewed by capitalist visionaries as a potential boon because it would free workers to spend more money as consumers and provide more time to buy the commodities they fabricated. Ewen (1976) noted that, "Shorter hours and higher wages were seen as a first step in a broader offensive against notions of thrift and an attempt to habituate a national population to the exigencies of mass production" (29).

In other words, if the capitalist economy was to expand, workers had to have sufficient income and time to purchase the products they made on the job. After all, capitalism suffers from periodic crises of overproduction, the most dramatic of which was the "The Great Depression" following the stock market crash of 1929, which lasted for more than a decade. The post-World War II period witnessed a dramatic increase in consumer culture. The "American way of life" was exemplified by an expanding economy, increasing leisure time, and upward mobility. Commentators of the time, David Riesman (1961) and C. Wright Mills (1951), both noted the emergence of "idols of leisure" over "idols of work." Baseball players and movie stars replaced industrial magnates and politicians as the subjects of magazine biographies. Even when the latter were featured, the focus was on their tastes in consumption.

The cultural contradiction of capitalism between the values of production and consumption was brought to its head in the 1960s and was resolved, inevitably, in favor of consumption (Bell 1976). With the constraints of bourgeois culture buried, the marketing industry danced on its grave. Sexual hedonism of the 1960s and early 1970s was yoked to volatile consumption. Although pretty women and mesomorphic men had always been used to sell commodities, sex itself was now being used to sell products, including products such as cigarettes and alcohol, which actually impair sexuality. Sexual imagery was so rampant in advertising that Wilson Bryan Key (1973; 1976) advanced the notion that sexual imagery was being implanted in advertisements subliminally.

The cultural revolution of the 1960s, divested of its social conflict, was divided into its constituent parts—sex, hipness, human potential, mysticism, Nature and the organic produce thereof, drugs, music—and turned into competitive struggles or new product fads. Meanwhile, the traditional competitive struggle for occupations raged more fiercely because of the declining availability of good jobs that compensated well. The price of labor declined throughout the labor force and the means of obtaining good jobs through higher education became increasingly expensive.

The reimposition of the competitive struggle in the post-1960s era led to intensified interpersonal competition. Within the land of plenty, success has been redefined such that material wealth is necessary but not sufficient. The subjectivism that defined movement mentality in opposition to bureaucratic rationalism was transformed into a commodity that was sold to upper-middle-class consumers in the human potential psychology movement, the spiritual supermarket, and therapy cults such as Werner Erhard's est, Dianetics (Scientology), and any number of localized organizations, such as Jim Kweskin's Family in Boston, the Sullivanians on the Upper West Side of New York City, Victor Barranco's Institute of Human Abilities in California, and Jim Jones's People's Temple in the San Francisco Bay Area (Felton 1972).

In the counterculture of the 1960s, beauty extended from Twiggy on one extreme to Mama Cass on the other. Today, somatic norm images have been redrawn to exclude most of the population for the purposes of selling diets, gym memberships and equipment, and new clothing lines. The trend has also been extended from an emphasis exclusively on women to include both genders. Sophisticated urban hipness is the mode of the day. Increasingly, brand-name images have emerged as talismans of appropriate buying habits. Today, it is absolutely necessary for adolescents to be dressed in clothes that have appropriate name brands: North Face, Nike (Just do it!), Reebok, Adidas, Polo, and Abercrombie and Fitch (these are subject to rapid change). Only in postmodern society would young people kill to steal a piece of clothing for its brand name.

The realienation of the liberated sensibilities of the 1960s gave rise to postmodern culture, which emphasizes multiculturalism, feminism, tolerance of cultural differences, subjectivist notions of reality, and contingent identity. Postmodern culture is urbane, hip, permissive, and sophisticated. Not surprisingly, postmodern culture has generated a backlash among large segments of the American population who are defined in postmodern culture as rural, unhip, and unsophisticated, or worse, as losers. From the American hinterlands has emerged a militant Christian fundamentalism, reassertion of patriarchal norms, cultural monism, and advocacy of puritanical sexual behaviors (Dyer 1998; Stern 1997). Advocates of these positions view postmodern culture as the playground of the devil.

Yet, as they decry postmodern culture, they are highly influenced by it. The Christian right, an amalgam of fundamentalist, evangelical, and traditionally conservative churches such as Mormons and Baptists, has built a parallel society replete with its own publishers, television networks, televangelists, megachurches, consumer products, and rock stars (Talbot 2000). The rise of a Christian counterculture is itself a postmodern phenomenon and is part of the multiculturalism of American society. Many deep Christians, evangelicals, and fundamentalists have taken the subjectivism of the 1960 counterculture one step further to irrationalism. They believe that they have the Truth, the whole Truth, and nothing but the Truth, which is contained in a literal reading of the Bible, even though there is no such thing as a literal interpretation of anything, because we all choose what to emphasize and what to ignore. They believe that all knowledge is revealed by God in the Bible, especially in the New Testament. They are anti-science and have no use for facts when they conflict with ideology. Faith trumps knowledge.

The subjectivism of the 1960s, although subversive of rational calculation, was not necessarily antirational. In many ways, it took a rationality to a new level as suggested by William Irwin Thompson (1971). Value free rationalism was called into question over the issue of ends. Functional rationalism, the use of rational means, could be devoted completely to irrational ends. These irrational endeavors included the Nazi use of technology and bureaucratic organization to exterminate millions of people with great efficiency and the American military's use of agent orange to wipe out an entire ecosystem in the Mekong Delta so that the Vietcong had no place to hide. Subjectivism was used by dissidents to raise questions about ends and value choices. The antirationalism of the Christian right is not subversive of conventional reality, but uncompromisingly stands in opposition to it; abortion is murder, a priori.

Postmodern culture is also characterized by the penetration of capitalist social relations into the production of cultural artifacts. Although such industries as motion pictures, publishing, and tourism predated postmodernism, not until the early 1970s was the majority of American workers employed in the creation, recording, and transmission of information. Moreover, as Gamson (1994) has noted, cultural reproduction has been penetrated by capitalist social relations. What was once left to institutions outside the marketplace, such as communities, subcultures, and educational and religious institutions, has been taken over by corporate-dominated media organizations directed at making a profit.[2]

One of the hallmarks of contemporary postmodern culture is the rise of an intensely competitive struggle within the cultural realm that can be distinguished from economic and political competition. Sitting at the top of this competitive struggle is the celebrity. Celebrity status is a modern phenomenon to be distinguished from fame in the following ways (Gamson 1994; Giles 2000; Marshall 1998): It is more ephemeral and fleeting, with some personages rising from nobodies to celebrities and falling to has-been status in a matter of months; it has little to do with character or with extraordinary feats, skills, or talents; and it is merely the phenomenon of being known (Boorstein 1962).

One of the major cultural emphases of postmodernism is the cult of celebrity. Modern society obviously had its sports figures, movie stars, and radio and TV celebrities, but they were not as important as celebrity in postmodern culture. Celebrities are the royalty of the postmodern era. They are the ones people fawn over, read about, and want to touch for magical reasons (Marshall 1998). They are not allowed private lives because the eyes of the media are always upon them. They are the staple of talk shows, TV insider-reports, and gossip columns. As a marketing device, their names are associated with numerous products, either through endorsements or the establishment of their own product lines, such as Jacklyn Smith's K-Mart clothing line, Michael Jordan's Air-Jordan Nike shoe line, and Britney Spears's Elizabeth Arden cosmetics line. Super-celebrities must be protected from the public; their houses must have sophisticated security systems, and they must appear in public with bodyguards (Gamson 1994). They are afforded special privileges in society, from exemptions from obeying laws to access to unearned wealth.

Faludi (1999), referring to postmodernism as "ornamental culture," described it as "constructed around celebrity and image, glamour and entertainment, marketing and consumerism, it is a ceremonial gateway to nowhere. Its essence is not just the selling act but the act of selling the self..."(35). In contemporary postmodern culture, the new class system can be categorized as celebrities, has-beens, and nobodies. The culture of the modern high school reflects that same sort of stratification in the microcosm. The jocks, the soches, and the school celebrities are the privileged minority. Within the culture of the school and the peer group, everybody else is a nobody. Those who have been jettisoned from the in-group are the adolescent equivalent of has-beens.

YOUTH IN A COLD NEW WORLD

For young people, the 1980s were dismal. In my study of suburban youth in the mid-1970s, I characterized them as struggling to get by in a world that ostensibly made little sense to them; they had to convince themselves that going to school and getting a degree would give meaning to their lives. Most students thought that the worst thing that could happen to them would be to live lives like their parents. Yet all indicators suggested that this was exactly what was going to happen to them (Larkin 1979). If one looks at the cultural products of adolescent subcultures in the 1980s and 1990s, one would have to conclude that the generation of the 1970s was relatively well-off. If adolescents of the 1970s were confused and uncertain about their futures, those of the 1980s and 1990s were frightened and dispirited (Hersch 1998). This was especially true for students who were outcasts (Wooden and Blazak 2001).

In 1976, a group of kids from Forest Hills, Queens—Joey, Johnny, Dee Dee, and Tommy Ramone—formed a rock band. The Ramones hung around and played at CBGBs (Country Bluegrass Blues), a rock-and-roll club in a rundown section on the lower east side of New York City. It was there that they invented punk rock. Other notable punk bands that came out of this club were Richard Hell and the Voidoids and Blondie (Larkin 1988). Although rock- and-roll always had a critical edge, punk quite literally sharpened that edge, glorifying violence and self-destructive behaviors including suicide, sex without love (especially S&M), and alienation. In addition, they flirted with extreme politics of the left (anarchy) and the right (Nazism).

The major premise of punk rock was a response to the boredom, competitiveness, and the alienation of contemporary suburban living (Larkin 1988). Rock-and-roll was supposed to be for everyone. To be an authentic punk band, the members had to endorse the punk ethos of "do it yourself," or DIY. The ethic of DIY was that all you needed to do was buy or steal a guitar and learn three chords and you could be a punk rock musician. Many punk rock bands were self-consciously technically bad, emphasizing the accessibility of punk rock to anybody who wanted to play.

Punk rock also reduced the disparity between the band and the audience. It was not unusual for audience members to spit on the band or throw bottles at them, which in turn would be thrown back. The audience could also fight with band members and destroy their instruments. Punk rockers invented stage diving, crowd surfing, pogo dancing, and slam dancing, which were the forerunners to the less violent mosh pit. Stage divers would jump off the stage, trusting that the dancers would catch them before they hit the ground. Crowd surfing occurred when members of the band or fans floated through the mosh pit as they were passed around over the heads of dancers. Pogo dancing was literally jumping up and down as if one was on a pogo stick. Slam dancing was similar to pogo dancing, except that dancers pushed each other, slammed others into the ground or up against walls, or otherwise engaged in violence to the beat of the band.

Strangely, rather than spreading to the hinterlands of America, punk rock took root in Britain, where in addition to the critique of everyday life found in American punk rock, it adopted an overt political tone, attacking Margret Thatcher's neoliberal project of shrinking the welfare state. In 1978, the premier

British punk rock band, The Sex Pistols, toured the United States. Although the band split apart, seeds of its effects on punk rock bands and punk culture sprouted up all over the United States. It was renamed "hardcore," a double entendre referring to graphic pornography and extreme disaffection from American culture, as in "hardcore criminal."

While the majority of Americans either celebrated or acquiesced to the neoliberal project of the Reagan Administration, punk rockers rebelled against it in perhaps the only way they could. Punk culture held up a mirror to American society and celebrated its ugliness. If their upper-middle-class peers were going to wear prep clothes, they wore T-shirts and jeans that were cut and ripped, often held together with safety pins, or black leather sadomasochism (S&M) outfits studded with spikes. Doc Marten boots and spiked Mohawk haircuts were sported by both males and females. Already designated as losers by their peers, they celebrated their failure by flaunting it as loudly and as brashly as they could. They were "in your face." They publicly engaged in self-destructive behavior. They smoked cigarettes and took drugs that destroyed consciousness; they sniffed glue ("Sniffin' Glue" was a popular song of the Ramones). They ditched school, purposely failed classes, engaged in senseless violence (a punk rock concert tended to take the form of a riot), and engaged in senseless and anonymous sex (message to the jocks—we can get laid too). To the extent that they had a political consciousness, they tended toward anarchy.

Punk rockers carved out social spaces where kids who were losers and did not fit in with the dominant and conservative jock/rah-rah crowds could find like-minded peers and surcease from the harassment they experienced because they were different (Gaines 1994). Since the 1980s, punk culture has continued to exist, changing several times, and, in the 1990s, becoming incorporated under the generic term "Goth."

If punk rock appealed to upper-middle-class kids and had a leftist political identity, skinhead subcultures appealed to working-class white kids, especially those who were downwardly mobile and had a right-wing political identity. Skinhead culture was detailed in the previous chapter in terms of the normative structure and its association with neo-Nazi and racist organizations (Ridgeway 1995). As punk celebrated their failure with self-destructive behavior, skinheads projected their violence outwards toward ethnic minorities whom they perceived as threatening their white-skin privileges.

The "indicative minorities" (Foss 1972) of youth subcultures of the 1980s and 1990s had despair as their central theme. In a culture where interpersonal competition had been intensified, they quit. Punks were losers, and they knew it. Their form of resistance was to celebrate a culture of failure in opposition to the sexual, hip, and status struggles. As an indicative minority, their products, cultural styles, and clothing were picked up by hip urban merchandisers and sold to the middle class, ironically projecting them as cultural innovators. Malcolm McLaren, the manager of The Sex Pistols, ran clothing stores that sold punk outfits and was one of the developers of the grunge look that was later popularized by Seattle garage bands, such as Nirvana. Skinheads also celebrated a culture of failure. However, their form of resistance was random and hate-filled violence. Their style, however, was not nearly as inventive as punk. Nor were there styles commercially viable. They tended to wear military fatigue pants, braces (suspenders), and T-shirts and to shave their heads. The one thing they had in common with the punks was the wearing of Doc Marten or combat boots.

The cultural studies of youth in the 1980s and 1990s revealed a profound malaise. William Finnegan (1998) in his aptly named book, *Cold New World*, chronicled the struggles of black and Hispanic, poor and working-class adolescents in cold, heartless, uncaring environments, where parents were relatively powerless to help them, even though some tried. It was a period of declining opportunity and increasing poverty, especially for children. Family incomes stagnated while the cost of higher education increased dramatically, pricing economically marginal students out of the educational marketplace (Males 1996). Patricia Hersch (1998) intensively studied the lives of six upper-middle-class adolescents. She found them isolated and alone, living in a world unknown to their parents, learning to play a game in which false appearances substituted for a known reality. They all attended the same suburban high school which, given the cultural trends, was hardened in anticipation of violence that had not yet occurred. She wrote:

> This year the administrators in the school are trying to toughen up all around. Expulsion policy is more exacting, rules are implemented more rigorously. School security is tighter, enforced by a full-time police officer in the school (304).

Students complained about the arbitrariness of the enforcement of behavior codes that meted out punishment to the innocent and guilty alike for fear of a student getting away with something (Hersch 1998). In a reversal of the American system of jurisprudence, students were assumed to be guilty until proven otherwise. Students perceived the sanctioning system of the school as unjust and absurd. They had great difficulty making sense of their lives, but they heroically tried to make some sense despite it all. The sense of arbitrariness—of sanctions being applied equally to perpetrator and victim—and the lack of distributive justice that Hersh reported were voiced by numerous Columbine students. All of Hersch's subjects, at one time or another, were depressed. One of her brightest, most dedicated subjects who appeared to work the hardest on himself to be a good and competent human being committed suicide shortly after she concluded her study.

In 1987, four high school students in suburban Bergenfield, New Jersey, suffocated themselves to death in a garaged car as part of a suicide pact (Gaines 1993). The students were described by locals as "losers," "burnouts," "druggies," and "dropouts." Gaines wrote:

> Throughout the 1980s, teenage suicide clusters appeared across the country—six or seven deaths, sometimes more, in a short period of time in a single community. In the Boomtown of Plano, Texas. The fading factory town of Leominster, Massachusetts. At Bryan High School in a white, working-class suburb of Omaha, Nebraska. A series of domino suicides among Arapahoe Indian youths at the Wind River Reservation in Wyoming. Six youth suicides in the county of Westchester, New York, in 1984; five in 1985 and seven in 1986 (8).

As a consequence of the Bergenfield suicide pact, Gaines (1993) conducted a participant observation study of a group of outcast students, known as "burnouts" or "dirt bags," in northern New Jersey. Their lives were aimless, boring, and depressing. They were shunned by their higher status peers; they were shipped off from their neighborhood school to the local vocational-technical high school. Among the powerless, they had even less power. Gaines described powerlessness of 1980s youth:

> Over the last 20 years kids kept losing ground as an autonomous power block. By the 1980s, they had virtually no voice. And without an effective national policy for youth, kids fell through the cracks in droves. It took awhile for adults to figure out that each new youth atrocity added up to a somewhat larger picture of societal neglect. …
>
> America's young people did their best to survive in a climate that was openly punitive toward the vulnerable. Yet they were consistently viewed as a generation of barbarians and losers, stupid, apathetic (239).

The disaffected students at Columbine High School were similarly viewed. They were perceived as trash, as potential threats of violence, as lacking in school spirit, and were blamed for their own outcast status. Even though many of them were bright and high achievers, they were perceived as a management problem

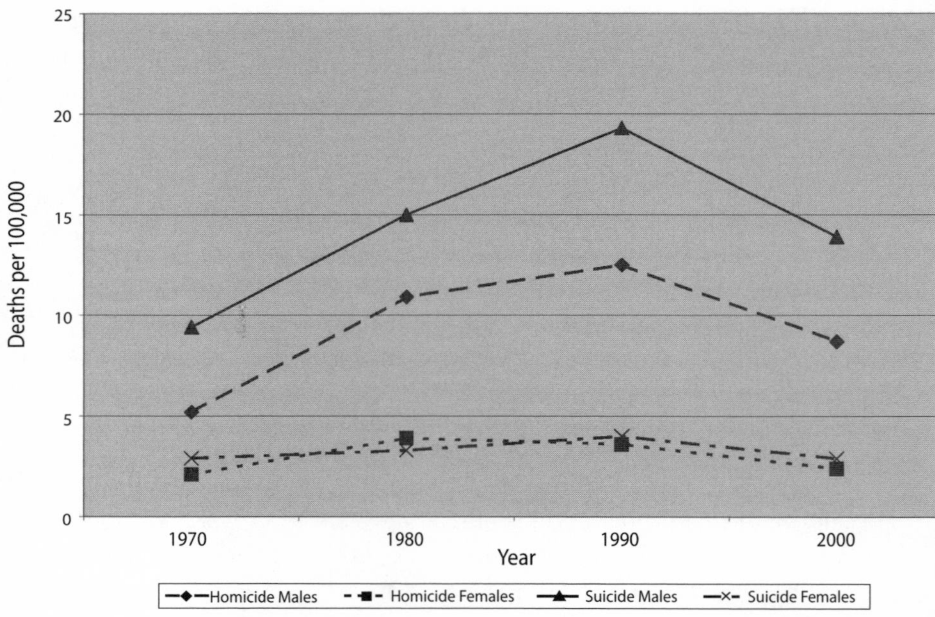

FIGURE 8.1: *Homicide and suicide rates for whites, age 15–19, 1970–2000*

for the school. Those who were victimized by the athletes were perceived by many other students and parents as deserving of the treatment they received.

Government statistics on homicide and suicide bore out the subjective and anecdotal observations of Gaines (1993), Finnegan (1998), and Hersch (1998). American adolescents, including white teenagers, were living in an increasingly violent world. Figure 8.1 contains the homicide and suicide rates for whites between the ages of fifteen and nineteen from 1970 to 2000 (Child DataBank 2005).

Between 1970 and 1980, homicide rate for white males between the ages of fifteen and nineteen doubled from 5.2 to 10.9 per 100,000 in 1980, rising to 12.5 in 1990, and peaking at 14.7 in 1995, and then declining to 8.7 in 2000. Suicide rates for white males jumped from 9.4 to 15.0 per 100,000 between 1970 and 1980, increasing to 19.3 in 1990, and then dropping to 13.9 in 2000. Rates for female adolescents were dramatically lower than males, but essentially followed the same trend, with homicides nearly doubling between 1970 and 1980 from 2.1 to 3.9 per 100, 000, declining slightly to 3.6 in 1990, and then declining to 2.1 in 2000. Female suicide rates showed a similar trend from 2.9 per 100,000 in 1970, increasing to 3.3 in 1980 and 4.0 in 1990, and dropping back down to the same rate of 2.9 that existed in 1970.

The spectacular rise in suicide and homicide rates among white males between 1970 and 1980 was stimulated, in part, by the end of the middle-class youth movement, resulting in a collective malaise among young people that has been explained in detail elsewhere (Foss and Larkin 1976; Larkin 1979). Briefly, many young movement participants burned their bridges to conventional society. When the movement came to an end, they were caught between lives that they had rejected and a vision that had been rendered impossible, resulting in a life construction crisis. Many joined post-movement groups that exercised discipline over their lives and provided bridges back to conventional society (Foss and Larkin 1976, 1986; Tipton 1982). Others lapsed into hedonism, excessive drug use, and otherwise dissolute lives. As noted above, a small minority joined terrorist organizations. Many who could not make the transition killed themselves. In 1973, two close friends of mine who were social movement activists committed suicide within six months of each other.

One would expect that such violence would subside as the time from the end of the movement increased and young people reconciled themselves to the reestablishment of the quotidian; however, suicides and homicides increased throughout the 1980s as the level of desperation among young people, especially those who were outcasts, also increased. Yet something else was going on. If the lives of marginal and outcast students were being degraded, as were the lives of all vulnerable Americans, the celebratory, triumphalist, and aggressive behaviors of the American upper class were being transmitted to adolescent leading crowds. After all, if capital could shove it to labor, and if the American superpower could beat up on weak Third World regimes in Grenada, Nicaragua, and Panama, why could student elites not do whatever they wanted without fear of retribution?

Because the increased aggressiveness of elites was hegemonic, it was invisible and grossly understudied. Gaines (1993), whose study focused on outcast students, noted, almost in passing, "The social order of Bergenfield High School was pretty normal except for one thing: the place was unusually polarized between jocks and the burnouts. There was not one conversation among the outcast that did not include de rigueur dissin' the jocks. ... So the vendetta between the jocks and the burnout was very serious in Bergenfield" (91).

Gaines (1993) also noted that because the Bergenfield High School football team was highly successful, they had provided the community considerable visibility and prestige. She described the jocks as "high-and-mighty," "the golden boys, the cream of the crop in a high school not known for producing many great scholars" (91).

At about the same time that Gaines was studying burnouts in Bergenfield, a news story broke about several members of the Glen Ridge High School football team raping a mentally retarded girl. The town of Glen Ridge, about twenty-five miles southeast of Bergenfield, is smaller and more upper-middle-class. Although news reports focused on the facts of the case and the police investigation, which was shocking enough, another story was being played out about the cover-up of the crime (Lefkowitz 1997).

The rape took place in the basement of two members of the football team who were neighbors and grew up with the victim. They were fully aware of her cognitive disabilities. Nevertheless, they lured her to their basement, where in the presence of thirteen members of the football, wrestling, basketball, and baseball teams, they had her perform oral sex on some of them, and they stuck a broom and a fungo bat up her vagina. The victim participated in the events because she idolized the athletes and thought that by doing what they wanted she would be included in their group (Lefkowitz 1997).

After hearing about the rape, Lefkowitz, a journalism professor at Columbia University, began investigating the crime. The investigation turned into a community study of Glen Ridge. What he found was a sports-crazed community that idolized its football team: "For the Saturday faithful, Glen Ridge was football. Without it, Glen Ridge was just another suburban town. Kids who didn't play football—and worse still, showed no enthusiasm for those who did—were treated as 'nobodies.' Adults who didn't find football and the hoopla surrounding it exciting were judged lacking in civic spirit. They would never be accepted as real Ridgers" (Lefkowitz 1997, 72).

In keeping with that normative environment, the jocks were privileged. Lefkowitz reported that parents alleged that the local police enforced underage alcohol regulations differentially, arresting nonathletes while being lenient in their treatment of athletes. Not surprisingly, those kids who were not interested in sports were stigmatized as losers and nobodies. Similarly to the Trenchcoat Mafia at Columbine High School, the outcasts banded together to form their own subculture, identifying themselves as, not surprisingly, "The Outcasts."

What Lefkowitz found in Glen Ridge was a normative pattern of nearly complete indulgence of the student athletes. Although a minority of parents and teachers were upset about the tolerance of immoral and illegal behaviors among the jocks, the rest of the community looked away. In Columbine, the jocks ruled the halls. Unlike Columbine, the aggression at Glen Ridge was specifically directed toward girls rather than anybody who got in their way. Numerous incidents were told of jocks pushing girls up against lockers and grinding their bodies against them, simulating sexual activity. Teachers were intimidated and afraid to sanction jocks because of their status.

Glen Ridge High School was essentially run by coaches. The principal was a former assistant football coach, the vice principal was a basketball coach, and the athletic director was a legendary former football coach. The coaches ran the school, and the jocks controlled the hallways. The school was effectively a "jock-ocracy." Although Glen Ridge High School was an upper-middle-class community and many of its graduates attended selective colleges and universities, the school looked more like a sports program with an academic track than an academic institution with sports programs. This is apparently a rather common phenomenon in the United States where coaches and former coaches dominate the school administration and teachers of academic disciplines are chosen not on the basis of academic and pedagogical skills, but on their abilities to coach sports teams.

In Glen Ridge and in Columbine, the school climate reflected the values of the community. The community wanted, in addition to a decent academic program, winning sports teams, especially winning football teams. Because these communities obtain their identity through the exploits of their high school football teams, football players received special dispensation. This meant that their high status provided them with access to girls and sex, adulation by peers and adults alike, lenient treatment for their misdemeanors, and a freedom to behave in a manner about which others of their age could hardly dream.

This particular group of Glen Ridge seniors, although their performance on the gridiron was less than spectacular with Glen Ridge High School achieving only three wins in eighteen games during their junior and senior years, tended to be more outrageous in their behaviors than their predecessors (Lefkowitz 1997). They seemed to be meaner, more aggressive, and more felonious than preceding classes. Under-aged jocks were caught buying alcohol, engaging in vandalism, instigating fights, and shooting BB guns at people in the township. At the winter prom, several jocks rifled through girls' purses and boys' wallets in jackets hanging over chairs as their victims danced. They stole several hundred dollars in cash. In nearly all of these escapades, when it was discovered that members of the football team were involved, restitution was made without punishment.

One of the most notorious and celebrated acts of the jocks, prior to the rape, was the complete trashing of a house in nearby East Orange. Just prior to the Valentine's Day weekend, a student who was trying to impress the in-crowd announced in the cafeteria that her parents would be away for the weekend and that she was going to have a party. Members of the Glen Ridge football team came to the party and began trashing the place, destroying everything they could, including all the furniture in the house, spray-painting graffiti on the walls, killing the fish in the fish tank, torching the pet cat, and ransacking dressers. Eleven juveniles from Glen Ridge were held by the police, including four former or present members of the football team, one of whom was later involved in the rape case. Lefkowitz (1997) indicated that they were questioned briefly and released to their parents without being charged with a crime. The high school administration acted as if nothing had happened.

One of the legacies of the 1960s middle-class youth movement was the creation of permanent dissident adolescent subcultures in predominantly white, suburban, middle-class high schools. Although they never challenged the jocks' domination of the school, they provided an important and valued space for outcast students. Although outcast subcultures were always at or near the bottom of the school status structure (Eckert 1989; Larkin 1979; Wooden and Blazak 2001), they provided a basis of cohesion for students who were rejected by the vast majority of their peers. They occupied their own space in the school, usually near a place where they could smoke, because one major source of differentiation was that outcast students smoked cigarettes whereas the vast majority of the other students did not. They listened to their own music (punk, heavy metal, industrial, ska, rap, hardcore), which separated them from the others. They also adopted their own clothing styles, especially dressing in black, which was an indicator of goth.

Even banding together in subcultures for protection and mutual support was insufficient for many outcast students. First, as indicated by the research of Gaines (1993) and Finnegan (1998), the peer group was incapable of providing for all the socioemotional needs of its participants. Adolescent peer groups are rife with rivalries, fights, and relationships that are labile and impermanent. Second, outcast student subcultures tend to be not only alienated from their peers but also from parent and adult authorities, including teachers and police. Aside from the occasional understanding parent or teacher, outcasts are pretty much left to their own devices, which are relatively few.

For adolescents more than for any other age group, the future looms as a source of anxiety. For outcast students, prospects seem particularly grim, to the point that thoughts of the future are to be avoided at all costs, and perhaps even suicide is considered (Gaines 1993). These are the kids in the community who evince a visceral dislike. They are the ones that "don't have school spirit," "give the community a black eye," on whom the police are supposed to keep an eye, even though they may be victims of predation by their higher status peers who play on the sports teams, wear clothing, including lettermen's jackets that have the school colors, and are vested with the reputation of the local community.

Meanwhile, bullying begins to emerge as a social problem in the early 1990s. The shootings at Columbine, because of the motivations of the shooters, brought bullying to center stage. Anecdotal, participant observational, and statistical data all indicate that in the post-1980s world, young people of all races and ethnicities were increasingly likely to experience violence. It is a colder, harder world that they faced compared to earlier generations. As noted in the previous chapter, working-class kids are no longer guaranteed a union job with a major corporation. For upper-middle-class kids, the taxpayer revolt resulted in the defunding of public higher education, which means that competition for selective universities intensifies and costs increase. The possibility of failure increases, raising anxiety levels.

Concomitant with the rise of public awareness about bullying, Americans began witnessing a new crime occurring not in overcrowded underfunded urban high schools but in rural and suburban middle and high schools: rampage shootings. According to Newman (2004), between 1974 and March 2001, twenty-five rampage shootings occurred. However, nearly eight years passed between the first shooting and the second. Between 1982 and 1988, five rampage shootings were documented, followed by a four year hiatus. Between 1992 and 1996, there were six rampage shootings, all in rural areas. Between 1997 and 2001, Newman documented thirteen rampage shootings, including the mass murders in Paducah, Kentucky, Jonesboro, Arkansas, Springfield, Oregon, and, of course, Columbine. All were committed by males. With the exception of one Asian and two blacks, the other twenty-four shooters were white. In nearly every case, the shooter had low peer status or was described as a loner. In every case where evidence existed, the shooter had been either teased or bullied. In every case where evidence existed, the shooter's masculinity had been challenged, and he felt marginalized in the peer group. In most cases, as in Columbine, the motive of the shooter was retaliation. One exception was Michael Carrneal in Paducah, Kentucky, who shot five fellow students in a prayer group in an attempt to impress members of the goth subculture in his high school.

The two decades leading up to the Columbine shootings were not particularly good ones for adolescents. Families had been under increasing stress, privatization mania and tax revolts by the propertied classes undermined national commitment to public education and required public universities to institute and increase tuition. As violence increased among teenagers, tough-on-crime legislators instituted increasingly draconian laws for juvenile offenders. The adolescent's world continued to grow harder, colder, and fraught with increasing probabilities of failure. Meanwhile, a minority of privileged students, especially those who played football, became adolescent culture's version of celebrities who seemed to be exempt from the misery that many of their peers experienced, especially the outcast students, who, because they thought and acted differently than the majority of students, became targets for violence down the social system. All too often, the violence and the bullying were excused and ignored by adults. High school sports heroes were exempted from punishment or received reduced or altered punishments that do not affect their eligibility to play. We witnessed in Columbine and in Glen Ridge that coaches effectively ran the school, wayward athletes committed crimes unpunished. In some cases, coaches abetted such behaviors, such as in the case of a coach bailing out a state championship wrestler and taking him to a meet directly from jail after he had been arrested for driving while intoxicated and smashing up his car, or the administration of Glen Ridge High School attempting to protect and excuse the behaviors of rapists because they were on the football team (Lefkowitz 1997).

Differential treatment of students for rule infractions creates cynicism below and arrogance above. It sends a message, in George Orwell's terms, that "some are more equal than others." Participant observational research indicates that the kids know what is going on, even if the adults deny it. A goth being harassed by a member of the football team as a coach stands by and snickers learns a message about justice very quickly. He also learns a lesson about powerlessness, humiliation, and adult corruption. He learns that it is much better to be a somebody than a nobody. The rules operate differently for somebodies.

Wealth is shifted up the social structure as the proportion of income for the top 1 percent of the population increases dramatically and the greater majority of Americans experience stagnating or declining incomes in real terms. While this redistribution of wealth takes place, the corporate media increasingly focus on the lives of celebrities. The phenomenon of the Reagan presidency represented the merging of celebrity with political power. Ronald Reagan became president of the United States because he was a celebrity. The opposite occurred with Bill Clinton, former Governor of a third world state who became a celebrity because he achieved the presidency. Americans are increasingly fed tidbits on the lives of celebrities as hard news reports diminish. The distinction between fact and fiction blurs, and a new genre called "infotainment" supplants journalism. To an impressionable adolescent, the message of postmodern American culture is that if you are not a somebody, then you must be a nobody, which is worse than being a has-been. At least if you are a has-been, you can be recycled on a "whatever became of ..." article or show. Gaines (1993) put it this way:

> Kids who go for the prize now understand there are only two choices—rise to the top or crash to the bottom. Many openly admit they would

> rather end it all now than end up losers. ... The big easy or the bottomless pit, but never the everyday drone. As long as there are local heroes and stories, you can still believe you have a chance to emerge from the mass as something larger than life ... kids try to play at being one in a million, some way of shining, even if it's just for a while (151).

WHO IS GOING TO MAKE MY MOVIE? THE KILLERS AND CELEBRITY STATUS

One can be a celebrity because of talent, beauty, athleticism, or personal achievements. Sports figures, movie stars, models, and assorted luminaries in various fields fit into this category. One can also become a celebrity by being in the right place at the right time (Gamson 1994). All one has to do is be in the eye of the camera at a critical moment. However, there is a third way to become a celebrity—and that is to do something so outrageous that one becomes notorious. For nobodies, this is the one sure route to celebrity; this is the road that Harris and Klebold took.

If their intent was to become celebrities, they were hugely successful. They commandeered the attention of all Americans, including the president of the United States, every high school principal in the land, researchers such as this writer, pundits, the clergy, and every kid in America capable of watching the news.

Harris and Klebold speculated that their act would generate a revolution. Harris said in one of the videotapes, "We're going to kick-start a revolution" among the dispossessed and despised students of the world. Although they did not engender a revolution, their acts resonated among those students who had been bullied and humiliated by their peers. In the weeks following the Columbine High School shootings, schools across the country experienced thousands of bomb scares, scores of attempted bombings, and several attempted copycat killings (Emergency Net 1999), partially achieving Harris and Klebold's apocalyptical vision of a nationwide revolt. The most serious incident occurred the day after Columbine in rural Alberta, Canada, where a high school student killed a peer and wounded another. Since then, numerous actual school shootings have occurred and potential attempts have been thwarted (Butterfield 2001). Several planned or actual attacks were inspired by Columbine: In 2001, Joseph DeGuzman, who was obsessed with the Columbine shootings, accumulated an arsenal of guns, bombs, Molotov cocktails, and 2000 rounds of ammunition. Two boys in Fort Collins, Colorado, a mere sixty miles from Columbine High School, planned a reenactment of the Columbine shootings. In a small town in Kansas, three boys collected white supremacy paraphernalia, guns, ammunition, and a book on how to make bombs, in what the press described as a "Columbine-like" planned assault that was foiled by a student tipping off authorities (Cable News Network 2001). An attempt uncovered in New Bedford, Massachusetts, was conspicuously modeled after Columbine. Three freshmen at the local high school planned an assault that they hoped would have a higher death toll than Columbine (Butterfield and McFadden 2001). In the summer of 2003, three outcast boys in southern New Jersey were arrested with a large arsenal that they planned to use in a mobile assault on their community (Campbell 2003). In March 2005, on the Red Lake Indian Reservation, Jeffrey Wiese killed his grandparents, five fellow students, a teacher and a security guard, in a rampage modeled after Columbine. With the protagonist claiming he was a goth and wearing a black duster, he asked one of his victims if he believed in God before killing him (Wilgoren, Pates, and Reuthling 2005).

The Columbine shootings were and continue to be media-driven. Harris and Klebold, especially Harris, had especially strong media savvy and awareness. The boys videotaped themselves prior to the shootings; Harris set up the "Trenchcoat Mafia" web page on AOL. The boys were quite facile in the use of video games. When they made their videotapes prior to the massacre, Eric Harris sat in a chair swigging a bottle of Jack Daniels and holding in his lap a sawed-off shotgun named "Arlene," after a favorite character in the Doom video game (Gibbs and Roche 1999).

Klebold was caught up in the pleasure of creating pain in those who had made his life so agonizing. He was also enamored by the social consequences of their actions. He seemed to be enthralled by the notoriety that they would receive. This appeared to be his major concern when talking with a journalist in a chat room about the Oklahoma City bombings. In the basement tapes, Klebold noted that people would take notice at the time and date of the videotapes they were making. He also considered what movie director could best be trusted with the script of their story; Quentin Tarantino topped their list (Gibbs and Roche 1999). They also wanted the story to have a lot of "dramatic irony." Instead, they got Gus Van Zandt's film, "Elephant," loosely based on the Columbine shootings, which was dramatically flat. However, the play, *Columbinus*, by P. J. Paparelli, which focused on precipitating events that led up to the shootings, toured the country and played off-Broadway in New York to rave reviews.

In November 2000, a year and a half after the Columbine shootings, my wife, Debra Larkin, conducted an investigation of Columbine-oriented chat rooms. She found memorial web sites dedicated to the victims, especially Rachel Scott and Cassie Bernall. In addition, countless web sites had sprung up as open forums for expressing opinions about issues related to the shootings: They included debates over gun control policies, bullying, guilt of the parents, proper actions of the police and school administration, the psychology of the shooters, and drug use. One of the most common themes on the web sites was whether or not Klebold and Harris should be forgiven for their deeds. Many students admitted that they felt sympathy and even empathy toward the boys. Several sites have been maintained as information clearinghouses on the shootings themselves. I have used these in my own research and have contacted, on occasion, the webmaster to provide information or correct misinformation.

Over five years after the shooting, there still exists the "Eric Harris Worship Site" ("Trench" 2005) on which the above-mentioned issues are still being debated. Dylan Klebold has a site devoted to his personage (www.DylanKlebold.com). The personages of Eric Harris and Dylan Klebold maintain an underground existence. For many young people who find themselves in positions similar to those of Harris and Klebold at Columbine High School, the boys strike a resonating chord. Some people in chat rooms regard them as heroes; most regard them as villains. In rare cases, they are exemplars. Since April 19, 1999, numerous rampage shootings have occurred in middle and high schools and colleges across North America; for every shooting that has been carried out, several have been discovered and thwarted before their execution. In most cases, the Columbine shootings were used as a template, an inspiration, or a record to be surpassed.

Although Eric Harris and Dylan Klebold did not jump-start a revolution, they provided outcast students with the possibility of an alternative to passive acceptance of abuse from their higher-status peers. Perhaps by now, most of America has forgotten their names. However, their memory lives on in the consciousness of what Brooks Brown aptly referred to as "loser students."

9

GIVE PEACE A CHANCE

IN THIS STUDY, I have examined school and community factors that prompted Eric Harris and Dylan Klebold to bomb their school and shoot their peers. Apparently, the most significant factor that generated the boys' aggression was the hostility directed at them by the jocks, especially the members of the football and wrestling teams. A second factor was the arrogance of the evangelical students who established themselves as a moral elite in the high school and who saw themselves as superiors who had the right to proselytize other students on campus. This practice especially affected the outcast students. Because many of the abusers and bullies were members of the evangelical community, many non-evangelical students, including Klebold and Harris, saw the behavior of the evangelical students as hypocritical and self-serving. The overlapping combination of athlete abusers and self-appointed evangelical moral elitists alienated many Columbine High School students. Clearly, Klebold and Harris possessed a powerful combination of anger and resentment which drove them to their heinous act.

I have explored the larger cultural context in which the Columbine shootings occurred and suggest that Harris and Klebold were influenced by the rise of paramilitary culture in the early-to-mid-1990s that culminated in the bombing of the federal building in Oklahoma City in 1996. American culture had become increasingly intolerant of deviation from the cultural norm. This intolerance was reflected throughout society in increased aggression by the American upper class against all lower classes, with special aggressiveness toward the poor and disfranchised. We witnessed a U.S. foreign policy that waged optional wars against weak, third world countries. The media played on these themes and celebrated the strong and the powerful, which both implicitly and explicitly reinforced existing power relationships. Resistance to the domination of corporate America and its unholy alliance with the Christian right was weak and ineffectual.

One of the few groups that resisted the increasing corporatization of America was in the adolescent youth culture. Musical genres such as punk, heavy metal, rap, hip-hop, and hard-core offered a critique of everyday life. Youths saw a consumer culture in which people are defined in terms of their social status and their ability to consume. By the 1990s, the white subcultures of resistance were generically characterized as goth. Young goths viewed the power exercised over their lives not as corporate capitalism but rather in terms of the predation they experienced at the hands of their higher status peers, the predator athletes, or jocks. Admired by the community for their physical aggression, the jocks were supported and protected by administrators and teachers, many of whom were coaches or former coaches.

In most cases, adolescent outcasts were powerless to resist harassment, physical violence, and stigmatization dealt out by their elite peers. The weaker students were labeled "losers" and "deviants." In turn, Gothic adolescent subcultures took an ironic position toward their situation; they praised that which was ostensibly antisocial. They listened to music that celebrated violence, misogyny, meaninglessness, anger, revenge, drugs, and being a loser. They took drugs to obliterate consciousness and engaged in interpersonal violence as an alternative to boredom. However, as the 1990s progressed, the most desperate, or as in the case of Columbine, the most desirous of fame, increasingly resorted to retaliatory violence. Many students brought weapons to school. Sometimes the weapons were tools of intimidation. Sometimes the outcast students shot at their tormentors. Ironically, in most of these cases, they simply attacked the most convenient targets. The Columbine shootings marked a cultural watershed in school violence.

Through a discussion of the issues related to the Columbine shootings in particular and rampage shootings in general, I want to offer an explanation of adolescent violence. From the outset, the evangelical community has attempted to define the Columbine shootings as a consequence of the secularization of society and the removal of religion from the schools. Most of the books written about Columbine have originated in the evangelical community. This book is the first attempt to analyze the Columbine shootings from a social science perspective. America is supposedly a democratic, pluralistic society in which freedom of expression is written into its legal structure. In that spirit, I will spend some time addressing issues raised by the evangelical community.

An essential element is the role of football and other sports in American communities and the methods by which sport programs can pervert the educational goals of local high schools. With the tacit acceptance of many adults and the active participation of a few, sports fever can generate a toxic environment for many adolescents.

We must evaluate the social stratification and goals of Columbine High School. What mistakes were made? What was done right? To what extent have the changes initiated by the school administration changed the environment of Columbine High since the shootings? Why is it important to study the causes of the shootings at Columbine? To what extent is the internal structure of Columbine applicable to the rest of American high schools?

Finally, I wish to address the relationship between the community and the well-being of its adolescents. Is the community responsible for the physical health and socio-emotional development of its youth? It has become clear to me that the middle school years are critical in the formation of adolescent subcultures. The question to be addressed is, How can middle schools and their communities facilitate the development of healthy adolescents?

We must examine what theories, research, and experiences have shown to be successful in the reduction of violence in high schools. First, we need to develop a theory that explains the existence of everyday violence in high schools. Second, we have to examine existing programs designed to reduce violence in terms of their empirical and theoretical efficacy. Third, we need to listen to high school students about their experiences and about what they think should be done about interpersonal violence among their peers.

GOOD AND EVIL AT COLUMBINE HIGH SCHOOL

The Christian right has taken upon itself the task of identifying the causes of the Columbine shootings in particular and school violence in general (Epperhart 2002; Huckabee 1998; Porter 1999; Scott and Rabey 2001; Watson 2002). They have cast the Columbine shootings in terms of good versus evil, with Dylan Klebold and Eric Harris as the agents of the devil. In view of this, it is necessary to address the following issues with spokespersons for the evangelical community:

1. Did Eric and Dylan target evangelicals in their rampage?
2. Why did evangelical commentators downplay or ignore bullying as a factor in the shootings?
3. Why did the evangelical commentators blame secular institutions and liberalism for the shootings?
4. Why did the evangelical community not engage in introspection about their culpability in the shootings?
5. Why did the evangelical community exploit the shootings for proselytizing and recruitment?
6. Why did evangelical commentators use blatantly counterfactual and spurious arguments to make their case?

Zoba (2000) maintained that Harris and Klebold targeted evangelical Christians in their rampage. Her evidence for this was the hostility toward evangelicals displayed by the boys in the basement tapes (see pages 91–92 for the text). She also claimed that evangelical students Rachel Scott, Cassie Bernall, and a third unnamed student were shot execution style. According to the police report, Harris and Klebold were standing approximately fifteen feet from Rachel Scott when they shot and killed her and wounded Richard Castaldo. Therefore, she could not have been shot execution style. Additionally, the description of the shooting of Cassie Bernall was confirmed by several witnesses: Eric Harris stuck his shotgun under the table in the library and said, "Peek-a-boo," and shot Cassie Bernall in the face. There is no evidence that Klebold or Harris knew Cassie Bernall or identified her as a Christian evangelical. As shown in Chapter 3, neither shooter talked to Cassie Bernall; Josh Lapp, the boy who originally stated that the shooters asked Cassie Bernall whether she believed in God, was across the room from her, near Valeen Schnurr, who was asked if she believed in God. Emily Winant, who was under the desk next to Cassie, testified that the boys did not speak to her, even though Emily was pressured by evangelicals to confirm the story that Cassie had died defending her beliefs. Cassie happened to be in the wrong place at the wrong time. Rachel Scott was unknown to Harris and Klebold. I cannot comment on the third unidentified person.

According to Zoba (2000), three of the twelve students killed by Klebold and Harris were evangelicals. Although the school keeps no statistics on the religious backgrounds of its students, I asked several students and staff members, including Principal DeAngelis (the latter would not comment) on the proportion of students at Columbine who were evangelicals. Estimates were between 35 percent and 45 percent. If Zoba's figures are correct, evangelical students were actually underrepresented among the dead. The only person who was singled out and executed was Isaiah Sholes, who was killed because he was African American. There is absolutely no evidence that Klebold and Harris sought out evangelical students to kill. They attacked targets of opportunity. Their original plan to set off bombs in the cafeteria would have been the ultimate act of random violence, except that they had placed the bombs where the student athletes usually sat.

When Bill Epperhart (2002) rhetorically asked, "Why did Columbine happen?" he answered his own question: "[P]eople have tried to come up with all kinds of reasons that it happened. But this is not a race issue, not a clique issue, not a jock issue. This is a spiritual issue, a heart issue" (91). Bruce Porter (1999), who claimed that he wanted to understand why this happened in his community did not even mention bullying. Zoba (2000) mentioned bullying in passing but did not explore it as a serious possibility.

Within a month of the shootings, several of the news media had reported on issues of "jock elitism," and bullying in the halls of Columbine (Adams and Russakoff 1999; Flynn 1999; Greene 1999; Von Drehle 1999). I think there are two reasons why the evangelical community overlooked the role that bullying played in the shootings. From the outset, the evangelical community scripted the shootings as a struggle between good and evil, with the evangelical community assuming the role of goodness and Klebold and Harris, along with secularism and political liberalism, in the role of evil. In this Manichean view, the evangelical community was cast as the innocent victim, which stood for God against the powerful forces of darkness. Once that frame became the defining image of the Columbine shootings, all data that did not conform to that image was regarded as irrelevant.

Second, the shootings rocked the community to its foundations. People were asking, "How could it happen here?" Although many people were asking the question out of pain and anguish, it was a valid question. It was also a question that made members of the evangelical community uncomfortable. Why did the worst shootings in the history of American education occur in their neighborhood? The response of the evangelical community was to point fingers elsewhere and engage in what can be described as reaction formation and projection. Since the evangelical community was a priori defined as good, the cause had to be an external agent, such as Satan, as manifested by the federal government or believers in secular humanism.

This, of course, leads to the next question as to why evangelicals blamed secular institutions for the shooting. Ironically, secular institutions, including the school, the federal government, and the media, played critical roles in the shootings but not in the ways suggested by spokespersons for the evangelical community. The school should shoulder some of the blame because of its laissez-faire attitude toward bullying and its failure to rein in the aggression of its athletes in the hallways and in its environs. It is not because it refused to display the Ten Commandments or required all students to recite a state prescribed prayer. The federal government played a role because it exemplified bullying with a foreign policy of aggression against weak and dependent nations and a domestic policy that rewarded wealth and blamed poverty on its victims. In the eight years leading up to April 1999, a hereditary upper class vilified the Clinton Administration and did everything it could to make it ineffectual and to drive Clinton out of the White House. The media played a role through its celebration of winners, its sensationalism of violent news stories, and the vilification of the powerless.

The evangelical community, and to a lesser extent school officials, denied the obvious. The major causes of the shootings could be located in their own community. Bill Epperhart (2002), quoted above, explicitly denied any role the jocks had in creating the conditions that gave rise to the massacre. Similarly, Principal DeAngelis denied that bullying by members of the wrestling and football teams was occurring in the halls of Columbine High School. He claimed that neither Klebold nor Harris came to him to complain about their treatment by the athletes (Garbarino and deLara 2002). Yet, as I have demonstrated in Chapter 5, any student complaining about their treatment by the jocks could not depend upon protection by the administration and would open themselves up to retribution. It was common knowledge around Columbine High School that "jocks ruled"—it was even written on the bathroom walls—and victims appeared powerless to do anything about it.

Protestantism, which posits that a believer has a personal relationship with an all-knowing, all-seeing God, has been traditionally a religion of deep personal introspection. I do not know what kind of introspection occurred among individuals, but collectively the evangelical community immediately distanced themselves from any culpability, as detailed in Chapter 3. Simplistically, Klebold and Harris were the agents of Satan. The only person to suggest that forces in the community were responsible for the rampage shootings was student Brooks Brown, who said that if Harris and Klebold were monsters, they were made that way by the school (Austin and Mendez 2004).

Nobody in the evangelical community suggested a prior cause for Harris and Klebold's evil acts. As we have seen, they even denied the possibility. This is a sad commentary. Several of the students I interviewed noted that several athletes who participated in the harassment of Klebold and Harris and other students were "deep Christians" or evangelicals. A number of students complained about the hypocrisy of evangelical students who, on the one hand claimed their spiritual superiority because they had been born again, while on the other hand, they seemed to party frequently, get drunk, take drugs, and engage in premarital sex along with the rest of their peers. [1] This apparent hypocrisy was also applied to violence, since some members of the evangelical community were absolved of any blame for creating the environment that led to the shootings in the first place. Take for example this explanation by Reverend Bill Oudemolen:

> When I was standing on the corner of Pierce and Bowles near Columbine High School [right after the shooting], I had the sense that there was only one way I could explain it. I believed I *did* smell the presence of evil—not that it alleviates the blame that I would place on Harris and Klebold. I believe they made choices and were responsible. But who is the author of the evil? My theological category for this is that Satan is the author of evil—a personal being, fallen angel Lucifer, a being of light who falls in the act of rebellion and devises all these plans (Zoba 2000, p. 167, emphasis in original).

Many pastors of the evangelical community, including Bruce Porter of Trinity Christian Center, Bill Oudemolen of Foothills Bible Church, and Jerry Nelson of Southern Gables Church used the shootings as an opportunity for evangelizing and recruitment, especially among young people (Cullen 1999a; Porter 1999). There is no doubt that the religious community in southern Jefferson County provided the students suffering the trauma of the shootings places where they could gather together and obtain spiritual sustenance in a supportive environment. But these were not the only places. A parent told me that in the weeks after the shootings large numbers of kids, maybe twenty or thirty in a group, would go from one kid's house to another and hang together. Parents would provide a safe, supportive environment and food for the kids to eat.

Behind the pain and anguish of the young people and their need to gather together in the wake of a tragedy, they desired a supportive community. There was a quest to have answers to difficult questions such as, Why do bad things happen to good people? Simultaneously, some leaders of the evangelical community exploited the situation for their own benefit. Chief among these was Bruce Porter, who blazed his Torchgrab Ministry at Rachel Scott's funeral (Porter 1999).

> At Rachel's funeral I was honored to issue a challenge to quite possibly the largest audience in the history of the planet to "pick up the torch" that Rachel and other believing kids at Columbine had carried in their

> school. I received so many responses from those across the world who had taken that challenge to heart that my mind reeled. … Spontaneously, scores of rallies began to spring up across the nation. I spoke at several of them. … One of these, held in San Jose and organized by Pastor Dick Burnal and dozens of churches in the San Francisco Bay area, had an attendance of more than 16,000 people. … A portion of Rachel's funeral, with my challenge to take up the torch Rachel carried, was presented. Thousands of youths leapt to their feet, held up their arms, and cheered. The powers of darkness were no doubt shaken that night!
>
> The messages shared during the Columbine Torchgrab Youth Rally in Littleton will go down in history as pivotal to the next wave of God's moving in our world … (84–85).

From Bruce Porter's perspective, he is doing God's work and hallowing the memory of Rachel Scott. He is heartened by the response of his audiences who seem to be dedicating their lives to her example. He claims that Rachel was carrying a torch symbolizing a spiritual revolution of compassion, mercy, and love; young people should pick up her torch and carry on her work. His book ends with the exhortation to stand up and declare:

> *I will live for Jesus Christ and not for myself! I will lift my voice in this generation and declare the truth and righteous standards of the Kingdom of God! I will carry, with bold proclamation, the martyr's torch!* (114; emphasis in original).

From the outside, despite Porter's professed intentions, his actions seemed crass and self-aggrandizing. Hyperbolic statements such as "the largest audience in the history of the planet" and "[t]he messages shared during the Columbine Torchgrab Youth Rally in Littleton will go down in history as pivotal to the next wave of God's moving in our world" reveal an astounding sense of grandiosity. That Bruce Porter could put himself at the head of a "movement" that expresses the will of God might strike an outsider as extremely arrogant. How is Bruce Porter's Torchgrab Ministry more valid an expression of God than Reverend Marxhausen's ministering to the needs of the Klebold family, for which he was reviled by many members of the evangelical community? Porter's sense of entitlement as one who speaks and does the will of God without question reflects the hubris of many in the evangelical community that alienates not onlynonbelievers and members of other religious traditions but other Christians as well.

Underlying the evangelicals' thrust into the spotlight as both a wounded community and a self-perceived source of spiritual redemption were the quests for fame and notoriety and a flood of donations. Although Cullen (1999a) suggested that the reaction of the evangelical community was, in part, a response to their own demonization by nonevangelicals and their exclusion from mainstream media, once the media focused on them, their response was telling.

Many of the local clergy were appalled at the behavior of some of the evangelical pastors in their attempt to grab the limelight, use public events for personal and political agendas, and exploit the death of children, all in the name of God (Cullen 1999a). In addition, the evangelical community was not afraid to use coercion to push their definition of the situation. Emily Wynant's family was inundated with calls urging her to confirm that Cassie Bernall was asked whether she believed in God before she was shot. The harassment was so extreme the family had to disconnect their telephone. When it became clear that the evidence did not support the claim that Cassie died defending her faith, the *Rocky Mountain News* sat on the story for two weeks, fearing to print it because of the backlash of the evangelical community. That lapse constituted a serious violation of journalistic ethics (Cullen 1999b).

Dave McPherson, the youth director of the West Bowles Community Church, said that the youth group had attempted outreach to the isolated and nonconformist students at Columbine. According to those nonconformist students, the outreach consisted of telling them that if they didn't change their ways, they would burn in hell. Reverend Marxhausen reported that in the wake of the shootings, evangelical students were using the shootings as a pretext for recruitment. Evangelical students at Columbine were telling other students that if they just accepted Christ as their savior, their sufferings would be alleviated. Marxhausen was outraged at such behavior because of its insensitivity to the feelings of others; furthermore, such a simplistic solution to the complex problem of coping actually interfered with the grieving process.

The evangelical community in the wake the Columbine shootings revealed itself as having compassion for their own members but not for those whose beliefs were different. After the shootings, all religious groups, whether mainline Protestant, Roman Catholic, or evangelical, opened their houses of worship to grieving members of the community. Parents, religious and secular, selflessly opened their homes to grieving students who huddled together in large groups. However, it was only the evangelicals who opportunistically took advantage of the situation to further their own ideological and material interests. It was only the evangelical community that attempted to take over and dominate the nationally televised memorial service. It was only the evangelical community that asserted its version of events in contradiction to the facts and attempted to coerce those who did not adhere to the party line. It was only evangelical ministers who claimed that their fallen children had a direct line to heaven while those who were not evangelicals were waiting in purgatory.

FOOTBALL AND TOXIC HIGH SCHOOL ENVIRONMENTS

For most students at Columbine High School, the hallways were commodious. For the athletes, they constituted a territory over which they rule to this day. For a small minority of students, they were sources of hidden terror. A student could be standing at his locker and get shoved into it. He could walk around the corner and come face-to-face with a nemesis who continually bullied him, whose eyes glowed with the knowledge of privileged opportunity. Minding his own business, a student suddenly might be grabbed by a couple of football players and stuffed into a trash can. While videotaping Eric Harris and another friend as they were walking down the hall, Dylan Klebold was hit by a fellow student wearing a Columbine football sweatshirt. All of these events occurred in the halls of Columbine High School. Judging by the content of talk shows in the wake of the Columbine shootings, such experiences were commonplace throughout the nation.

When I was interviewing in Columbine, a parent told me, "[T]he school is run by the coaches." I knew that Principal DeAngelis was a former baseball coach whose teams won two state championships. He was also an assistant football coach. Coaches were also deans, and, of course, many of the faculty members coached part-time. However, I had a hard time comprehending what she meant. Curriculum is determined by the state; departments have chairpersons; principals have a multitude of duties requiring their attention other than athletics, as Principal DeAngelis was anxious to point out to me. Additionally, Columbine had a strong academic reputation. Many of its teachers were inspirational and provided an alternative point of view for students. One of the great virtues of Columbine High School was that it offered most students a favorite teacher with whom they could talk.

What this parent meant was that the overwhelming tenor of the high school was sports related. The core of the most influential faculty members and administrators was formed of coaches and former coaches. DeAngelis was the formal leader of that collectivity. Although the school was certainly proud of its academic program and the accomplishments of its graduates, sports appeared to be first on the agenda. This emphasis was apparent in a number of ways: the tributes to DeAngelis in his office for his coaching accomplishments, the trophy cases at the east entrance of the school, the athletic Hall of Fame in the gymnasium corridor, the wall of sports pictures in one of the dean's offices. When I walked into the administration office on my first visit, two newly won state championship trophies, one for soccer and one for football, were sitting around apparently because the staff had to rearrange trophy cases in order to include them. But most of all, the athletes, especially the male athletes, controlled the hallways and had privileges beyond those of the average student.

Although there are no statistics, this pattern of sports domination of high schools is apparently the norm in America. Some high schools, such as Glen Ridge in northern New Jersey in the mid-1990s (Lefkowitz 1997) and Permian High School in Odessa, Texas (Bissinger 1990), seem to be run more like sports teams with academic programs as an afterthought. This was especially the case of Permian, where students were learning from textbooks that were fifteen years out-of-date and the football team spent $70,000 for a chartered jet airplane for visiting games. In the early 1980s, the school board spent $5.6 million for a state-of-the-art football stadium that held slightly under 20,000 fans in a city with a population of slightly under 90,000. The football coach, who also served as athletic director, taught no classes and earned half again as much as a teacher at the top of the pay scale.

In the previous chapter, I pointed out that over the past twenty-five years, postmodern culture has increasingly focused on the cult of celebrity. Baudrillard (1983) has characterized contemporary postmodern culture as celebrating the hyper-real. For advertisers to sell a product to a sufficiently manipulated audience, first they need to get the reader's or viewer's attention. They do this by sensationalizing or "hyping" the product, associating it with the trappings of what it is not: sexuality, existential meaning, and social status. Sometimes, advertisers merely place their product in an alien context so that it is out of place in a field/ground configuration.

Celebrity is used not only to sell products but to reinforce notions of superiority and inferiority in contemporary society. Celebrities are larger-than-life and, as noted in the previous chapter, are used as commercialized role models in popular culture. Different rules apply to their behaviors in much in the same way that the aristocracy operated according to different rules than the peasantry during feudal times. The culture of celebrity filters down to high schools. It is played out in the relationships of high school sports stars and students of substantially lower status. High school sports stars, popularly known as "jocks," are both adulated and despised. They are lauded for their achievements on the field and the approbation they bring their schools and communities. As Bissinger (1990) witnessed, Permian football players were continually given favors by members of the business community, accorded leniency by local police, and exempted from school work while being given passing grades by teachers.

In Columbine, as in Glen Ridge and Permian High Schools, football players, especially the stars, had easy access to sexual favors from any number of willing female peers. For some, this form of social wealth was insufficient. Bissinger (1990) noted that a sophomore girl was desperate to have sex with members of the football team. Team members, regarding her as a wannabe, photographed the encounter and showed pictures around school. The football players at Glen Ridge purposely had anonymous sexual liaisons with girls they hardly knew, preferring "circle jerks," where they would gather around and masturbate to see who would ejaculate first. Their sexual experiences culminated in the rape of a girl who was mentally retarded. They even tried to restage the rape, this time videotaping it.

In Columbine and in Glen Ridge, members of the football team jealously guarded their status as alpha males through intimidation of those of lesser status. They used physical abuse and sexual humiliation by publicly referring to them as "fags," "homos," and "queers." This probably occurred at Permian High School as well, but was not reported on by Bissinger, who was a sports writer and was more interested in the exploits of the football team on the field.

For high school athletes, such adulation is corrupting. It sends them a message that they are better than other people, that they can treat others any way they want without fear of retribution, and that there will always be somebody available to save them from their own worst impulses. To be a high school sports star is a heady experience from which some never recover. For example, several of the stars on the Permian High School football team were recruited by Division IA universities for their football teams. Some of them did not last very long as college players. It was not because of lack of talent but because college football did not provide the community status that high school did (Bissinger 1990).

Yes, there was easy access to sex with good-looking girls, as there was in high school. Yes, they received gifts and under-the-table payments from adoring alumni. However, unlike high school, instead of being kings of the campus, they were segregated, living together, practicing together, and playing together. Although they were celebrated on Saturdays, the real action on campus was elsewhere: in classes, in fraternities and sororities, in the dorms. Athletes, especially football players, were perceived somewhat like other nonacademic university employees. Football players were assumed to be stupid unless proven otherwise. In many ways, they had less status and less fun than the average undergraduate.

Several students from Permian High School who went onto college claimed that they were never happier than when they played high school football (Bissinger 1990). The letdown was so great for some, they quit playing college ball. This happened to a former Columbine High School football team member as well. In the middle of his senior season as starting safety for the Colorado State University Rams, Landon Jones abruptly quit the team, apparently burned out on football (Phifer 2003). Jones was a star player at Colorado State; he was selected twice to the Academic all-Mountain West Conference team. His future seemed bright, yet he quit football.

Football has become incorporated into a hyper-masculinized subculture that emphasizes physical aggression, domination, sexism, and the celebration of victory. One of the most revered coaches in the history of the game, Vince Lombardi, once said, "Winning isn't everything; it's the only thing." Football is one of the most violent sports that can be played. As mentioned in the previous chapter, being an American male requires that one must be able to deal with violence. This is why one of the major aphorisms of football, repeated by Ronald Reagan who played college football, is "Football builds character." More than in any other sport, defeat in football is associated with being physically dominated and humiliated. In other sports, such as basketball, soccer, and especially baseball, winning teams need not be physically dominant, although that may be the case. However, in football, the role of physical dominance in winning is much more important.

Football's close association with militarism has been mentioned by numerous commentators, including George Carlin (2000–2006) in his comedy routine where he compares baseball and football :

> In football the object is for the quarterback, also known as the field general, to be on target with his aerial assault, riddling the defense by hitting his receivers with deadly accuracy in spite of the blitz, even if he has to use the shotgun. With short bullet passes and long bombs, he marches his troops into enemy territory, balancing this aerial assault with a sustained ground attack that punches holes in the forward wall of the enemy's defensive line.
>
> In baseball the object is to go home! And to be safe!

In postmodern America, football has replaced baseball as the national pastime. Its celebration of aggression, territoriality, disciplined violence, and physical domination has been used as a metaphor for America's relationship with the rest of the world. Therefore, football is fraught with symbolic meanings relating to masculinity, militarism, discipline, obedience, patriotism, and glory. If ever there was a secular religious holiday, it would be Super Sunday when the NFC and the AFC play for the Lombardi trophy. While Thanksgiving is celebrated in elementary schools as a re-creation of the amity between the Pilgrims and Native Americans in appreciation of the harvest, by the time an American male reaches high school, the afternoon is taken up watching the Detroit Lions lose another football game.

In American postmodern culture, football has become war by alternative means. On Friday nights in the fall, communities are pitted against each other in a symbolic struggle of domination and subordination with the players on each team wearing the colors of their high school, struggling for victory on the fields of dreams. High school football players are soldiers on the battlefield where the identity of a school and the community are at stake.

The symbolic significance of football in American life strikes its most resonant chord in the high school football team. Quite literally, high school football teams fight over bragging rights. In most places across the United States, communities project their identity on the exploits of their football teams. In southern Jefferson County, the only institution that provides a communal basis of solidarity is the local high school. It achieves its identity primarily through the efforts of its football team. Therefore, resources are allocated to the football team far beyond those allocated for any other nonacademic activity. In some cases, such as Permian High School in Odessa, Texas, the imbalance of allocations is egregious.

In Columbine High School, the culture of hypermasculinity reigned supreme: the administration was dominated by coaches and former coaches; the football team controlled the hallways. This way of being was perceived as legitimate by the vast majority of the student body and the parent population. Columbine was a sports power, and the community took pride in its strong sports program. Ironically, Columbine High School had many other attributes of which parents and community members could be proud: a championship debating team, an award-winning marching band, a superior theater department, sportsmanship trophies, and a student body of which 85 percent went on to higher education. But the physical proof of these accomplishments is not nearly as evident throughout the building as is the evidence of football and other sports.

The heavy emphasis on football has corrupted many high schools. Too many high schools in America are dedicated to the pursuit of football glory instead of providing their students an education that will help them to become informed citizens of a democratic society and provide them with the basics for labor force participation. Too many high schools, such as Columbine High School, are run by former football coaches who obtain their positions through the old boy network. Too many faculty members in high schools are recruited and hired on their abilities to coach team sports and only secondarily on their ability to teach students academic subjects. Too many communities tolerate substandard academic programs as long as the football team has a winning season. In too many high schools, the football team, or a group within the football team, constitutes itself as little more than a community sanctioned gang.

Football is a game played by twenty-two young men on a field 120 yards long. It consists of running, passing, blocking, and tackling. Somewhere along the way, it became identified with masculinity, militarism, community identity, and nationhood. The national cult surrounding football has spun wildly out of control. It has undermined the purposes of many high schools, corrupted adults, and perverted children. At Columbine High School, sadly, it appears to have been instrumental in the death of fourteen students and one teacher. It is pure irony that in the year following the shootings, the Columbine High School Rebel football team won the Colorado State 5A (large schools) championship, and Principal Frank DeAngelis used the victory as a demonstration of how Columbine was recovering from the wounds inflicted by Klebold and Harris. Meanwhile, many students were saying that bullying was back at Columbine (Berkow 2003; Meadows 2003).

If we wish to reduce violence in high schools, we have to deemphasize the power of sports and change the culture of hypermasculinity. Football players cannot be lords of the hallways, bullying their peers with impunity, sometimes encouraged by coaches with adolescent mentalities. However, asking American high schools to deemphasize their football programs is like calling for a socialist revolution: it is not going to happen. As a matter of fact, high school football is receiving increased importance nationwide. Television sports channels routinely cover high school football on a local and national basis. High school football teams are nationally ranked despite the fact that there is no rational basis for doing so. Even worse, several sports companies feature high school all-American teams. In the July 25, 2005, issue of *Sports Illustrated*, Reebok presented its preseason all-American high school football team. High schools had not even begun fall practice, and Reebok predicted stellar performances from these adolescents. I wonder if the executives at Reebok ever considered what influence such expectations might have on a seventeen-year-old.

COLUMBINE RETROSPECTIVE

One of the more disheartening aspects of this study was that several years after the shootings, Columbine High School had, in many ways, returned to the *status quo ante*. In May 2003, I sat down with seven Columbine seniors (six boys and one girl) in a restaurant near the high school. They were finishing lunch, and I identified myself as a sociologist and asked if I could talk with them. It was clear from the outset that they understood that I was an outsider inquiring about the inner workings of the high school. I was assured by these students that everybody respected everybody else, that the administration was doing a wonderful job, and that bullying had disappeared. The following came from my field notes:

> One student said that Columbine HS has a zero tolerance policy for bullying on campus. The students repeated the phrase, "I'm offended; you're suspended." They lauded their teachers. One student said that they were all understanding. The consensus was that that was a bit of an exaggeration, but that it wasn't that far off the mark (Recorded May 9, 2003).

It was difficult to tell whether the students believed what they were telling me or whether they were appeasing yet another academic/reporter/snoop coming into their community with the intent of sullying the reputation of Columbine High School. My field notes indicated that the students were aware that they were painting an impossibly positive picture of the school. However, I could not determine their sincerity.

A couple of days later, I interviewed two parents, one who was an employee of the high school. Both parents told me that bullying had returned to the high school. Several students testified that in the weeks following the shootings, barriers had come down between student groups. There was a genuine feeling of solidarity among Columbine students, and people were sensitive to and caring of each other. However, the summer intervened, and when they returned to school in the fall, the lessons of the previous year had been forgotten. The football and wrestling team members resumed their domination of the halls, and the caste system reconsolidated itself with those at the top unafraid of defending their superior status through physical or symbolic violence, such as that delineated in Chapter 4. Several students claimed that their younger brothers and sisters who were presently attending Columbine High School told them that they either had been witness to or the victim of bullying. Six months later, after the Columbine High Rebel football team won the 2003 state championship, *Newsweek* published a retrospective article (Meadows 2003). *Newsweek* reporters were told by students that bullying had returned to the school.

Columbine High School had reverted back to a system where two contradictory realities existed: the reality from above, supported by Principal DeAngelis, the rest of the administration, and the athletes, affirmed that students respected each other, that homophobia was at a minimum, and that, with the exception of a few bad apples who had graduated years earlier, bullying did not exist at Columbine. The reality from below ran counter to this claim and suggested that privileged students and the administration were in denial; students were routinely harassed and humiliated by the same students who claimed that bullying did not exist. The athletes whom I met in the restaurant, when asked about calling other students "fags," "homos," "queers," or "cock suckers," claimed that, yes, they used those terms, but only in fun among friends and, of course, they were just kidding.

Before discussing the shortcomings of the Jefferson County School District and Columbine High School in their efforts to prevent rampage shootings, I would like to discuss some of the positive steps that they did take. First, they did not lock down the high school. On my first visit to the school in the spring of 2003, an armed police officer greeted me at the door. This was because the school had received a bomb threat that day; it was finals week. On my other visit to the school in the spring of 2004, I saw no armed uniformed officers. It was school policy not to have armed officers on campus. Security had been enhanced in several other ways: increased security cameras monitoring the hallways, closer liaison with the sheriff's office, three on-campus unarmed security officers, and the sharing of information about students who were in trouble with the law. With the exception of a memorial tablet at the entrance of the new library, there was no evidence that horrible shootings had taken place in that school. Although my observations of students in the school were extremely limited, I did see students going about their business in a relaxed and informal manner.

In the wake of the Columbine shootings, students, especially girls (Meadows 2003), upon hearing plans of their peers to attack their school or shoot a fellow student or teacher, were much more likely to break the peer code of silence and inform an adult authority, as in the case of the DeAnza College (California) and New Bedford, Massachusetts, incidents. This new willingness to tell on peers has been referred to as "the Columbine effect" (Newman 2004). In the hall by the gymnasium, Principal DeAngelis maintains a tip box. Any student who is aware of a potentially dangerous activity is encouraged to inform the administration about it anonymously. DeAngelis checks the tip box every morning. He testified about its importance:

> Some of the leads that I get from [the tip box] are just phenomenal. We probably over the past four years have had other students concerned about their friends followed up on it. They have legitimate concerns; their friends were thinking of hurting themselves (Recorded May 12, 2003).

DeAngelis expressed great pride in his counseling program. Two components were described: the Links program and the peer counselors. The Links program was a long-standing program at Columbine High that existed prior to the shootings. High school juniors and seniors were trained over the summer as big brothers or big sisters, each responsible for six or seven incoming freshmen from Ken Caryl Middle School. Their job was to help with the transition between middle school and high school. Each incoming freshman would have an upper class student who would provide them with advice and help as they acclimated themselves to high school. One of the major functions of the program was to protect the incoming freshmen from hazing by older students. The program was very popular, and the students and parents with whom I talked regarded it highly.

Somewhat less successful than the Links program was the peer counseling program. Peer counselors were attached to the guidance department. They were supposedly trained in conflict resolution. However, their major function was to provide advice to students about normal problems of being an adolescent or problems in school. If students seemed to be having serious problems, peer counselors would refer them to an adult counselor. Both DeAngelis and a parent who was familiar with the program indicated that the students who were recruited were excellent. However, their roles were highly circumscribed, and they could not deal with issues related to teachers. Although they may have been trained in conflict resolution techniques, they were apparently used rarely. In my interviews with students, they were vaguely aware that the peer counselors had mediation skills. However, I did not encounter a single student whose conflicts with other students had been mediated by a peer counselor or anybody else, for that matter, with the exception of the disaster described by CL in Chapter 5. Interpersonal conflicts were dealt with primarily by counselors or deans; most students with whom I talked were not particularly satisfied by the outcome of the problem-solving efforts of school officials.

Principal DeAngelis viewed himself as supportive of all extracurricular efforts in the school. He was understandably sensitive about media reports regarding the emphasis on sports at Columbine. He stated to me:

> People say boy, you support football. I say football, time out! You know about football because you're covering the game. But you didn't see me at the art show. Where were you? I mean, you're criticizing me for supporting football, but how come you're not there when I invite you to our art show, or when I invite you to come and see a play? I never see a reporter there, and yet you're criticizing me and you don't see me because you're not there.

> And that's what drives me crazy. The other night, and I'm one of the few principals at the art show, we have all these pieces of art around, I went on the band trip a few years ago, and I said, "As reporters, you're criticizing me for the exact thing you're doing. At least I'm there, but you won't even come and cover some of the things. Show up at a play; show up at a band concert. Why aren't you there, reporting on that? (Recorded April 28, 2004).

DeAngelis is correct when he avers that there was no way that he could have anticipated the assault on Columbine High School. He pointed out that he had absolutely no information about Dylan Klebold's and Eric Harris's arrest and remand to a diversion program, although his ignorance has been disputed by others. Until after the shootings, he was unaware of the existence of Eric's Trenchcoat Mafia web site that contained threats directed at the school. He was not privy to the threats that Eric made on the life of Brooks Brown. Even given the security changes, it would be difficult to anticipate a school assault. Over the past twenty years, there have been approximately thirty rampage shootings in American middle and high schools, an average of about 1 ½ per year. They are extremely rare occurrences. Yet for every rampage shooting, there are literally thousands of verbalized threats and millions of discussions among students in which they fantasize about trashing their schools, as in the case of Melissa Sowder, a disaffected Columbine High School student quoted in Chapter 5 (Cloud 1999).

DeAngelis stated that he was in touch with FBI profilers. The problems associated with profiling of school assaults are manifold: first, it individualizes what is essentially an issue of social relationships. Of the twenty-seven rampage shooters documented by Newman (1999), nineteen were socially marginalized among their peers compared to fifteen who evinced severe psychological disorders and fourteen who were abused or neglected or had other home-related problems. These findings were corroborated by Meloy, Hempel, Mohandie, Shiva, and Gray (2004). Second, and worse, is that profiling ignores the etiology of rampage shootings. Inferring from Newman's list and from media reports, minimally fifteen and perhaps as many as twenty of the rampage shootings were retaliatory. That is, the shooters perceived themselves as punishing peers or teachers who had done them wrong. Third is the problem of labeling. The major problem with profiling is the false positive. Certainly the Columbine shootings were retaliatory violence. For every rampage shooter, however, there are tens of thousands, perhaps hundreds of thousands, of students who fit the profile. It further victimizes students who, for whatever reason, dislike or are alienated from the school and are otherwise socially marginalized. As noted by Gaines (2001), outcast students have enough problems without being labeled as potential rampage shooters. Once a student fits the profile, the perceptions of adult authorities are influenced by the expectations that the student will engage in violence. It becomes a self-fulfilling prophecy, because authorities suspect the student of harboring violent tendencies. Therefore, the behavior of such a student is increasingly surveyed in expectation of uncovering violence.

The greatest problem with profiling is that it ignores entirely the context that generates the retaliation. DeAngelis and the profilers are looking through the wrong end of the telescope. However, the profiler perspective fits in with the dominant view of the problems at Columbine High School; they primarily reside in the persons of a small minority of disaffected students who bear watching. The dominant elites are absolved of any responsibility. Issues related to ostracism, defense of social privilege, homophobia, harassment, humiliation, and violence directed at lesser status peers are defined out of existence. Many people assume that because outcast students dress and behave differently than the majority of students, do not support the sports teams, have different tastes in music, and are otherwise different from the vast majority, they deserve what they get.

As a consequence of the shootings, Columbine now has a threat assessment team. The threat assessment team evaluates the seriousness of threats made to students or the school and crafts a response based upon the perceived seriousness of the threat (O'Toole 2000). Although the threat assessment team is supposed to evaluate the climate of the school, the evidence from this study suggests that adult authorities tend to be unaware of tensions between groups of students until threats are made or violence breaks out. A threat assessment team is a valuable tool for maintaining safety in the school. However, threat assessment is negatively focused and is brought to bear after a threat is made. The major emphasis of a school safety program should be the reduction of threat so that the threat assessment team does not have to meet in the first place. Positive approaches to school safety will be addressed in the next section.

As long as Principal DeAngelis and his supporters, who are manifold, believe that the Columbine shootings were the work of a couple of deranged outcasts (see, e.g., Cullen 2004) and had nothing to do with the internal climate of the high school, the vulnerability of the school to rampage shootings is as high after April 20, 1999, as it was before. In addition to security changes, the school instituted one other innovation of which DeAngelis was particularly proud, called "The American Students' Funding Program," in which students selected thirteen character traits: the Golden Rule [*sic*], compassion, confidence, courage, determination, generosity, integrity, justice, leadership, loyalty, respect, responsibility, and teamwork. Volunteer students are divided into four groups: one that does community outreach, one that tries to improve student life, one that raises funds, and one that selects students who best exemplify each virtue and who are each given a $1,000 scholarship. There is absolutely no evidence to indicate that this program helps to reduce school violence.

Delbert Elliott, Professor of Sociology at the University of Colorado, Director of the Center for the Study and Prevention of Violence, and perhaps America's leading expert on school violence, pointed out that one of the most important contributing factors to school violence is the perception among the students that rules are enforced differentially:

> One of the big issues we know exists [in] schools is [that] kids perceive the policies are not enforced uniformly—some kids get away with everything; some kids can't get away with anything. That undermines a sense of safety in the school. [K]ids start bringing [weapons] to school ... when they don't think the school is going to protect them. [T]hey have to protect themselves (Recorded May 13, 2003).

One of the main complaints of students at Columbine High School was that athletes were subject to a different set of standards than other students. The school was rife with rumors about coaches protecting athletes engaged in even felonious behavior. Students told stories about how they were harassed, embarrassed, or humiliated by athletes in the presence of coaches who either ignored or supported such behaviors. One student admitted that after being beaten up by a jock, he began taking a weapon to school, corroborating the observations made by Professor Elliott.

Ironically, Columbine High School sits within easy commuting distance of the Center for the Study and Prevention of Violence. The Center operates as a clearinghouse for research on violence and reduction of violence in schools. In addition, the Center sponsors and conducts research on school safety. The Center is a national resource of information about school violence and about programs that can ameliorate it. Yet, no administrator from the Jefferson County School District has set foot in the Center. When I interviewed the superintendent of the school district, as soon as I asked her a question about violence prevention, she told me that the interview was terminated and escorted me from the premises. Professor Elliott had this to say about Columbine's antiviolence initiatives:

> To my knowledge, Columbine is not implementing any proven programs. ... At this point in time all I know is that ... they have not

> implemented any programs which have high credibility with respect to effectiveness (Recorded May 13, 2003).

PEACE EDUCATION

American high schools are both more and less violent than the public perceives. It is true that schools are safer than the streets and home (Brooks, Schiraldi, and Ziedenberg 1999). A child is less liable to be injured or killed in the school than practically any other place. Yet, schools, especially middle and high schools, are venues in which there is a great deal of hidden physical and psychological violence (Garbarino and deLara 2002; Greene 1999; Pankratz 2000). Although nearly all violence is low level with only a minuscule portion of it being observed or brought to the attention of authorities, it can be psychologically deleterious to the victims, dehumanizing to the perpetrators, corrosive for the social climate of the school, and can lead to an escalation of hostilities, usually fistfights. DeAngelis, the principal of Columbine High School told me, "I've been here twenty-five years, and I'll bet you that I can count on the fingers of two hands the number of fights we've had in school" (Recorded April 28, 2004). I have no reason to doubt his testimony. However, Columbine High School, like other high schools, has had substantial amounts of low-level violence. Klebold and Harris were never involved in a fight in their high school. Yet every male Columbine High School student I interviewed could recall at least one incident where he was physically intimidated by another student or had a physical confrontation with another student on campus, including the trading of punches. Every female student could relate at least one incident where she was humiliated, verbally abused, or witnessed physical violence on campus. I do not think that Columbine is any more or less violent than the average American high school. As I stated earlier, such violence is normative. It is so common that students do not even recognize it as violence until it is pointed out. Rampage killings are the extreme tip of the adolescent violence pyramid.

So how can violence be reduced in schools? First, the thesis of this study is that the prime source of conflict at Columbine High School, as it is among nearly all high schools in America, is the distribution of power within the school. The testimony of the students indicated that the vast majority of the violence was perpetrated downward from higher status to lower status students. Even outcast students like Klebold and Harris found students of lower status than themselves to bully. Second, the distribution of power and its exercise to protect and reinforce already existing social barriers generate two diametrically opposing perspectives: the assumption on the part of high status students of their inherent superiority over the rest of the student body, and the perception by the rest of the student body of a lack of justice. Third, the faculty and the administration of the school, because of a lack of a systematic plan and an inherent bias in favor of high status students, reinforce the arbitrariness of power relationships among the students, leading victimized students to feel that they have no alternative other than to endure their punishment. For them, school is a place where absurdity reigns, predators are rewarded, and victims are punished. Even if they play by the rules, there is no guarantee that they will be better off than if they do not. Several Columbine students told me stories about going to the authorities to complain about being victimized in which the best outcome was that nothing happened. Students related stories about how their complaints were mishandled, resulting in greater ostracism and targeting by bullies. Students also indicated that retaliatory violence was treated the same as or harsher than the original violent act that lead to retaliation. This problem is not unique to Columbine High School; Garbarino and deLara (2002) found similar stories when talking to students about bullying. School authorities tended to be indifferent or incompetent when dealing with interpersonal violence among students. All students knew that by making their complaints to authorities, they were taking a huge risk and that the outcome was anything but assured.

The most serious problem in attempting to reduce violence in the school like Columbine is misdiagnosis. To this day, Principal DeAngelis has no viable explanation of the rampage shootings in his high school. He essentially accepted the Manichean explanation of the evangelical community that Klebold and Harris were instruments of Satan, committing evil against the good people of Columbine High School. As late as spring 2004, he insisted that bullying had nothing to do with the rampage shooting at Columbine, but rather, blamed the incident on the characteristics of the shooters. Most rampage shootings, including the ones at Columbine, have been retaliatory (Magee and DeBernardo 1999). As long as DeAngelis denies that the attack in his school was retaliatory, he will be unable to develop a viable antiviolence program. Because rampage shootings are such a rare occurrence, it is likely that he will never see a recurrence at Columbine. However, it is also true that once a norm is broken, it is likely to be broken again.[2] This means that there is a higher probability of a similar, copycat style shooting occurring in the halls of Columbine than elsewhere. Therefore, it is in the interests of residents of southern Jefferson County, Colorado, that antiviolence programs should be seriously considered.

If educators and the Jefferson County school system understand and accept that the shootings at Columbine were retaliatory, then they can design antiviolence programs to reduce the probability of another recurrence. However, educational inertia, lack of public support, and cognitive indolence militate against the institution of positive solutions. The good people of southern Jefferson County, for the most part, have refused to understand that although Klebold and Harris were victimizers, they were themselves victims of long-term and intense bullying. It is easy to see the dynamic that underlies this perspective. It is much easier to blame others than to assume any sort of collective responsibility. Members of the football and wrestling teams who control the halls of Columbine share responsibility; parents and community members who revile and loathe nonconforming students share responsibility; religious leaders who preach the superiority of their own creed rather than the common suffering of humanity share responsibility; coaches and administrators who ignored, tolerated, or actively encouraged bullying by the athletes share responsibility.

For an antiviolence program to work, it must be systemic, and it must change the internal social climate of the school. By systemic, I mean that it must extend below the high school to elementary and middle grades. Changing the climate of the school means altering the way in which administrators, teachers, and students interact in a school setting. The research is clear that top-down, zero-tolerance programs do not work and can produce counterproductive results (National Association of Attorneys General 2000; Skiba and Peterson 1999).

Researchers have demonstrated that bullying almost exclusively occurs when there are no adult witnesses (Garbarino and deLara 2002; Skiba and Peterson 1999). At Columbine, this was certainly true. Students were physically assaulted in the halls, in locker rooms, and during unsupervised play in the gym. Verbal harassment could occur anywhere. Therefore, any worthwhile antiviolence program must change the way in which students interact and change the climate of the school. This means that the school needs a critical mass of students involved in peacekeeping activities.

I also think that an effective antiviolence program must reach beyond the schools to the local community. A large portion of Columbine students belong to a variety of youth groups, many of which are associated with local churches. Because of the strength of religious institutions in southern Jefferson County, they have an important role to play in the reduction of youth violence. It is no leap from the worship of Jesus Christ as the savior of humanity, the Prince of Peace, to the institution of nonviolent conflict resolution programs or character education programs that emphasize tolerance, empathy, and compassion. As a matter of fact, the Society of Friends, or Quakers, has been involved in peace education and conflict resolution for many years. They have established institutes, programs, and workshops on peaceful conflict resolution. In addition, they have produced numerous books, pamphlets, curricula, and resource guides. Conflict resolution programs need not be limited to a church youth groups; they can also be employed by secular or quasi-religious youth organizations such as scouting organizations and YM/WCAs. For example, the Boy Scouts of America should have a conflict resolution merit badge that would be required for the rank of Eagle Scout. Scouting organizations heavily emphasize citizenship and character development. It is surprising then that one can get a merit badge in riflery but not in conflict resolution.

A number of antiviolence programs have been implemented and evaluated. For my purposes, they can be classified into three major categories: (a) those for at-risk students, such as bullies, aggressive children, and children with emotional difficulties (Gregg 1998); (b) curricular initiatives, such as restructuring learning in the classroom (Aronson 2000), character education, violence awareness and avoidance, and the teaching of negotiation skills (Samples and Aber 1998); and (c) those that are directed at the resolution of interpersonal and intergroup conflicts (Wilson-Brewer, Cohen, O'Donnell, and Goodman 1991). The first category involves programs that may incorporate social skills training, guidance, psychotherapy, and family involvement. Although certainly important in the reduction of violence by targeting perpetrators, they are beyond the scope of this study because they are individualized.

The Jefferson County School District has treated the Columbine shootings as an aberration, which they were. However, the problem is that the violence that perpetrated the shootings is so common that it has become routine. Law enforcement solutions described to me by Principal DeAngelis are only a small part of the antiviolence picture. The response of Jefferson County has been reactive with few in the way of proactive programs, at least at the high school level. Numerous antiviolence programs exist that have been evaluated and have shown positive results in the reduction of interpersonal violence, teaching children nonviolent problem solutions, reduction of bullying, and changing school climates so that they encourage harmonious interpersonal relations (Aber, Jones, Brown, Chaudry, and Samples 1998; Cockrane and Saroyan 1997; DeJong 1993; Olweus, Limber, and Mahalic 1999; Samples and Aber 1998; Wilson-Brewer, Cohen, O'Donnell, and Goodman 1991). In addition, there are curricular interventions that reduce interpersonal competition and emphasize cooperation, such as the jigsaw method of organizing classroom learning (Aronson and Patnoe 1997).

Several comprehensive violence reduction programs have been developed and show promise. Programs developed by the Child Development Project, the Office of Juvenile Justice and Delinquency Prevention of the U.S. Department of Justice, Big Brothers/Big Sisters, and The Peace Foundation, have been directed at building caring communities, cooperative education, respect for others, understanding of the law, teaching social skills and prosocial behavior, and anger management (Gregg 1998). Project Schools Teaching Options for Peace (STOP)/Safe Harbor is a multifaceted program that uses peer mediation, teacher training, parent education, and an antiviolence curriculum that has been shown to reduce feelings of helplessness related to violence and promote peaceful ways of resolving conflicts (National Institute of Justice 1995).

Perhaps one of the most successful antiviolence programs is the Bully Prevention Program, created by Olweus and Associates (Olweus 1993; Olweus et al. 1999) in response to a growing awareness of widespread bullying in Norway. The program was implemented countrywide and focused on reducing opportunities for bullying behavior and social rewards for engaging in bullying by creating a normative environment in the school that discourages bullying. The program begins by establishing a committee that plans to change school conditions and monitors those changes. Bullies and their parents are targeted for intervention. Firm limits are established for unacceptable behavior, and adults act as authority figures and positive role models. Students are actively involved in the program through a curriculum that uses role-playing, modeling, and classroom discussion to teach children how to cope with bullying. They become the first line of defense in generating an environment that does not tolerate bullying. Herein lies the key to the reduction of violence. Students must be actively involved in the solutions to violence; they must learn to practice nonviolent conflict resolution actively.

Most antiviolence programs, including those enumerated above, focus on bullying in the elementary and middle schools. This is as it should be because students should be taught how to deal with violence at a young age, and antiviolence programs should be taught from kindergarten through twelfth grade. However, beginning in middle school, a qualitative change occurs in the nature of bullying and interpersonal violence as the peer group assumes ascendancy as a reference group among young adolescents (Harris 1999). Bullying and harassment become less the aberrant behavior of an individual child and more institutionalized and collectivized as a method by which peers subcultures communicate dominance and establish hierarchies.

Columbine High School is an example of the meshing of bullying and peer group hierarchies. Everyone in Columbine High School was very much aware that a particular student was a bully and could turn on anybody at any time. Even though he was sanctioned by the administration for some of his misdeeds, he was protected by coaches. Because of his physical virtuosity and athletic prowess, he was a member of the leading crowd. He and his coterie of friends terrorized the rest of the student body with relative impunity. His egregious behavior was tolerated by his high-status peers as long as he was targeting "loser students" and not focusing on his status-equals. Additionally, his bullying of lower-status students helped to reinforce the peer social structure and emphasize the dominance of the student elite through physical intimidation. Within the social structure of Columbine High School, the tepid attempts of the administration to control his behavior could not match the social rewards he received from his peers for his bullying. He graduated from Columbine in 1998. In the subsequent year, bullying did not abate because it was part of the structured social relations within the school. Outcast students such as Klebold and Harris adhered to the pattern by harassing students of even lesser status than they, such as students with disabilities.

Although researchers in bullying have acknowledged some of the qualitative differences in adolescence, their solutions have not really taken these differences into consideration (Aronson 2000; Garbarino and deLara 2002; Samples and Aber 1998). The special quality of adolescent bullying must be addressed in any antiviolence program or else it is doomed to failure or only marginal success. Any program to be successful must (a) change the climate of the school, (b) alter the relationships among peer subcultures, and (c) cede adult power to the students so that they can positively enforce antiviolence norms.

This latter aspect, I believe, is one of the most serious stumbling blocks to the implementation of a successful antiviolence program among adolescents. It is a necessary component of conflict mediation among peers. In Colorado in general and in Columbine in particular, discussions with educational administrators and law enforcement personnel revealed a lack of awareness and openness to conflict mediation programs using peer mediators. My interview with the superintendent of the Jefferson County Schools was abruptly terminated by her when I asked a question about what the district was doing to reduce violence in the schools. Principal DeAngelis, whom I thought would be interested in successful antiviolence programs, was unresponsive when my wife, a seasoned conflict mediator in the New York City Schools, who had established the conflict resolution program in a high school that was approximately the same size as Columbine, told him of the successes of the program in her own school.

The program has two components: conflict negotiation and conflict resolution. The conflict negotiation portion is an antiviolence curriculum that is designed to teach students negotiation skills so that they can avoid interpersonal conflicts. It makes use of proper speech and the logic used by a trained individual to turn potential conflict into peacemaking. It uses compromise and movement to a win/win situation.

The second component is conflict mediation, which involves learning the steps of nonviolent conflict resolution, interviewing, brainstorming, role-play, and modeling (DeJong 1993). The skills that are emphasized are active listening, assertiveness, expression of feelings, empathy, negotiation, and the airing of positions. These skills are taught in many antiviolence programs. They are usually instituted in the second year of the program, primarily because teachers (or administrators) have to be trained in the program. In 1993, in New York City, each high school had one teacher trained in conflict mediation, who would establish and run the program, and one teacher trained in conflict negotiation to teach students violence prevention. The conflict mediation coordinator was responsible for recruiting and training student (peer) mediators, establishing a room or site where mediations could be conducted confidentially, supervising and documenting mediations, and evaluating mediators. All students in the school must know that there is a place where they can talk out their differences in strict confidence.

Although conflict negotiation is important in an antiviolence program, the conflict mediation component offers the best possibility to confront already emerging conflict and change the climate of the school. With a critical mass of peer mediators who take their jobs seriously—and nearly all of them do—the school has a presence of students who are committed to antiviolence in the halls at all times. If they see fights brewing, they can intervene and offer mediation. Given the alternative of suspension, many students will opt for mediation. If students have disputes or feel that they are being victimized, they can go to the mediation coordinator and ask that the problem be mediated. In most New York City high schools, when students were suspended for fighting, they were required to have their dispute mediated upon entry back into the school.

Conflict mediation programs have been evaluated with promising results (Cassels 1993; DeJong 1993; Gregg 1998; Hawkins, Farrington, and Catalano 1998). The main problems with conflict resolution programs have been half-hearted support by administration and lack of willingness on the part of teachers to fully implement them (Bickmore 1999). One of the major problems of implementing conflict resolution programs is that it requires school officials to adhere to democratic values, empower students to be active participants in the solution, and provide them the resources for peaceful resolution of interpersonal conflicts. It means trusting students and ceding to them a certain amount of autonomy and control. In this writer's observations of over forty years in education, most educators are hesitant to cede power to students, even for issues that are beyond the classroom.

Even with teachers patrolling the halls, the locker rooms, and the playfields, if the culture of school is conducive to violence, violence will occur. Therefore, if the school wishes to reduce the level of interpersonal violence among its students, it must empower the students to solve their own problems. Obviously, students cannot be used to police other students. They do not have legitimate authority. However, with an effective conflict mediation program, student mediators can help their peers to resolve potentially violent conflicts in a peaceful manner.

I will discuss the program developed by the International Center for Cooperation and Conflict Resolution at Teachers College Columbia University because I have seen it in operation firsthand at a New York City high school. In this particular instance, my wife, Debra Larkin, was trained as a conflict mediator and ran a successful program for over ten years at Murry Bergtraum High School, in lower Manhattan, New York City. Over that period, the student population was 99 percent minority, with varying mixtures of Asian, black (Caribbean, African, and African American) and Hispanic (Puerto Rican, Dominican, and Central and South American) students. As the coordinator, Ms. Larkin promoted the program, recruited and trained students, and supervised and documented all mediations. In an eight-period day, mediations were conducted during six of those periods. The last two periods were used to train mediators and teach them English writing and literature in which the major theme was conflict and its resolution. The school allocated a room for conflict mediation, which was Ms. Larkin's classroom. Students knew that if they had a conflict they could go to the mediation room and schedule mediation.

The conflict mediation program was supported by the principal in the school and the high school superintendent, especially in the early days of its operation. The program was instituted in 1992 at the high school level in reaction to a gunfight that broke out in Thomas Jefferson High School and resulted in the death of a student and the wounding of a bystander and a teacher who tried to intervene (McFadden 1991). Mayor David Dinkins instituted a Safe Schools, Safe Streets initiative that funded conflict resolution programs in all New York City high schools (McKinley 1992). The central Board of Education established an Office of Conflict Resolution that coordinated the program in the five boroughs of the city. The board passed a resolution that required that all students who had been suspended for fighting had to go through conflict mediation before they could reenter their school. Each borough had a coordinator for conflict resolution programs who oversaw the operation of the programs in each high school, arranged conferences and training, and linked the program with other advocates of nonviolent conflict resolution, such as the United Nations and the Southern

Christian Leadership Conference. The New York City program was linked to national and international efforts at peaceful conflict resolution.

As the program grew over the years, the Murry Bergtraum High School maintained a critical mass of 100–150 peer mediators in a school of 2800 students. Mediations focused on pairs of students who had a dispute and could include as many as twenty or twenty-five or more students who were involved in the conflict. If all persons involved in the conflict were not included in the mediation, it could not be adequately resolved. In the vast majority of cases, upwards of 95 percent, the conflicts were resolved peacefully. In a small number of cases, disputants needed more than one mediation to resolve their conflict. Approximately two or three mediations per year failed to achieve a satisfactory conclusion. In this particular school, approximately 150–175 mediations were conducted each year. Although school district policy mandated that the program was not to deal with gang violence, it was clear that in some cases, local gangs used the mediation process to resolve differences and misunderstandings among opposing gangs.

Students for the program were recruited through promotions in the school by making presentations at school assemblies, distributing flyers, making announcements over the public address system, and gathering staff recommendations. Prospective mediators were interviewed by Ms. Larkin and peer mediators to assess their qualifications, fitness, and motivation. After the initial semester, student mediators began recommending their friends. In addition, Ms. Larkin discovered that some of the best potential mediators were students whose conflicts had been brought to the mediation room. Some of the most troublesome students in the school, upon being mediated, expressed desires to become mediators themselves. Not surprisingly, some of those students discovered hidden talents as mediators and became advocates for mediation and peaceful resolution of conflicts.

The vast majority of peer mediators took the program very seriously. Several students told Ms. Larkin that without the peer mediation program they would have been dead. They learned how to negotiate solutions to problems and how to deescalate and defuse confrontations. In addition, participation in the conflict mediation program gave mediators status among their peers. They were helpful, positive, and resourceful, and they helped people avoid violence and personal injury.

Peer mediators staged mock mediations in assemblies so that the other students understood the process. A group of students established a rap group and created raps that extolled nonviolent conflict resolution. In addition, the mediators visited elementary and other high schools to conduct mock mediations or teach conflict mediation/negotiation skills. They met with other students to advocate for the program. Each year, anywhere from twenty-five to forty mediators would take a trip to the state capital to advocate for gun control legislation under the sponsorship of the New Yorkers against Gun Violence. Many of those students had seen the destructiveness of gun violence firsthand and worked to rid their environment of guns.

The program generated a critical mass of peace advocates in the student population. This critical mass of students altered the climate of the school, making it less violent. Students in the school felt safer because of the presence of the conflict mediation program. Confrontations were less likely to escalate to violence because of the necessity of one or more of those in conflict to protect their image or their egos. The mediation process allowed students to deescalate the conflict in a nonthreatening way. When mediators saw fights brewing, they brought the disputants to the conflict resolution room or informed the mediation teacher of the pending conflict so that she could intervene and offer mediation before the fight erupted.

Increasingly, programs are being offered at higher education institutions in conflict resolution. Stokes (2002) documented approximately fifty undergraduate and thirty graduate programs in the United States and Canada that offer degrees or certification in conflict mediation. Therefore, conflict resolution is not only a voluntary activity but also offers students a vocational option that they may not have considered. Several students from the Murry Burgtraum program have pursued careers in conflict resolution as either undergraduates or graduate students. Many law schools now offer conflict resolution programs, and many corporations employ conflict mediators as an alternative to litigation (Riskin 1993).

Although the above example is from an inner-city school that has few white students, the research has indicated that conflict mediation can be used successfully in rural, suburban, and urban schools for literally all students from prekindergarten to graduate school, staff members, for adults in the workplace, and for family conflicts. However, adaptations must be made for suburban high schools (Cassels 1993; DeJong 1993; Gregg 1998; Hawkins et al. 1998; Samples and Aber 1998). All of the extant research on suburban high schools indicate that the dominant adolescent peer group is organized around athletics and is almost universally identified as jocks and their female counterparts (Bissinger 1990; Coleman 1961; Eckert 1989; Gordon 1957; Larkin 1979; Wooden and Blazak 2001). As with any subculture, a great variety of orientations, attitudes, and behaviors exist within it. If the peer mediation program is to work in such schools, it must have significant representation among peer mediators from male and female members of the leading crowd, especially members of the football team. Without such representation, the program will lack legitimacy. Any student who wishes to be a quarterback of the football team or captain of any interscholastic sports team should be required to have a minimum of one semester's experience in conflict resolution training. Not only will this provide them with important leadership skills, it would link nonviolent conflict resolution with sports participation.

As important, the peer mediators must be representative of the school population. With any school, the person in charge of mediation must be sensitive to and aware of all of the various affinity groups, racial and ethnic categories, and subcultures within the school and make sure that each one is represented among the peer mediators. It is especially important that students will be included who are members of subcultures that are antischool. This means that in suburban high schools, peer mediators should include goths, stoners, skateboarders, bikers, and skinheads, if they can be recruited.

PEACE

This book was written because of a destructive act that killed fifteen Americans. It is postmortem because we are looking backward to examine why it occurred. In this chapter, we also look forward to see what can be done to prevent such attacks from happening in the future.

There is a substantial research base that provides important clues about how to reduce violence (Elliott, Hamburg, and Williams 1998; Mihalic, Fagan, Irwin, Ballard, and Elliott 2002), but sadly there is little political will to implement positive peace education policies in high schools. If this inquiry into the shootings at Columbine High School can be generalized, and I think it can, a large portion of incivility, harassment, and physical intimidation that occurs in the halls of the local high school is perpetrated by athletic elites in the defense of their own social privilege. The vast majority of rampage shootings, including those at Columbine, are retaliatory violence by the victims of such physical and psychological violence. If educators wish to stop the cycle of violence in American high schools, they have to begin at the top of the student status structure and provide students with the political, human, and physical resources to participate actively in the solution to the problem of violence.

Because a substantial proportion of high school violence is perpetrated by student elites associated with sports, the problem has been kept invisible. One of the major purposes of this study is to make the violence that is perpetrated by student elites visible. The first step in solving a problem is an accurate diagnosis.

For too long, the issue of rampage shootings in middle and high schools across this country has focused on individual pathologies to the detriment of contextual factors. In many cases, including Columbine, rampage shooters have demonstrated signs of personal pathology. It is entirely true that Dylan Klebold was depressed and Eric Harris had a serious personality disorder, most likely bipolar disorder. Yet it was not the disorders that caused the rampage shootings. Rather, it was the interplay between psychological factors and the social context that gave shape to their behavior.

Sadly, America prides itself on its violence. It has a whole mythology of gunfighters that is especially predominant in the South and West where, not surprisingly, most middle and high school rampage shootings occur. America adheres to the cult of masculinity in which personal vulnerability is masked by violence. Within that cult, men are encouraged to avenge insults with physical and psychological violence in order to maintain their self-respect and image. Perhaps even more viciously, males are encouraged to demonstrate their dominance over others through violence and intimidation. This is clearly the modus operandi of the athletic elites. They defend their dominance and hegemony over the peer structure by erecting invisible walls between themselves and lesser males through intimidation, harassment, and violence. Once those boundaries are established, woes betide those who violate them. Wannabes, hangers on, and those who reject the status system in its entirety, usually at the bottom of the peer structure, are targeted because they either transgress the boundaries or call them into question.

Although not as physically violent, a parallel process occurs among adolescent women. The violence, although rarely physical, is every bit as vicious and psychologically debilitating to the victims. Instead of physical combat, barriers are maintained through gossip and shunning. For males, the criteria for elite membership are personal achievement, especially in sports, personal attractiveness, and social skills. For females, the criteria are family social status, physical attractiveness, and the status of males who will date them. It is still a sexist world, and female status is still attached to the status of the males they attract.

Adolescence is probably the time of life during which humans are involved in more competitive struggles than at any other time. In addition to the struggle for peer status, there are the associated struggles around sexuality and one's future. The lives of high school students are being sorted out. Who gets the awards, accolades, and recognition? Who gets the hot girl or guy? Who gets into the elite universities, and who ends up at the local community college? Who has a future, and who does not? All of these struggles pit teenagers against one another. One can be a winner in one arena and a loser in others. One can be a football star, a loser with women, and a poor student. One of the enduring themes of American culture is the revenge of the nerd, the central themes of such diverse offerings as the movies "Heathers," "The Revenge of the Nerds," "Broadcast News," "Election," and the Bruce Springsteen song, "Glory Days."

Historically, American culture has vacillated between dreams of domination and visions of utopias. The nineteenth-century vision of manifest destiny, realized, if necessary, through genocide, has expanded to fantasies of world domination. Americans have attempted to build intentional utopian communities from the nineteenth-century Mormons and Oneida communities to the communal movement of the late 1960s through the early 1970s. There is a strain in American culture that yearns for connectedness and living in harmony with ourselves, our community, our neighbors, and our environment. We cannot possibly achieve such harmony without acknowledgment and appreciation of human diversity. It is, therefore, necessary for us, as Americans, to develop human technologies that help us to live in harmony with others and resolve disputes and conflicts peacefully. There is no way we can do this without being able to put ourselves in the place of others. Without empathy, there can be no peace, only shortsighted self-interest. Schools are social institutions that, as their major function, teach people from different backgrounds to get along together. It is time that schools took this function seriously.

Some of us suffer for the sins of others. Sometimes innocents are slaughtered and the guilty die peacefully in their sleep blissfully unaware of the pain and suffering they have caused others. Surely this was the case with the following innocents:

Cassie Bernall
Steven Curnow
Corey DePooter
Kelly Fleming
Matthew Kechter
Daniel Mauser
Daniel Rohrbough
Rachel Scott
Isaiah Sholes
John Tomlin
Laura Townsend
Kyle Velasquez
William "Dave" Sanders

Although they have been memorialized, to this day, there has been no concerted effort to build a viable antiviolence program at Columbine High School worthy of their memory. As the famous antiwar song, "Where Have All the Flowers Gone," asks, "When will they ever learn?"

METHODOLOGICAL APPENDIX

The research reported herein was conducted without financial support from any institution. It was conducted as an act of love. In the spring of 2000, my wife, in anticipation of her own retirement as a New York City English teacher and conflict mediator, asked me what I would like to do in the near future. I responded by saying, "I want to study the Columbine shootings." Because I had no academic position, I realized that I had only my own resources at hand. However, those resources were considerable: an abiding interest in adolescent social development, my skills as a research sociologist, and an understanding and supportive wife and family.

However, I could conduct a study without academic credentials. I approached David Brotherton at the John Jay College of Criminal Justice of the City University of New York and asked him if the sociology department would sponsor me with an unpaid research position that would allow me legitimacy as a university-based academic researcher. The department granted me the position and provided me with department letterhead stationery. The department has been very supportive of my research efforts, with various members reading over drafts of my work, inviting me to colloquia, and asking me to make presentations in faculty members' classes. Department members in addition to David Brotherton who have been supportive of my work are Michael Flynn, Maria Volpe, and Barry Spunt.

I began reading media accounts of the Columbine shootings and ordering books that had been written about them in preparation for developing a research grant proposal. Because of the recency of the shootings, explorations of the relevant databases, including ERIC, Psychinfo, and SocSciSearch revealed no original research on the shootings. I was surprised to find that by the end of 2001, the only books published on the Columbine shootings were from the evangelical community, interpreting the shootings in distinctly Manichean terms of the struggle between good and evil, with Harris and Klebold cast in the role of Satan and the evangelical community as the defenders of virtue. In addition, there were numerous hagiographies of two of the victims, Rachel Scott and Cassie Bernall.

Perhaps even more disturbing was the subsequent publication of numerous books and magazine articles that had used media reports about the Columbine shootings as a jumping off point for their own authors' agendas. Two such examples blamed the Columbine shootings on lax and indulgent parenting within the middle class with absolutely no knowledge of how Dylan Klebold and Eric Harris were raised (Coleman 2002; Shaw 2003).

In 2000, after collaborating with my colleagues at John Jay, I submitted a research proposal to the Spencer Foundation, which was not funded. About that time, the economic bubble of the 1990s collapsed, and foundations found themselves having to cut back grant monies severely. At that point, I figured I was wasting my time attempting to obtain research funds and began to execute a research plan based on a shoestring budget. From a variety of sources, I began compiling a list of possible interviewees in anticipation of a data collection trip to southern Jefferson County in the fall of 2000. Prospective interviewees were primarily Columbine High School students but also included reporters, investigators from the attorney general's office, scholars and colleagues in the Denver area, and police investigators. In addition, I included educators, including Frank DeAngelis, principal of Columbine High School, and Jane Harman, the Superintendent of Jefferson County School District.

The responses from those most closely involved with the shootings were resoundingly negative. Prior to calling the high school, I wrote the principal a letter introducing myself and the nature of my study; I informed him that I would be calling within a few days. When I called the high school, I was referred to the public information officer who scolded me and told me that the school community was still in the process of healing and that my investigation would interfere with that process. He inferred that my investigation was part of a ghoulish fascination with the shootings, and he informed me that the high school was constantly being visited by tour buses filled with picture-snapping curiosity seekers.

My attempts to interview the students also met a dead end. Columbine residents who were closely associated with the shootings had learned from their negative experiences to screen their calls. Nearly all telephone inquiries ended with my leaving messages on answering machines, messages that were never returned. In some cases, parents would answer the phone and would refuse access to their children. A common response was, "We've had enough of that Columbine crap," and they would hang up.

Nevertheless, my wife Debbie, and I traveled to Denver in November 2000 for our first data collection trip. We interviewed several reporters for the *Rocky Mountain News*, an investigator at the state Attorney General's Office, a representative of the Center for the Study and Prevention of Violence in Boulder, and drove around the Columbine High School catchment area in southern Jefferson County. We also scheduled an interview with Kate Battan, the lead investigator for the Jefferson County Sheriff's Department. She canceled, citing overwhelming job responsibilities. Although Battan seemed sympathetic to the investigation and almost always returned my calls, I was never able to interview her for the study.

From the Attorney General's office and at the Center for the Study and Prevention of Violence, we received valuable information on the investigations relating to high school violence. We were given the recent report on bullying from the assistant attorney general and were provided several monographs on school violence produced by the Center for the Study of Violence and Violence Prevention.

The data collected from the trip provided two benefits: first, we were able to talk to people who had a close-up view of the shootings and their aftermath; second, we were provided with contacts inside the Columbine community from cooperative reporters. One of the major sources of information about the Columbine shootings was the Brown family. Their son, Brooks, was a close friend of Dylan Klebold and had an on-again-off-again relationship with Eric Harris. The Brown family was victimized by the Columbine shootings on several levels. First, because Brooks was linked to Harris and Klebold, he was suspected of having participated in the shootings or having foreknowledge of them. Second, because Brooks was close to both shooters and victims, he was in the unenviable position of mourning for both his friends who were killers and his friends who were their victims. Because of his position as an outcast student, he had a visceral understanding of why Klebold and Harris perpetrated their horrendous act. This put him at odds with the vast majority of Columbine residents who viewed the shootings as causeless or as pure evil, further isolating him. Third, the Brown family had repeatedly attempted to alert the Jefferson County Sheriff's Department of the danger of Eric Harris's actions prior to the shootings. When the Brown family went to the media to complain about the in action of the Sheriff's Department, the sheriff engaged in a personal vendetta against the Brown family. He tried to frame Brooks Brown as a coconspirator in the shootings. The sheriff also engaged in personal attacks against the Brown family, calling them liars. It was only later that the ignored complaints were discovered in the department's files.

Because of the closeness of Brooks to Eric and Dylan and because of the viciousness of the attacks on their family, the Browns became deeply involved in the shooting investigations. They served as witnesses and as information sources. Brooks (Brown and Merritt 2002) wrote *No Easy Answers* with Rob Merritt, a book about his experiences, which was published in 2002. I attempted to contact him through his publisher. I was given his email address but never received a response to my inquiries. I was provided the Brown's phone number by a reporter. I called the number and left a message explaining to the Browns the purpose of my investigation. I received a call back from Judy Brown, who gave me a great deal of inside information and names to contact for possible interviews. She also gave me Brooks's cell phone number. Any time a significant event occurred relative to the shootings, such as the release of the Sheriff's Department's report, I would receive a call from Judy that would last minimally an hour during which she would update me on what was happening and provide me with leads to follow up.

In the meantime, I had to devise a strategy to get access to Columbine students. I used several strategies. By that time, the 11,000-page report on the shootings had been released by the Jefferson County Sheriff's Department. I began to scour the report for names of students who had been interviewed by the police. I was able to identify several members of the Trenchcoat Mafia whom I subsequently interviewed. In addition, a colleague at John Jay indicated that he had a student who was a former Columbine High School student who was in attendance on the day of the shootings. She agreed to an interview and became a resource for other interviewees. I began searching the Internet for names of and contact information for former Columbine High School students. By far the best source was alumni.com, which lists high school graduates from high schools across United States. I tapped into the Columbine High School alumni list and was able to recruit six or seven students who had listed their names on the web site and who were in attendance on April 20, 1999. I interviewed them by telephone and asked if they could recommend any other students for interviews. I was unable to recruit any other students from this pool. Interviews were about an hour long and covered their experiences as Columbine High School students: what their typical days were like; whether they had experienced or observed any harassment; if so, a description of it. I asked them about the social structure of the high school and where they fit into it. What was their knowledge of the Trenchcoat Mafia, Eric Harris, and Dylan Klebold? What were their experiences on the day of the shootings? None of the students from this source knew Klebold or Harris personally, but all could identify the Trenchcoat Mafia. All were in the school the morning of the shootings, and none was injured. They all knew at least one of the victims.

On my second visit to southern Jefferson County in May, 2003, I visited the Brown's house, interviewed Judy Brown and a friend of hers who was a district employee. The Browns had an entire room filled with records and documentation of investigations of the shootings. I also met Brooks for the first time, who introduced me to some of his friends, whom I was able to interview. In one case, a female friend of his arranged an interview with her and three of her friends who had returned to the area from college. All four had been in school on the day of the shootings.

During this data collection trip, I interviewed Principal Frank DeAngelis for the first time. I also visited the West Bowles Community Church, where Cassie Bernall and her family were parishioners. I attended services and interviewed the youth minister and six members of the youth congregation, most of whom attended Columbine High School. It was during this trip that I began collaring students on the run for interviews. I was also able to interview football team members. I attempted to interview the new superintendent of schools for Jefferson County, Dr. Cindy Stevenson, and was thrown out of her office when I made inquiries about antiviolence programs instituted by the school district. During this trip, I made a second visit to the Center for the Study and Prevention of Violence to interview Del Elliott, the center's director, a world-renowned expert on high school violence and violence prevention.

During this time, I had been writing the book. In addition to the interviews, I used census and economic data to develop a demographic profile of the area served by Columbine High School. Interviews were transcribed, read over, and were reorganized by topics. I read newspaper and journal articles and read about rampage shootings as they occurred. All books on the topic were purchased and read. I conducted periodic searches of academic databases to see if other studies have been conducted. I also contacted other scholars working in related areas. I viewed television shows and movies related to Columbine, adolescent violence, and bullying. Friends and colleagues alerted me to materials that they had seen. I received envelopes with clippings about Columbine and related issues from my friend and colleague, Peter Freund. My wife, Debbie, would also inform me when she came across any information that she thought would be relevant to the study. Meanwhile, I began writing the book, chapter by chapter, although not in the order they would eventually appear in the book. My first and most critical reader, Debbie Larkin, would read over the manuscript, focusing on style, syntax, and grammar, but also keeping an eye to the cogency of the argument. She would discuss with me issues relating to my argument and supporting materials and the direction in which the study was going. After making corrections, I would send the chapter off to my sociologist colleagues, Peter Freund, Ray Calluori, Stanley Aronowitz, and Glenn Mushert. Peter would always provide me detailed feedback, usually in a restaurant with Asian cuisine. Ray would call me on the telephone and discuss conceptual issues and point me in directions related to adolescent subcultures, the music scene, and criminological perspectives. Emails from Stanley would say something like "Keep going." I sent Glenn Mushert copies of papers written from the study and he would provide detailed and trenchant critiques. He and Peter Freund were always raising issues about the relationship between the data and my analyses and corrected my tendencies toward arguing beyond the data.

In April 2004, Debbie and I again visited Columbine. This last trip to the Denver area was for the purpose of plugging holes in the data. Interviews were conducted with Principal DeAngelis, the Reverend Don Marxhausen, Brooks Brown, a former Columbine High School teacher and coach, and several other students. The interviews focused on issues related to harassment by elite students. After returning from the third trip, I concluded that I had sufficient data to complete the study. By that time, I had interviewed approximately thirty students from all strata of the student body, religious leaders, community members, scholars, investigators, educators, and reporters. I sat down and completed writing the book.

As I wrote and revised according to the feedback of my professional colleagues, I began sending chapters to interested friends and family members. Because I viewed the book of interest to what professionals referred to as the "lay community," I gave my friends Harvey Markowitz and Richard Breier copies of the documents to read. Their responses provided several hours of spirited dialogue. In addition, my son, Tom Larkin, and my brother-in-law, Gerald Douglass read the completed manuscript and provided comments. The chapter on Eric and Dylan was read and critiqued by my friends and clinical psychologist, Elliot Selighan. Early drafts of the manuscript were read by Vioki Sudhalter. The completed manuscript was also sent to Ray Calluori, David Brotherton, and Glenn Mushert. Ray provided suggestions for several important improvements, and Glenn went over the manuscript and provided a much-needed close reading. David Brotherton provided me with valuable insights derived from a newly emerging cultural criminology paradigm among British sociologists. I also sent copies to the Brown family. Randy, Judy, and Brooks all separately read the manuscript, primarily checking it for factual errors, but also commenting on the overall direction of the argument. Prepublication copies were also sent to the Center on the Study and Prevention of Violence and to Frank DeAngelis, Principal of Columbine High School. No responses were returned from them.

Although this has been a cooperative venture and I have used the help of the numerous individuals named above, I made the final decisions about what to include and exclude; therefore the responsibility for errors and biases are my own. I would like to thank all those persons who contributed to the writing of this book including the reporters who were generous with their time, Randy and Judy Brown for their help in the research and editing, Brooks Brown, who introduced me to numerous friends who were willing to talk about Columbine, Mr. DeAngelis, who granted the time for two interviews, knowing that he would be the subject of criticism, and the staff at the Center for the Study and Prevention of Violence. I would also like to thank Stanley Aronowitz, who is like an intellectual godfather to me, providing encouragement, guiding me to a publisher, and supporting me behind the scenes. I would particularly like to thank the faculty of the Sociology Department at John Jay College of Criminal Justice who were so supportive and provided me an intellectual home. I especially would like to thank David Brotherton for his support in this endeavor.

Finally, I wish to express my enduring gratitude to and love for my wife Debbie, without whom this project would have been impossible. It was through her that I met David Brotherton, developed an interest in techniques of violence reduction, and observed firsthand how a top-flight conflict mediation program could permanently change the lives of adolescents. She has been a steadfast and supportive partner through this entire process. She helped collect the data and conducted interviews with a skill and sensitivity beyond my capacities. She reviewed every word of this book. Material had to pass muster with her before I would send it out to anybody else. Family time and financial resources were invested in this project. I greatly appreciate her acceptance of these sacrifices.

REFERENCES

Brown, B. and R.Merritt. 2002. *No easy answers: The truth behind death at Columbine*. New York: Lantern Books.

Coleman, D. L. 2002. *Fixing Columbine: the challenged to American liberalism*. Durum, NC: Carolina Academic Press.

Shaw, R. 2003. *The epidemic: The rot of American culture, absentee and permissive parenting, and the resultant plague of joyless, selfish children*. New York: HarperCollins.

NOTES

CHAPTER 1

1 The data for the descriptions of the attack had been derived from several sources: the Jefferson County Sheriff's Department report (Jefferson County Sheriff's Office 1999), Zoba (2000), and newspaper reportage.

CHAPTER 8

1 The social movements of the 1960s created a cultural revolution that affected all of Western society. Modernism, with its emphasis on the values of production, rationality, scientism, cultural monism, sexual repression, and traditional gender roles was attacked by African Americans, white middle-class youth, feminists, and gays in tandem (Foss and Larkin 1976). After the civil rights phase of the black movement of the 1960s, blacks engaged in a period of nationalism, asserting Afrocentric culture as an alternative to assimilation into white society. White middle-class youth attacked the work ethic, the capitalistic notion that the ultimate goal in life was the accumulation of material goods, the intrinsic value of the status struggle, sexual repression, and the barrier between the personal and political. Feminists challenged traditional gender roles, the patriarchal power structure, and enlarged upon the concept of personal politics originally espoused by white middle-class youth. The women's movement also opened new areas for sexual expression, especially in their defense of lesbianism. Gays also countered traditional gender roles, enlarging the critique of sexual orientation opened up by the women's movement. Within the social movements of the 1960s, cultural revolutionaries saw their efforts at attacking bourgeois modernist culture as acts of liberation whereby those persons excluded from the dominant culture were able to claim space within society on their own terms. By the mid-1970s, the United States was experiencing a dramatic cultural crisis as increasing portions of the old culture were stripped away and the institutions supporting them were losing legitimacy.

President Jimmy Carter felt it incumbent upon himself to declaim the "cultural malaise" (Kennedy 1979; Willis 1999).

2 Postmodern culture is impossible without the intrusion of the electronic media into everyday life. Capitalism, however, has an insatiable ability to appropriate liberated aspects of culture and realienate them by turning them into commodities that are sold for profit in the marketplace. Foss (1972) reported:

> [I]t is absolutely amazing how quickly the vocabulary and other superficial features of even the most dissident youth cultures becomes absorbed into the hucksterism of mass culture. "Plymouth is tripping out this year"; "Chevrolet is happening"; Dodge offers a "groovy ride"; while Ford offers a sort of mystical illumination: "You're feeling uptight/Then you see the Light/Those better ideas from Ford/See the Light/See the Light/See the Light." (115)

The fundamental purpose of commercial media is to deliver a suitably conditioned audience to an advertiser (Barnouw 1975, 1978). In the final analysis, the only meaningful criterion on which media advertising is evaluated is its ability to generate increased sales. It is insufficient that more people will be exposed to advertising; they must go out and buy the product. Therefore, not only must the advertisement, "create more desire" (Henry 1963), but the programming itself must soften the audience so that it will be susceptible to the advertising pitch. This is done through a variety of means, including product placement; associations with status, sex, and other desires; and technically by juxtaposing shots of longer duration with advertisements containing rapid cuts or changes or alterations in sound volume.

For electronic media outlets, the prime currency is the size of the audience, along with audience demographics (Gitlin 1983). Therefore, outlets compete for audience size and "quality," with prime audiences being those with the most disposable income. Therefore, in the competition for audiences in ratings, media outlets hype their products. Given the fevered pitch of a myriad of advertisers attempting to harness the attention of populations of potential buyers, postmodern culture becomes increasingly commercialized and directed at generating false consciousness.

The term "false consciousness" is derived from Marx's theory of commodity fetishism, in which the commodity form takes on a symbolic value above and beyond that of its "use value." Marx (1967) posited that in capitalist society, commodities, in addition to the value generated by their utility, were also given exchange values in the marketplace by virtue of how much money they could demand. Marx regarded money as the ultimate commodity form, the commodity by which all other commodities could be measured. Because human labor is also a commodity that is bought and sold in the marketplace, one aspect of false consciousness is the treatment of a living human subject as nothing more than a source of labor. Thus, we are given the notion of factory "hands" in reference to the labor force.

With the extension of capitalist social relations into the manufacture of culture, where increasing numbers of cultural artifacts and services are sold in the marketplace by profit-seekers, the notion of false consciousness takes on new meaning. As Americans spend increasing amounts of their time in the marketplace buying, selling, persuading, and being persuaded to buy products, the commodity form assumes a facticity of its own, giving it a taken-for-granted status. Yet, because of the need to sell, commodities are enhanced with transcendent values, such as power, status, sexuality, love, peace of mind, acceptance, community, and so forth, ad infinitum.

If the nineteenth century was the century of the industrial revolution, the twentieth century witnessed a revolution in communications media. As so many commentators have noted (e.g., Peter Drucker, Daniel Bell, Arthur Toffler), the age of industry has given way to the age of information. Each new medium developed in the twentieth century, with the possible exception of television—radio, sound recording, moving pictures, computers, and the Internet—was developed for noncommercial purposes but was quickly appropriated by commercial interests. The dramatic expansion of the mass media over the twentieth century has allowed commercial interests unprecedented control over cultural reproduction. For any given product, there are literally thousands of venues that can be used to advertise it.

The expanse of the mass media and their harnessing by commercial interests have lead to what Baudrillard has referred to as "hyperreality" (1983). He was referring to a media-constructed reality of simulacra that substitute for unmediated experience. In its consequences, it competes with and shapes lived experience. Because the hyperreal is a constructed reality that emphasizes the unusual, the spectacular, and the consummatory, it always generates expectations that it cannot fulfill. Although the advertising for, say, the Lexus automobile may promise status, power, and sexual fulfillment, the actual purchase of the car does not automatically grant any of those. That is why irony is a classically postmodern attitude. The postmodern individual understands that the hyperreal emphasizes the hype over the real and is in on the joke. Therefore, the ironic posture assumes that one understands that hyperreality has the same relationship to reality as "weapons of mass destruction" has to the invasion of Iraq. Postmodern culture, with its emphasis on the hyperreal, the intentional generation of false consciousness, and the worship of the commodity form, combines them all in the persona of the celebrity, which is simultaneously everything and nothing. It is nothing because it is a cipher into which desires, mythologies, and public relations are used to craft an identity. It is everything because it embodies the society-wide desire for fame and recognition.

3 A check of the *Reader's Guide to Periodical Literature* indicated that between 1984 and 1989, fifty-five articles were published on bullying, between 1990 and 1994, 119 articles, between 1995 and 1999, 372 articles, and between 2000 and 2005, 499 articles. A similar pattern is revealed in the ERIC files, which lists journals and research reports in education, where just three articles were published prior to 1986, seventeen between 1986 and 1990, forty-six between 1991 and 1995, 254 between 1995 and 2000, and 229 after 2000. One would expect that awareness of a social problem would appear first in the popular literature, followed by the professional literature.

CHAPTER 9

1 It is important to point out that the students whom I interviewed tended not to moralize about partying, taking drugs, having sex, or drinking alcohol. What upset them was that evangelical students would take moral positions against such behaviors while engaging in them themselves.

2 The "emergent norm" theory was first introduced by Ralph Turner and Lewis M. Killian (1957) as an explanation of social contagion. That is, when people see other people engaging in deviant activities that do not result in negative sanctions, they are more likely to engage in such behavior. The theory also underpins James Q. Wilson's (1982) "broken window" theory of crime contagion in a community. He noted that when somebody throws a rock through the window of an abandoned building and it remains broken, it is merely a matter of time until all the windows in the building are broken. This presents a visible indicator of social decay and the loss of the community's ability to enforce norms of decorous behavior.

REFERENCES

Aber, J. L., S. M. Jones, J. L. Brown, N. Chaudry, and F. Samples. 1998. Resolving conflict creatively: Evaluating the developmental effects of a school-based violence prevention program in neighborhood and classroom context. *Development and Psychopathology* 10: 187–213.

Abrahams, R. D. 1962. Playing the dozens. *Journal of American Folklore* 75: 209–18.

Adams, L., and D. Russakoff. 1999. High schools' "cult of the athlete" under scrutiny. *The Washington Post*, 13 June, 1ff.

AllPsych online. 2004. *Psychiatric disorders*. Retrieved 26 September 2004, from http://allpsych.com/disorders/personality/antisocial.html

Aronowitz, S. 1973. *False promises*. New York: McGraw-Hill.

———. 1996. *The death and rebirth of American radicalism*. New York: Routledge.

Aronson, E. 2000. *Nobody left to hate*. New York: W. H. Freeman.

Aronson, E., and S. Patnoe. 1997. *The jigsaw classroom: Building cooperation in the classroom*. 2d ed. New York: Longman.

Austin, A., and T. Mendez. 2004. *Life after Columbine*. Retrieved 9 July 2005, from http://www.csmonitor.com/2004/0420/p11s01-legn.html

Barnouw, E. 1975. *Tube of plenty: The evolution of American television*. New York: Oxford University Press.

———. 1978. *The sponsor: Notes on a modern potentate*. New York: Oxford University Press.

Bartels, L. 1999. *At "perfect" school, student sat next to a bomb but Elsa Coffey-Berg wants to know where the positive stories about Columbine are*. Retrieved 3 November 2003, from http://ask.elibrary.com/printdoc.asp?

Bartels, L., and C. Crowder. 1999. *Fatal friendship: How two suburban boys traded baseball and bowling for murder and madness*. Retrieved 27 November 2004, from http://denver.rockymountainnews.com/shooting/0822fata1.shtml

Baudrillard, J. 1983. *In the shadow of the silent majorities*. Translated by P. Foss, P. Patton, and J. Johnston. New York: Semiotext(e) Inc.

Bell, D. 1976. *The cultural contradictions of capitalism*. New York: Basic Books.
Berger, P., and T. Luckmann. 1966. *The social construction of reality*. New York: Doubleday.
Bergin, P. R. 1999. *Eric Harris was taking Luvox (a Prozac-like drug) at the time of the Littleton murders*. Retrieved 1 November 2005, from http://www.breggin.com/luvox.html
Berkow, I. 2003. Coping, one championship at a time at Columbine: Successful football team helps community heal. *The New York Times*, 26 September, D1–D5.
Bernall, M. 1999. *She said yes*. New York: Pocket Books.
Berry, V. 1994. Redeeming the rap music experience. In *Adolescents and their music: If it's too loud, you're too old*, edited by J. S. Epstein. New York: Garland Publishing, Inc.
Bickmore, K. 1999. *Student conflict resolution, power "sharing" in schools, and citizenship education*. Paper presented at the annual meeting of the Citizenship Education Research Network at the Canadian Society for Studies in Education, Sherbrooke, Québec, Canada. (ERIC Document Reproduction No. ED 437328)
Bissinger, H. G. 1990. *Friday night lights: A town, a team, and a dream*. Cambridge, MA: Da Capo Press.
Boorstein, D. 1962. *The image*. New York: Atheneum.
Brand, M. 2004. Five years later: The lessons of Columbine. On *National Public Radio*. Washington, DC.
Brooks, K., V. Schiraldi, and J. Ziedenberg. 1999. *School house hype: Two years later*. Washington, DC: The Center on Juvenile and Criminal Justice.
Brown, B., and R. Merritt. 2002. *No easy answers: The truth behind death at Columbine*. New York: Lantern Books.
Bugliosi, V., and C. Gentry. 1974. *Helter skelter: The true story of the Manson murders*. New York: Norton.
Butterfield, F. 2001. Students, mindful of Columbine, break silence to report threats. *The New York Times*, 10 February. 1ff.
Butterfield, F., and R. D. McFadden. 2001. Three teenagers held in plot at Massachusetts school. *The New York Times*, 26 November, 16.
Cable News Network. 2001. *Kansas town in shock over Columbine-style plot*. Retrieved 2 August 2005, from http://cnnstudentnews.cnn.com/2001/US/02/06/kansas.students/
Campbell, D. 2003. Teenagers held for attack plan. *The Guardian*, 8 July, 15.
Carlin, G. (2000-2006). *Baseball and football*. Retrieved 19 July 2005, from http://www.baseball-almanac.com/humor7.shtml
Cassels, J. R. 1993. *Decreasing physical and verbal aggression in fifth grade students to conflict resolution training*. North Miami Beach, FL: Nova Southeastern University. (ERIC Document Reproduction No. ED 370031)
Cassie Bernall–Her faith has touched us all. 1999. Retrieved 9 July 2000, from http://home.columbus.rr.com/drq/cassie/
Cavan, S. 1972. *Hippies of the Haight*. St. Louis, MO: New Critics Press.
Chase, A. 2001. Violent reaction: What do teen killers have in common? *In These Times*, 25 (16): 16–27.
Child DataBank. 2005. Retrieved 12 June 2005, from http://www.childrendsdatabank.org
Christian Coalition. 2003. *Christian coalition of America's agenda for the 108th congress (2003–2004)*. Retrieved 9 December 2003, from http://www.cc.org/issues.cfm
City of Littleton. 2004. Major employers (over fifty employees). Littleton, CO: Author.
Clark, B. R. 1962. *Educating the expert society*. San Francisco: Chandler Pub. Co.
Cloud, J. 1999. The Columbine effect. *Time Magazine* 154 (23): 12ff.
Cockrane, L. J., and A. Saroyan. 1997. *Finding evidence to support violence prevention programs*. Paper presented at the annual meeting of the American Educational Research Association, Chicago, IL (ERIC Document Reproduction No. ED 409359)

Coleman, J. S. 1961. *The adolescent society: The social life of the teenager and its impact on education*. New York: Free Press of Glencoe.

Colorado Department of Education. 2003. *Columbine High School: Jefferson County R-1*. Retrieved 8 March 2004, from www.state.co.us/schools

Columbine High School. 2001, 11 December. Retrieved 11 July 2002, from http://jeffcoweb.jeffco.k12.co.us/profiles/high/columbine.html

Columbine Research Site. 2003. Retrieved 25 July 2003, from http://columbine-research.info/index.html

Cooley, C. H. 1902. *Human nature and the social order*. New York: C. Scribner's Sons.

Cooper, M. 1995. God and man in Colorado Springs. *The Nation*, 2 January, 9–12.

Cullen, D. 1999a, 15 May. *I smell the presence of Satan*. Retrieved 17 November 2003, from http://archive.salon.com/news/feature/1999/05/15/evangelicals/index.html

———. 1999b, 23 September. *Inside the Columbine High investigation*. Retrieved July 2004, from http://www.salon.com/news/feature/1999/09/23/columbine/print.html

———. 1999c, 23 September. *Kill mankind. No one should survive*. Retrieved 10 July 2004, from http://www.salon.com/news/feature/1999/09/23/journal/index.html

———. 1999d. *The rumor that won't go away*. Retrieved 17 November 2003, from http://archive.salon.com/news/feature.1999/04/24/rumors/print.HTML

———. 1999e, 7 October. *Rutherford Institute sues Columbine officials*. Retrieved 17 November 2003, from http://archive.salon.com/news/feature/1999/10/07/columbine/print.html

———. 1999f, 30 September. *Who said "yes"?* Retrieved 14 February 2003, from http://www.salon.com

———. 1999g. *Who said "yes"?* Retrieved 2 October 2005, from http://www.salon.com/news/feature/1999/09/30/bernall/print.html

———. 2004. *The depressive and the psychopath*. Retrieved 18 September 2004, from http://slate.msn.com/id/2099203/

Culver, V. 1999. *Klebolds called "loneliest people."* Retrieved 28 January 2005, from http://www.baptiststandard.com/1999/5_5/pages/klebolds.html

DeJong, W. 1993. *Building the peace: To resolving conflict creatively program (RCCP)*. Washington, DC: Department of Justice. (ERIC Document Reproduction No. ED 379562)

Domestic Violence Project. 1998. *Arkansas school shootings gender hate crime, say domestic violence experts*. Retrieved 24 November 2003, from http://csf.colorado.edu/forums/femisa/98/0132.html

Downs, A. 1998. Up and down with ecology—The "issue-attention cycle." In *Political theory and public choice: The selected essays of Anthony Downs*. Vol. 1, edited by A. Downs, 100–112. Northampton, MA: Edward Elgar.

Duberman, M. 1993. *Stonewall*. New York: Penguin.

Durkheim, E. 1956. *Education and sociology*. New York: The Free Press.

Dyer, J. 1998. *Harvest of rage*. Boulder, CO: Westview Press.

Eckert, P. 1989. *Jocks and burnouts: Social categories and identity in the high school*. New York: Teachers College Press.

Elliott, D. S., B. A. Hamburg, and K. R. Williams, eds. 1998. *Violence in American schools*. New York: Cambridge University Press.

Emergency Net, N. 1999. Summary of real-time reports concerning a shooting at the Columbine High School in Littleton, Colorado. *ERRI Emergency Services Report*, 3.

Enlissen, J. C. 1999. *Shooting memories creep into rally Columbine students joyously celebrate football championship*. Retrieved 3 November 2003, from http://ask.elibrary.com/printdoc.asp?

Epperhart, B. 2002. *Columbine: Questions that demand an answer*. Tulsa, OK: Insight Publishing Group.

Evans, S. 1979. *Personal politics: The roots of women's liberation in the Civil Rights movement and the new left*. New York: Vintage.
Ewen, S. 1976. *The captains of consciousness*. New York: McGraw-Hill.
Faludi, S. 1999. *Stiffed: The betrayal of the American man*. New York: William Morrow.
Felton, D. 1972. *Mindfuckers*. San Francisco, CA: Straight Arrow Books.
Finnigan, W. 1998. *Cold new world: Growing up in a harder country*. New York: Random House.
Flynn, K. 1999. Columbine killers strike chord on net. *Denver Rocky Mountain News*.
Foss, D. A. 1972. *Freak culture: Lifestyle and politics*. New York: E. P. Dutton & Co., Inc.
Foss, D. A., and R. W. Larkin. 1976. From "The Gates of Eden" to "Day of the Locust": An analysis of the dissident youth movement of the 1960s and its heirs in the 1970s—The post-movement groups. *Theory and Society* 3: 45–64.
———. 1986. *Beyond revolution: A new theory of social movements*. South Hadley, MA: Bergen & Garvey.
Freeman, J. 1975. *The politics of women's liberation*. New York: Longman.
Freud, S. 1952. *The ego and the id*. Translated by J. Riviere. In *Freud*.Vol. 54, 697–717. Chicago: William Benton.
Gaines, D. 1993. *Teenage wasteland: Suburbia's dead-end kids*. New York: HarperCollins.
———. 1994. The local economy of suburban scenes. In *Adolescents and their music: If it's too loud, you're too old*, edited by J. S. Epstein, 47–66. New York: Garland Publishing, Inc.
Gamson, J. 1994. *Claims to fame: Celebrity in contemporary America*. Berkeley, CA: University of California Press.
Garbarino, J., and E. deLara. 2002. *And words can hurt forever*. New York: The Free Press.
Gibbs, N., and T. Roche. 1999. The Columbine tapes. *Time Magazine*, 20 December, 4ff.
Gibson, J. W. 1994. *Warrior dreams*. New York: Hill & Wang.
Giles, D. 2000. *Illusions of immortality: A psychology of fame and celebrity*. New York: St. Martin's Press.
Gillis, J. R. 1974. *Youth and history*. New York: Academic Press.
Gitlin, T. 1983. *Inside prime time*. New York: Pantheon.
Gonzales, M. 1999. Jeffco schools study charge of athlete's special treatment. *Denver Rocky Mountain News*.
Gordon, C. W. 1957. *The social system of the high school: A study in the sociology of adolescence*. Glencoe, IL: Free Press.
Graves, A. B. 1999, 10 May. *ACLU swamped with complaints*. Retrieved 4 June 2002, from http://www.thedailycamera.com/shooting/10caclu.html
Green, S. 1999. *Teen described school life filled with taunts, abuse*. Retrieved 18 July 2004, from http://63.147.65.175/news/shot0424f.htm
Gregg, S. 1998. *School-based programs to promote safety and civility. AEL policy briefs*. Washington, DC: Office of Educational Research and Improvement. (ERIC Document Reproduction No. ED 419180)
Hare, R. D. 1999. *Without conscience: The disturbing world of the psychopaths among us*. New York: Guilford Press.
Harris, E. 1998. *Journal entries*. Retrieved 4 October 2004, from http://www.westward.com/special_reports/columbine/files/index_html?file=02.gif
Harris, J. R. 1999. *The nurture assumption: Why children turn out the way they do*. New York: Touchstone.
Hawkins, J. D., D. P. Farrington, and R. F. Catalano. 1998. Reducing violence of the schools. In *Violence in American schools*, edited by D. S. Elliott, B. A. Hamburg, and K. R. Williams,188–216. Cambridge, England: Cambridge University Press.
Henry, J. 1963. *Culture against man*. New York: Random House.
Hersch, P. 1998. *A tribe apart*. New York: Ballantine.

Hodkinson, P. 2002. *Goth: Identity, style and subculture*. New York: Oxford University Press.

Holtz, R. 1999. Shootings fuel debate over "jock elitism" at Columbine. *Denver Rocky Mountain News*.

Hubbard, B. 1999. Researchers say Harris reconfigured video game. *Denver Rocky Mountain News*.

Huckabee, M. 1998. *Kids who kill*. Nashville, TN: Broadman and Holman.

Huerter, R. 2000. *The culture of Columbine*. Denver, CO: Governor's Columbine Commission.

Jankowski, M. S. 1991. *Islands in the street: Gangs and American urban society*. Berkeley, CA: University of California Press.

Jefferson County Public Schools. 2004. *Columbine High*. Retrieved 2 February 2004, from http://jeffcoweb.jeffco.k12.co.us/profiles/high/columbine.html

Jefferson County Sheriff's Office. 1999. *Time line on Columbine shootings*. Retrieved 9 July 2000, from http://www.denverpost.com/news/colreport/Columbinerep/pages/TOC.htm

———. 2003. Harris and Kebold video clips [Videotape]. Golden, CO.

Johnson, K. 1999. *Boss saw Harris' bomb, didn't report it*. Retrieved 19 December 2004, from http://www.usatoday.com/news/index/colo/colo155.htm

Kennedy, E. 1979. Carter agonistes. *The New York Times Magazine*, 5 August, 7ff.

Key, W. B. 1973. *Subliminal seduction*. New York: Signet.

———. 1976. *Media sexploitation*. New York: Signet.

Kimmel, M. 1996. *Manhood in America*. New York: The Free Press.

Kotarba, J. A. 1994. The post modernization of rock 'n roll music: The case of Metallica. In *Adolescents and their music: If it's too loud, you're too old*, edited by J. S. Epstein, 141–164. New York: Garland Publishing, Inc.

Kurtz, H. 1999. Columbine like a hologram: Life at school depends on angle of one's view. *Denver Rocky Mountain News*, 25 July, 4A.

Laing, R. D. 1999. *The divided self : An existential study in sanity and madness*. London; New York: Routledge.

Larkin, R. W. 1979. *Suburban youth in cultural crisis*. New York: Oxford University Press.

———. 1988. Lurching toward the millennium: Youth in the next decade. *The World and I* 3(11): 535–49.

Lefkowitz, B. 1997. *Our guys*. New York: Vintage Press.

Longman, J. 2003. Drugs in sports; an althlete's dangerous experiment. *The New York Times*, 26 November, D1.

Magee, J. P., and C. R. DeBernardo. 1999. Offender and defense characteristics of a nonrandom sample of adolescent mass murderers. *Journal of the American Academy of Child and Adolescent Psychiatry* 40(6): 16–18.

Males, M. A. 1996. *The scapegoat generation: America's war on adolescents*. Monroe, ME: Common Courage Press.

Marijuana Policy Project. 1996. *Marijuana prohibition has not curtailed marijuana use by adolescents*. Retrieved 27 June 2004, from http://www.ukcia.org/research/adolescents.htm

Marshall, P. D. 1998. *Celebrity and power: Fame in contemporary culture*. Minneapolis, MN: University of Minnesota Press.

Marx, K. 1967. *A critical analysis of capitalist production*. Vol. 1 of *Capital*. New York: International Publishers.

Massacre foreshadowed by gunmen's videos. 1999. *USA Today*, 22 April, 1.

McFadden, B. D. 1991. Sixteen-year-old is shot to death in a high school in Brooklyn. *The New York Times*, 26 November, A1.

McKinley, J. C. 1992. Diversion plan: "Safe streets" as budget aid. *The New York Times*, 25 March, B4.

Mead, G. H. 1964. *On social psychology*. Chicago: University of Chicago Press.

Meadows, S. 2003. Ghosts of Columbine. *Newsweek*, 3 November, 54–57.

Mehnert, K. 1976. *Twilight of the young: The radical movements of the 1960s and their legacy*. New York: Holt, Rinehart & Winston.

Meloy, J. R., A. G. Hempel, K. Mohandie, A. A. Shiva, and B. T. Gray. 2001. Offender and offense characteristics of a nonrandom sample of adolescent mass murderers. *Journal of the American Academy of Child and Adolescent Psychiatry* 40, no. 6: 719–28.

Merton, R. K. 1957. *Social theory and social structure* (Rev. and enl. ed.). Glencoe, IL: Free Press.

Mihalic, S., A. Fagan, C. Irwin, D. Ballard, and D. S. Elliott. 2002. *Blueprints for violence prevention replications: Factors for implementation success*. Boulder, CO: Institute of Behavioral Science, Regents of the University of Colorado.

Mills, C. W. 1951. *White collar*. New York: Oxford University Press.

Moore, J. B. 1993. *Skinheads: Shaved for battle*. Bowling Green, OH: Bowling Green State University Popular Press.

Morgan, R. 1970. *Sisterhood is powerful*. New York: Vintage.

Murphy, J. F., Jr. 2001. *Day of reckoning: The massacre at Columbine High School*. Philadelphia, PA: Xlibiris.

Muschert, G. 2002. *Media and massacre: The social construction of the Columbine story*. University of Colorado, Boulder, CO. (UMI Order No. AADAA-I3043550)

National Association of Attorneys General. 2000. *Bruised inside: What our children say about youth violence, what causes it, and what we need to do about it*. Washington, DC: Author.

National Institute of Justice. 1995. *Evaluation of violence prevention programs and middle schools*. Washington, DC: US Department of Justice, Office of Justice Programs.

Newhouse, J. 1966. *A prophetic minority*. New York: Signet Books.

Newman, K. S. 2004. *Rampage: The social roots of school shootings*. New York: Basic Books.

Niewart, D. A. 1999. *In God's country: The patriot movement and the Pacific Northwest*. Pullman, WA: Washington State University Press.

Nimmo, B., and D. K. Klingsporn. 2001. *The journals of Rachel Scott*. Nashville, TN: Thomas Nelson, Inc.

Nimmo, B., D. Scott, and S. Rabey. 2000. *Rachel's tears: The spiritual journey of Columbine martyr Rachel Scott*. Nashville, TN: Thomas Nelson Publishers.

O'Harrow, R. J., and E. Wee. 1996. Marijuana users' air of defiance. *The Washington Post*, 3 August, A1.

Olweus, D. 1993. *Bullying at school: What we know and what we can do*. Cambridge, MA: Blackwell.

Olweus, D., S. Limber, and S. F. Mahalic. 1999. *Bullying prevention program*. Boulder, CO: Center for the Study and Prevention of Violence, Institute of Behavioral Science, University of Colorado at Boulder.

O'Meara, K. P. 2001. *Prescription drugs may trigger killing*. Retrieved 1 November 2005, from http://www.happinessonline.org/BeTemperate/p1.htm

O'Toole, M. E. 2000. *The school shooter: A threat assessment perspective*. Quantico, VA: FBI Academy.

Pankratz, H. 2000. Columbine bullying no myth, panel told victims' parents, teacher rebut principal's words. *The Denver Post*, 3 October, A-1.

Parsons, T. 1951. *The social system*. New York: The Free Press.

Phifer, T. 2003, 4 September. *Safety Jones quits team*. Retrieved 19 July 2005, from http://www.coloradoan.com/news/coloradoanpublishing/CSURams2003/season/090403_jonesquits.html

Porter, B. 1999. *Martyr's torch: The message of the Columbine massacre*. Shippensburg, PA: Destiny Image Publishers, Inc.

Prendergast, A. 1999. *Doom rules: Much of what we think we know about Columbine is wrong*. Retrieved 13 June 2004, from www.westword.com

———. 2000. *The missing motive*. Retrieved 8 June 2002, from www.westword.com

Ridgeway, J. 1995. *Blood in the face*. 2d ed. New York: Thunder's Mouth Press.

Riesman, D. 1961. *The lonely crowd: A study of the changing American character*. Abridged ed. New Haven, CT: Yale University Press.

Riskin, L. L. 1993. *Integrating dispute processing in the first-year law school courses: The videotape series and evaluation. Final report*. Columbia, MO: Missouri University School of Law. (ERIC Document Reproduction No. ED 415764)

Roth, A. 2001. Dad says bullying drove son to act. *San Diego Union-Tribune*, 6 September.

Rubin, J. 1970. *Do it!* New York: Simon and Schuster.

Sale, K. 1974. *SDS*. New York: Vintage Books.

———. 1976. *Power shift: The rise of the southern rim and its challenge to the Eastern establishment*. New York: Vintage Books.

Salzman, M. 2001. Backtalk: Disappointed in Denver. *Phi Delta Kappa* 82.

Samples, F., and J. L. Aber. 1998. Evaluations of school-based violence prevention programs. In *Violence in American schools*, edited by D. S. Elliott, B. A. Hamburg, and K. R. Williams, 217–52. Cambridge, England: Cambridge University Press.

Sanko, J. 2000. School bell rings bullies, drugs across Colorado, kids paint unsettling picture of student life for touring Salazar, Elliott. *The Rocky Mountain News*, 18 September, 1A, 8A.

Savidge, M. 1999. *Littleton mourns the victims of the Columbine shooting*. Littleton, CO: LexisNexis. (Transcript no. 99042502V54)

Scanlon, B. 1999. Principal describes fateful day: DeAngelis says he was never alerted to signs of violence by gunmen. *Rocky Mountain News*, 24 April, 6A.

Scott, D., and S. Rabey. 2001. *Chain reaction: A call to compassionate revolution*. Nashville: T. Nelson.

Shepard, C. 1999. *4-20-99: A Columbine web site*. Retrieved 27 November 2004, from http://columbine.free2host.net/index.html

Sherif, M., and C. W. Sherif. 1964. *Reference groups: Exploration into conformity and deviation of adolescents*. New York: Harper and Row.

Skiba, R., and R. Peterson. 1999. The dark side of zero tolerance. *Phi Delta Kappan* 80, no. 5: 372–82.

Stark, J. 1999. *We called it "little fun."* Retrieved 8 March 2004, from http://www.salon.com/news/feature/1999/04/21/littleton_graduate/index.html

Staten, C., Sr. 1999. Littleton: Who's to blame. *EmergencyNet News Service* 3, no.119.

Stern, K. 1997. *A force upon the plain*. Norman, OK: University of Oklahoma.

Stokes, H. 2002, 6–9 March. *Education for conflict—Education for peace*. Paper presented at the Annual meeting of the Comparative and International Education Society, Orlando, FL. (ERIC Document Reproduction No. ED476602)

Stout, D. 1999. Terror in Littleton: The president; Clinton, "Shocked and Saddened," hopes for prevention. *The New York Times*, 21 April.

Talbot, M. 2000. A mighty fortress. *The New York Times Magazine*, 27 February, 34ff.

Thompson, W. I. 1971. *At the edge of history: Speculations on the transformation of culture*. New York: Harper.

Tipton, S. M. 1982. *Getting saved from the sixties : Moral meaning in conversion and cultural change*. Berkeley: University of California Press.

Tobias, L. 1999. School has history of excellence. *Denver Rocky Mountain News*.

"Trench". 2005. *Trenchcoat chronicles*. Retrieved 2 August 2005, from http://www.thetrenchcoat.com/archives/2003/07/14/eric-harris-worship-site/

Turner, R. H., and L. M. Killian. 1957. *Collective behavior*. Englewood Cliffs, NJ: Prentice-Hall.

United States Army MPs in Vietnam, 1962-1975. (n.d.). Retrieved 6 August 2003, from http://home.mweb.co.za/re/redcap/vietcrim.htm

Vaughan, K. 2004, 16 September. *Frustration, anger and sadness*. Retrieved 18 December 2004, from http://www.rockymountainnews.com/drmn/local/article/0,1299,DRMN_15_3188744,00.html

Vaughan, K., A. M. Washington, and A. Carnahan. 1999. Harris told of ambition to blow up Columbine. *Rocky Mountain News*, 29 April.

Verhovek, S. H. 1999. Terror in Littleton: The overview. *The New York Times*, 22 April, 1ff.

Von Drehle, D. 1999. To killers, model school was cruel. *The Washington Post*, 25 April, A1.

Watson, J. 2002. *The martyrs of Columbine: Faith and the politics of tragedy*. New York: Palgrave.

Weinstein, D. 1994. Rock: Youth and its music. In *Adolescents and their music: If it's too loud, you're too old*, edited by J. S. Epstein, 3–24. New York: Garland Publishing, Inc.

Weller, K. 1973. *The Lordstown struggle and the real crisis in production*. Retrieved 6 August 2003, from http://flag.blackened.net/revolt/disband/solidarity/lordstown.html

West, V. 1999. *Inside the Columbine High School shootings*. Retrieved 26 November 2004, from http://www.members.tripod.com/~VanessaWest/columbine-4.html

Westword. 1999. *Crossing the line on Rebel Hill*, from http://www.westword.com/issues/1999-08-19/offlimits.html/1/index.html

Wilgoren, J., M. Pates, and G. Reuthling. 2005. Shooting rampage by student leave ten dead on reservation. *The New York Times*, 22 March, 1.

Willis, E. 1999. *Don't think, smile!* Boston: Beacon.

Wilogoren, J. 2005a. Eerie parallels are seen to shootings at Columbine. *The New York Times*, 23 March, A1.

———. 2005b. Shooting rampage by student leaves ten dead on reservation. *The New York Times*, 22 March, A1.

Wilson, J. Q., and G. L. Kelling. 1982. Broken windows: The police and neighborhood safety. *The Atlantic Monthly*, 29–38.

Wilson-Brewer, R., S. Cohen, L. O'Donnell, and I. F. Goodman. 1991. *Violence prevention for young adolescents: A survey of the state of art*. Cambridge, MA: Education Development Center. (ERIC Document Reproduction No. ED 356442)

Wooden, W. S., and R. Blazak. 2001. *Renegade kids, suburban outlaws*. Belmont, CA: Wadsworth.

Zoba, W. M. 2000. Day of reckoning: Columbine and the search for America's soul. Grand Rapids, MI: Brazos Press.

INDEX

Ralph W. Larkin, Ph.D. is owner of Academic Research Consulting Service and a Senior Research Associate, John Jay College of Criminal Justice, City University of New York. He is the author of *Suburban Youth in Cultural Crisis and* (with Daniel A. Foss) and *Beyond Revolution: Social Movements in Historical and Comparative Perspective*.